For Elissa

Praise for *All Tomorrow's Parties*

"Truly exceptional memoirs have to do something more than recount a good origin story: they have to test the author's youthful understanding of the world, and break down that world, even as it's being built upon the page. *All Tomorrow's Parties* is such a memoir . . . A thrill to read."
—Christopher Bollen, *Interview*

"Spillman is happiest when he is betwixt and between—on the road, crossing borders, running long distances. This is a realm he knows intimately and documents beautifully in *All Tomorrow's Parties*, a yearning, restless memoir about a lost boy looking for home."
—Erika Schickel, *Los Angeles Review of Books*

"A completely relatable and unique coming-of-age story . . . [Spillman's] desire for an exciting life can be infectious, and his ultimate pursuit of it makes for an exhilarating read."
—Alexandra Karina, *Electric Literature*

"Wondrous . . . every page [is] an ecstatic celebration of this thing called life in all of its weird and short glory."
—Jason Diamond, *Vol. 1 Brooklyn*

"A kind of meditation on place and placelessness, and the thrilling, dangerous, necessary place that both art and the artist occupy in the world."
—Jason Sheehan, NPR

"A compelling memoir . . . [it] says exactly the right things in the most engaging way." —*Minneapolis Star Tribune*

"Artful and irreverent." —Aditi Sriram, *Brooklyn Rail*

"An engrossing memoir of self-discovery through the arts that spans two continents." —David Gutowski, *Largehearted Boy*

"A culturally saturated, Technicolor account of the author's unusual up-bringing and the intentional adventures of his young adulthood . . . It quivers with the type of honesty it takes to admit your deepest, most damning secrets. But Spillman isn't angling for sympathy. Instead he is bold and almost defiant. *All Tomorrow's Parties* is a major achievement."

—Kea Krause, *Rumpus*

"It is a portrait of the artist as a young man, retracing the steps that led him to a deeper truth, which (of course) lay outside himself. Spillman brilliantly—thrillingly—captures the velocity and the changing sounds of youth as it simultaneously hurls away from, and toward, home. This memoir rivets me to the page."

—Nick Flynn

"A deeply personal work about love, art, and authenticity . . . The emotional risks Spillman takes in his life and in this book pay off. Readers will relate to his struggle toward vulnerability and presence, and the unexpected satisfaction he finds in a more rooted idea of family and home."

—Amy Gall, *Barnes & Noble Review*

"Captivating . . . A Hunter S. Thompson-esque journey."

—Sue Carter, *Toronto Star METRO*

"An engrossing coming-of-age story about a guy who did his level best to avoid coming of age." —Douglas J. Johnston, *Winnipeg Free Press*

"Rob Spillman's story of rarefied opera culture as a child, and East German nightlife as an adult, is limpid and lively in its telling, and it covers fascinating ground. Spillman is endearing and frank in his various adventures."

—Rachel Kushner

"It's impossible to not become utterly immersed in [Spillman's] journey toward artistic self-discovery . . . His search for identity, home, and his inner spark will echo with anyone who's longed to make a creative mark on the world." —Anna Chandler, *Connect Savannah*

"Revealing and energetic . . . a captivating story of both personal awakening and the cultural upheaval that accompanied the fall of the Berlin Wall."

—Harvey Freedenberg, Bookreporter.com

"Part survivor's manual, part travelogue, part cultural history, it's a story of an arts-mad, idealistic, brave young man struggling to make his way—and find a place in the world. Set in large part against the backdrop of Berlin in the raucous months after the wall was torn down and people struggled with re-unification, Spillman unspools a story that will resonate with everyone who's ever searched for home."

—Michael Hainey

"In this carefully wrought coming-of-age memoir, a young American writer searches for home in an unlikely place: East Berlin immediately after the fall of the Wall . . . His is a quest of roots and writerly authenticity—and his evocation of East Berlin's days is exquisite and revealing."

—*Publishers Weekly* (starred review)

"Lifelong exposure to passionate artists may have fueled [Spillman's] creativity, but an existential dread that he won't find passion in his own life gnaws at him . . . This is the story of formative years spent struggling to fully embrace life at the crossroads of history, art, home, and family."

—*Booklist* (starred review)

"[A] lively debut . . . Musically and culturally astute, this well-structured book is a delightful coming-of-age story couched within a travel narrative that deftly evokes one of the major historical moments of the 20th century. A richly detailed and always engaging memoir on artistic discovery."

—*Kirkus Reviews* (starred review)

"Rob Spillman's memoir is built out of an extraordinary and extraordinarily powerful and significant paradox: Spillman wants only art; at every juncture he chooses only life; the book succeeds precisely because we love Spillman for what he decries in himself. An achingly beautiful and brilliantly structured book."

—David Shields

All
Tomorrow's
Parties

A MEMOIR

Rob
Spillman

To Ann,
Saved the most you
in Boston. I hope
you enjoy.
Best,
Rob Sp

Grove Press
New York

Note from the author:
Though this book is a memoir, I've changed names and certain background details to preserve the privacy of characters who aren't members of my immediate family.

First Grove Atlantic hardcover edition: April 2016

First Grove Atlantic paperback edition: February 2017

Published simultaneously in Canada
Printed in the United States of America

FIRST EDITION

ISBN 978-0-8021-2626-9
eISBN 978-0-8021-9040-6

Grove Press
an imprint of Grove Atlantic
154 West 14th Street
New York, NY 10011

Distributed by Publishers Group West

groveatlantic.com

17 18 19 20   10 9 8 7 6 5 4 3 2 1

1

"Art should be life. It's an imitation of life. It should have some humanity in it."

—John Lydon

Soundtrack: Sex Pistols, "Holidays in the Sun," 1977

"THIS MUST BE THE PLACE." I point to the street signs above us, then back down at the flyer.

"If you say so," Elissa says.

"Where else should we possibly be?" I ask, and raise my glass.

Four months before reunification, we are drinking a previously impossible-to-obtain West German wine at a makeshift sidewalk café stumbling distance from our illegal coldwater flat. Although the Wall has "fallen" the previous October, West German authorities don't yet have authority to cross into the East. When the German Democratic Republic (GDR) police's wages vanished, so did they. The only authority left here is the elite riot police and the remnants of the GDR's army. They keep order by bashing the skinheads and anarchists in running street battles every night. We haven't seen many other Westerners on this side of the Wall. Most are staying away until reunification. Young East Germans have looked out for us, twenty-five-year-old Americans, married less than two years, self-proclaimed bohemians crazy enough to live in the midst of their chaos. But to us it doesn't feel crazy; there is something alive and magical in the air, what it must have been like in the twenties when Marlene Dietrich was roaming the risqué drag clubs in men's clothes, when culture and politics collided and the possibilities were revolutionary.

Now, for East Germans, Berlin is reborn and in the month we've been living here everything feels possible. Two weeks ago, this wine bar was a boarded-up food market. Young locals pooled their money and drove through a gap in the Wall in a battered Wartburg which they filled with cases of West German wine, then smashed down the market's door and served the wine on the sidewalk on upturned cable spools scavenged from abandoned warehouses along the Eastern side of the Wall. Thus the Prenzlauer Berg Wine Bar was born and thus we became regulars, doing what was unthinkable only a year ago—publically downing a whole bottle of cold 1989 *Pfälzer Landwein* from the Rhine. Not that there aren't still risks. Almost every night the sirens sound, blaring like World War II air-raid warnings, winding up louder and louder, signaling that the riot police are coming in to clear the skinheads who are trying to firebomb the *Autonomen* (anarchist) squats nearby. All up and down our block the anarchists have taken over abandoned buildings and have painted them pink and are flying old East German flags with the hammers and compasses cut out of the centers. When the riot police charge in, they bust any and all heads they see. If the clashes aren't on our street, we'll wait out the alarm in our bullet-pocked archway, unrepaired since World War II, and if the melee is on our street we'll flee up the four flights to our apartment.

The sun is bleeding down, streaking East Berlin's grays and browns with fiery orange and red, warming the cold, gray buildings to create a pocket of calm, an oasis perfect for sharing our nightly bottle of wine before we head off to the CV, our other regular neighborhood bar, just across the park. I pick up the hand-drawn flyer that the young East German has dropped on our table, try to make sense of it. Black and red concentric circles telescope down to a black X, with the names "Duncker-strasse" and "Lettestrasse" written below. We are sitting directly under the street signs for Dunckerstrasse and Lettestrasse.

"Thanks," I tell Michael. He's one of the earnest Bat Theater Studio guys who are still putting on plays and happenings in appropriated ex-government buildings despite, or to spite, the vanished socialist subsidies.

"But what is it?"

"A rave," he replies, all business.

" 'Rave'?"

"*Ja*, rave. A big dance, mostly illegal, held in big, illegal spaces."

"Like here?" I ask, not getting it. I look to Elissa, but she also doesn't understand.

"How do you mean?" Michael asks.

I point to the street names on the flyer and his confusion cracks into a smile. "No, no. We meet here. Tomorrow night, starting at midnight, every half hour, one of us will come here and take you to the place of the rave."

"Which is where?" I ask.

"You Americans are funny, yes?"

We debate going to the rave, whatever a rave is, but it isn't much of a debate. Of course I'm going to jump into the abyss. That's what I do—throw myself into the unknown. So, twenty-four hours later, flyer in hand, at exactly midnight I jump on the back of the sparkling blue Vespa, driven by a young East German I hardly know, who has promised to take me someplace secret and spectacular. Michael takes off before the other Vespa, sparkling red, pulls to a stop in front of Elissa. She scrambles behind the unknown woman and they set off after us. I hold tight and we fly the two-block length of Helmholtzplatz park, then past the even smaller Kollwitzplatz park, weaving our way through scattered cobblestones and torched Communist cardboard cars, Wartburgs and Trabants, stacked like charred logs under the dead street lamps. I feel like I'm in *Fellini's Roma,* a camera mounted on a scooter gliding through Rome at night, the Vespa's soft, sweeping light illuminating ancient fountains and statues. But in reality, in the here and now, this Vespa's narrow beam of weak white light is cutting through the stark blackness, catching obstacles so that we don't crash out on the cobbles.

Last night's battle between the skinheads and anarchists has coated the streets with smashed Molotovs. Michael tries to avoid the bigger shards as we zigzag out of Prenzlauer Berg and toward the Wall. Around the corners I check behind for the trailing Vespa's yellow beam. I briefly wonder if Elissa is scared or thrilled—she doesn't speak German and I don't know how much English her driver has. I shelve that worry, as we are now heading straight for the Wall, but a short block away, Michael lurches us hard right along a road that parallels the clean gray slabs of concrete.

We cruise past long-abandoned warehouses and industrial buildings and at each intersection I see the Wall, a hundred feet to the left, its faintly iridescent whitish gray visible for a second, then gone, glimpsed, gone again.

"Hang on," Michael says, and switches off his light. He drives blind for a bumpy minute, then swings the Vespa left, toward a warehouse, a large dark door coming into focus. It opens right before we reach it, then slams shut as soon as we are inside. Pitch black. Where is Elissa? Should I run out? Before I reach full-on panic, the door flies open and the second Vespa coasts in. The door bangs shut with a metallic clang and several flashlights click on.

"Here. You will need this," Michael says, and hands me a small plastic flashlight.

I aim the light at Elissa, who gives me a questioning look, and I shrug.

"*Bitte, gehen sie jetzt,*" a young man says, impatiently pointing his flashlight toward the water-stained back of the room. His eyes are all pupil and he is sweating, his jaw fiercely working over a piece of gum.

I wave goodbye to Michael and follow the sweating man to the other side of the small, white-tiled room and through a set of steel doors that lead to a stairwell. *Banish all bad thoughts— we're not going to get rolled. It's all good. Follow the signs.* I squeeze Elissa's hand to reassure her, and myself. We skip down one flight of steps, then another, trying to keep up with our hopped-up leader. Two floors below street level, our Orpheus pushes open a creaky black metal door, revealing a vast, flooded basement, strewn with rubble and industrial detritus.

"*Was gibt's?*" I ask, and our guide snorts. He explains, in German, which I quickly translate for Elissa, that we are in an old ball-bearing factory. He tells me this as he dances across long, sagging boards stretched between cinder-block islands. Our flashlight beams ricochet off the oily water, which has a ferrous, noxious reek, and I picture my foot dissolving in it as if it were sulfuric acid. A faint, far-off beat—a fast, steady *thump, thump, thump*—matches the pulse in my ears.

"Is there another room to the factory?" I call after our guide, repeating the question in English for Elissa.

"No, no," he replies. "The party isn't in here. This is only the passageway."

Before I can begin to think about where we are heading, on the other side of the waterlogged basement a six-foot-wide hole opens into a dank tunnel. The *thump, thump, thump* of music is now clear. And up ahead a bright light pulls me forward.

"*Entschuldigung*, excuse me," my new friend says, shining his flashlight over my shoulder. I turn around and Elissa catches up to us. She gives me her "What have you gotten me into?" look and I give her my "You agreed to this" look back. I also silently give her what I hope is reassurance, and I think she's on the same page, but I really don't care because we're obviously on the cusp of something weird and quite possibly wonderful.

"Where *are* we?" I once more ask our guide, who snorts again and moves aside so that we can be the first to step through the hole and into a cavernous space constructed of gray granite blocks, the vaulted ceiling sweeping up a good hundred feet. People are dancing everywhere—on piles of paving stones and railroad ties, and in the long trench that runs through the center of the giant space. They are dancing to the loud, steady, bass-heavy electronic music, something that sounds like Kraftwerk crossed with Donna Summer. The dancers cast huge shadows from the low, icy-white strobe lights ringing the room. Atop a Lincoln-Log-like construction of scavenged railroad ties perch two sets of turntables and two young men with black-bubble headphones who are bobbing along to the music.

"Where *are* we?" I shout.

"Under the Wall," our guide yells. "This is an old subway station, from before the war, closed off for forty years. Now we break through and have a rave."

"I never want to leave," I say—out loud, I think. I can't believe this. We are literally between countries, under two countries.

I close my eyes and let the concussive bass vibrate through my body. I can feel the beat of my heart aligning with the beat of the music. I'm dissolving, breaking into a million particles. I am nowhere. I am home.

2

"The world is teeming. Anything can happen."

—John Cage

Soundtrack: John Cage, *Concerto for Prepared Piano and Chamber Orchestra,* 1951

MY FIRST CLEAR MEMORY is of my father being booed. This happened when I was four, twenty-one years before the rave but only four miles away, in the newly opened Mies van der Rohe–designed Neue Nationalgalerie, where my father performed in an avant-garde contemporary music series. Swallowed up in a deep, plush red seat, I was surrounded by West Berlin's cognoscenti, many of whom were booing my father, who was onstage coaxing discordant, grinding sounds from a big black piano.

The lid of the concert grand was open and my father was leaning inside, pulling on the strings. There were bolts and pins jammed in between and around the strings to alter the sound. My dad was wearing black pants, a black turtleneck, and a black beret, and was smoking a cigarette, which I found funny because he never smoked. Nor, for that matter, did he ever wear a beret or black sweater. He never went in for affectations, even in the fall of 1969 when all of the other artists in our orbit had outward-flaring bell-bottoms and bright paisleys, ascots, and heeled boots. West Berlin at that moment was a creative Mecca, or more accurately, an artistic oasis, a multicultural playground situated two hundred miles inside of East Bloc territory, ringed in by a double-rowed concrete wall punctuated by guard towers with machine-gun turrets, outside of which were several hundred thousand heavily armed East German and Soviet troops. The Wall had gone up on August 13, 1961, only three years and five months before I was born. The postwar treaty stipulated that West Berlin was not formally part of the Federal Republic of Germany, which meant that if you were a citizen of the city, you were exempt from compulsory military service. Because of this, young artistic Germans, along with foreign artists and musicians, flocked to this safe haven at the very heart of the Cold War.

My parents had come over in the summer of 1964, on Fulbright scholarships after having attended the Eastman School of Music. For American classical musicians, Europe—particularly Germany, with its hundreds of big and little concert and opera halls, each with voracious, supportive audiences—was a much easier place to launch a career than back home. My parents had started off in Stuttgart, where my mother was building her opera credentials, and from where my father could scramble around Europe playing prestigious, high-pressure contests that could make his career while also cobbling together paid work as an opera coach and accompanist. After I was born, in December, my mother took little time off and managed to sing the role of Mimi in *La Bohéme* thirty times in one year. Yet they lacked consistent, reliable work and when my father was offered a job as accompanist for legendary voice teacher, Madame Mauz, in Berlin, my mother had little choice but to put her ambitions behind my father's, and we all moved to the place I have always called home.

I have no memories of my parents being together. They separated six months before the concert at which my father was booed. It is hard for me to imagine them as a couple. Temperamentally, they are opposites—she logical and always in control of her environment and emotions, he impulsive, impractical, and driven by emotion. At the time, he was in turmoil over his sexuality, resisting what he knew to be true but which went against his conservative, central Kentucky upbringing.

After they separated, even though my mother was still in Berlin, I lived primarily with my father, and tagged along with him to rehearsals, lessons, and performances. I loved watching him play the piano, especially up onstage where he would unfurl his broad six-foot-two frame, sway and nod along to the music, and sometimes even cry. The music possessed him, animated him, and watching him play concerts, I felt buoyant, my stomach fizzing with happiness. But as the boos and whistles started that day, I wanted to sink through the cushy red seat. How could they be so mean to him?

As soon as the concert ended, I rushed backstage to comfort my father, but when I found him in the dressing room he wasn't upset. Instead, he was joking and drinking beer with the other musicians. He took me outside to explain that the turtleneck, beret, and cigarette were called for in the "John-Cage-wannabe" score and that he had to give everything he could to the piece, even though he didn't like it, but it was his job, and he loved his job, which was performing. He also explained that the audience wasn't booing him. German audiences care deeply for music, so they were "booing the pretentious piece of you-know-what."

"If I was out there," my father said, "I would have booed it myself."

3

"The more I see, the less I know for sure."

—John Lennon

Soundtrack: The Beatles, "Nowhere Man," 1965

ON THURSDAY, NOVEMBER 9, 1989, I was in Joe's Bar on Sixth Street in the East Village, staring at the TV mounted over the bar, watching young East and West Berliners swarm around the Brandenburg Gate. Perestroika had loosed communism's grip on the East Bloc, but the Wall remained as both symbol and reality of division and repression. Young and old were taking crowbars and sledgehammers to the Wall, and were at first met by water cannons from the East, but the authorities quickly realized the inevitability of the moment. Germans from both sides danced atop the Wall while kids punched holes through the four-inch-thick concrete, shaking hands with the dazed East German soldiers. Four thousand miles away in Manhattan, I was stunned. The impossible was happening. In the smoky din, I couldn't hear what the exuberant kids on the Wall were yelling, but I felt like they were calling me: *Come home, Rob. Come home.*

I was possessed by what the Germans call *Sehnsucht*, one of those wonderfully untranslatable words that combines longing and nostalgia for a home that one doesn't even know is one's home. English has no precise equivalent, but the Portuguese have *saudade*. My *Sehnsucht*, or *saudade*, was for Berlin, and I could think of nothing else but how to get there. Like the Allied forces in World War II, I needed a plan. If I parachuted right into the heart of Berlin, I wouldn't last a minute. It was too daunting, what with no friendly troops already on the ground; I hadn't lived there in over a dozen years, had no family left there, hardly knew anyone there from when I was young. And my wife, the logical one, would insist that we have some kind of sustainable plan.

My Normandy would be Zambujeira do Mar, a small Portuguese fishing village on the Atlantic coast two hours south of Lisbon. We had stumbled upon it a year and a half before, on our honeymoon. We had flown to Lisbon, driven down the coast, and at the dead end of a six-mile-long dirt road we fell in love with the rugged little town that wasn't even on our map.

The November night the Wall fell, as we walked past the homeless camps in Tompkins Square Park to our tiny apartment on East 8th Street between Avenues B and C, I told Elissa, "I *have* to go there."

"We will, we will," she said. "Soon."

She was imagining a visit. I was envisioning dropping out and living there. But no way was she walking away from her dream job as a reporter at *Spy* magazine. And no way would I want her to. She was surrounded by wickedly clever peers, and her own wicked cleverness was fully embraced. These were her people, and they were paying her to be a wiseass. This tapped one part of her creative self. Her wilder, storytelling self she fed by writing stories, late at night on yellow legal pads and a sticky old Olivetti typewriter. I was freelancing as a writer and factchecker, while also attempting to write fiction, but not with the same intensity as Elissa. We were doing what we had vowed to do together—live for art in the creative capital of the world. We were scraping by with an exuberant, drunken group of writer friends willing to put up with high rents, low pay, and shaky prospects.

I, however, was restless. With steady work and a steady do-
mestic life, I felt like I was locked into the publishing-industrial
complex and marriage. Is this how true artists lived? Even though
I wanted to transform myself as Berlin was transforming itself, I
was resigned to watching Berlin from afar. Then, over the winter,
Spy fell apart. The owners put the magazine up for sale and core
staffers jumped ship. So I once again said, "Let's drop out, let's
live the dream, go to Europe and be expat writers with a capital
W." When she said yes I was surprised, though I shouldn't have
been; we were both besotted with romantic visions of our literary
forebears, from Fitzgerald to Stein to Baldwin, who had run off
to Europe to live large and write novels. So why not us?

Elissa, unlike me, was more than just in love with the
continuum of art. She was really writing and risking herself on
the page. I was dipping my toe in from the riverbank, afraid of
dark waters. I was in love with my ideas, but was afraid to risk, to
fail. I was working on a novel called *Coffee and Absinthe*, which
was about two competing spirits—wild, in-the-moment Coffee
and soulful, dreamy, idealistic Absinthe. These were, naturally,
my two competing spirits—the social one who wanted to live
to the fullest, in the moment, and the artistic one who wanted
to create. I burned with desire to write and read as much as I
could. I would crank out ten handwritten pages a day while
working as a freelance fact-checker and researcher.

At the time I was doing research for the *Spy Who's Who*,
which meant compiling salacious details about *Spy's* favorite
celebrities, so I was reading a dozen celebrity biographies a week,
plus hundreds of gossip-column items on the likes of Michael
Jackson and Donald Trump. It was a paycheck. And morally I
justified this work to myself as part of *Spy's* greater mission to
stick it to the powers that be. I balanced my steady diet of crap

celebrity bios with Greil Marcus's *Lipstick Traces: A Secret History of the Twentieth Century*, in which he connects the Sex Pistols back through the Situationists and Dadaists all the way back to the Gnostic Gospels. I carried *Lipstick Traces* around like a bible, hoping to inoculate myself against the celebrity fluff.

I read hungrily, desperately, and likewise felt insatiable for visual art. I repeatedly dragged Elissa to Gerhard Richter's *October 18, 1977* series at NYU's Grey Art Gallery. Richter's Baader-Meinhof paintings were based on police photos taken in the prison cells of three Red Army Faction leaders who were either murdered or committed joint suicide on the same day. The slightly blurred black-and-white paintings felt realer than real, all the more immediate in the face of the fall of the Wall. I was obsessed with the painting of Andreas Baader's jail-cell record player (what did he listen to in isolation?), while Elissa spent hours in front of the painting of teenage Ulrike Meinhof, the journalist turned Red Army Faction soldier, the good girl who went from reporting on terrorism to being a terrorist. I wanted to be Richter and Marcus, to be at the crossroads of art and politics. Politically engaged art—that's what I was after.

I thought of myself as fearless, but reckless and voyeuristic are not the same as fearless. Elissa was fearless, both in her work and out in the world. I joked that she had a "psycho magnet," that the crazies, the slightly off, the unfiltered, the socially challenged were drawn to her wherever we went. But she never flinched; she always engaged and was fully present with them. While I threw myself into any social situation, could put on any mask—punk, preppy, artist—I also put masks on everyone I met, instantly judging them. I inhabited my masks, adopted the personas. Perhaps it was self-preservation, and stemmed from my itinerant childhood, which had forced me to form friendships quickly, potential allies or foes judged in an instant. Elissa, on the other hand, was open to the universe. While she also had masks, she used them to put others at ease. I marveled at and was frequently jealous and resentful of her willingness to talk, really talk, to anyone.

Even with my limited self-awareness, I was completely confident about Elissa's passion and creativity. It wasn't just that I was in love with her, or that she was the first person to ever challenge and deeply engage me—she once threw her engagement ring at me outside CBGB's after I had ducked an argument (she'd called me an elitist snob after I bit a can of beer at her rich college friend's loft, spraying her immaculate white Shabby-Chic sofa) and we spent an hour digging through the Bowery gutter looking for the modest ring. No, it was obvious that as in real life, in her fiction she would say the things that people were afraid to say out loud. I knew that if we could get away and she had time to write, she would produce miracles.

While a romantic, I wasn't completely delusional—we had saved up three thousand dollars, and I did have a solid lead on work abroad. After I wrote a piece for *Sports Illustrated* about running across the Grand Canyon—North Rim to South Rim in five hours, twenty-three miles with eight thousand feet of elevation drop and gain—my editor there told me that I could do some stringing for them from Portugal, especially about Portuguese track and field stars. Rosa Mota and Carlos Lopes had recently won the Olympic marathons. I'd run track in college and was a student of the sport, so I knew I could do the job.

I told Elissa that we could live in Portugal for nothing. We would work on our Great American Expat Novels and I would do enough stringing to establish myself. As soon as we were set up we would visit Berlin. That's what I said, but in the back of my mind I was hoping that we could find a way to stay in Berlin, that it would welcome me back like a long-lost native son.

How easy it is to upend your life. To restless, heedless me it was nothing. To Elissa, it was everything. While we packed, sweating over which cassettes to include, Sonic Youth or Mudhoney, Elissa kept asking if this was the right thing to do, if we would be safe, if I really could get work overseas, if we'd be able to jump back into the hamster wheel when we returned to New York. "Yes, yes, yes, yes," I would reply, increasingly impatient and annoyed that I would have to worry if she could handle living off the grid. For me, this wasn't a big leap—our fleeing known New York for the uncertainty of life in Europe was within the continuum of leaps I had been making my entire life. What if this adventure failed spectacularly? Oh, well. There would always be other adventures. "Remain true to your art, be open to the world" were two of my mantras. This optimism, this faith that the world would provide for us made me insensitive to the leap Elissa was making. I could intellectually understand why she was nervous, but I had little empathy for her bourgeois, nonartistic attachments and baggage.

4

"If I'm free, it's because I'm always running."

—Jimi Hendrix

Soundtrack: Jimi Hendrix, "Crosstown Traffic," 1968

MY FATHER AND I were regulars at New York Pizza, a Lichterfeld neighborhood bar and pizzeria that catered to American soldiers from the nearby Andrews Barracks. Black-light psychedelic posters on every wall, the jukebox blasting Jimi Hendrix, Cream, Stones, Janis Joplin. We started going there at the end of the summer when my parents split. It was the time of Woodstock and collective hope, but with the flip side of Manson's Helter Skelter murders. Now, months later, Hells Angels had stabbed a kid to death at Altamont with the Rolling Stones onstage. Gimme shelter, indeed.

The nearby tables were filled with clean-cut guys in their late teens and early twenties, many of whom were being cycled in and out of Vietnam. The jukebox pumped out the music of the social revolution and the antiwar movement happening across the ocean. I liked the beat and energy, but didn't know the social significance; the sounds reached me on a primal, cellular level. Mitch Mitchell's unnerving drumming underneath Hendrix's blues wail was vibrant and sloppy and made me want to jump and scream. Basically, it was everything that classical music wasn't. It was a fitting soundtrack to what was the only news that mattered to me—my parents were living apart.

There's a disconnect between my memories of the time and the photographic evidence of the era. I see myself as a kid with the run of concert halls and opera houses. I was the equivalent of Eloise in the Plaza: unsupervised, skedaddling backstage, through the dressing rooms, up into the catwalks, then back down through the set-building shops, oblivious to being at the center of the Cold War and thrilled to be in the wake of my indulgent father. But shortly after we married, I showed Elissa the few photos I have from that time—one where I am clutching a worn-down brown teddy bear and battered book on a beige sofa, another where I am startled next to a thin, undecorated Christmas tree, and one where I am holding and peering through an empty picture frame.

"Jesus, I want to give that poor kid a hug," Elissa said. Through her eyes, it was hard not to see a sad, frightened child. He looks lost, staring past the camera as if there are answers to questions somewhere out there, questions that would haunt him well beyond Berlin.

As my father shuffled our Gothic German playing cards, I wondered, not for the first time, when he or my mother were going to tell me why they had been living apart. But they rarely acknowledged the other's existence. When either of them did, usually during a discussion about the logistics of getting me between homes, something unpleasant and unspoken lurked below the thin façade of civility. Or maybe this was me projecting my desperate need to understand why they were apart. Maybe they had both processed their split and didn't want to talk about it. I, however, did want to talk about it. Yet, at the same time, I was too afraid to ask.

My mother stayed in Berlin for two years after they split, then returned to the states, to New Orleans to get her master's degree at Tulane. This would allow her to teach and to get herself emotionally and financially back together after the separation from my father. I could say that I stayed behind with him, but that would imply volition on my part. You could say my mother left me behind with him, but that would imply blame on my part. I knew nothing of their arrangement except that she disappeared. Her absence was a void, an unexplained vacancy. It was always there, but never acknowledged. Not by my father, and not by me, for fear of driving my father off as well. I felt responsible for her absence. And if she could disappear, so then could my father.

I tapped my feet to "Crosstown Traffic," concentrating on our game of Crazy Eights. Some alchemical mix of Coca-Cola and Hendrix made me blurt out, "Dad, why isn't Mom living with us anymore?" My father looked up from his slice of pizza, a rarely seen flash of anger in his eyes. I flinched. He pursed his lips, then slowly exhaled, regaining his usual Buddha-like calm.

"We couldn't live together anymore," my father said. He paused. I waited for more. "Want another Coke?"

"Sure, Dad." Subject closed. Terrified, I wondered, *Is he mad at me?* I vowed that I would never ask again.

My father went to the bar and came back with a tall Berliner Weisse beer for himself and a tall, curved glass of Coke for me. He shuffled the cards and dealt out another hand. I was trying to be careful with my top-heavy glass of soda, to not spill it like I frequently did. I was a good boy. I'd never give my father an opportunity to ever be mad at me. I was a little adult with impeccable manners and a genius for social camouflage. I was safe with my father. I was safe in Berlin. When I reached for the discard pile I once again knocked the glass over. My father sighed, then helped me clean up the mess. After another trip to the bar, Dad said, "Still your play."

5

"Madame Bovary, c'est moi."

—Gustave Flaubert

"Madame Bovary, c'est moi."

—Rob Spillman

Soundtrack: Erik Satie, *Gnossiennes No. 2,* 1890

WHILE ON THE SUBWAYS in Berlin, my father and I would spot Americans and whisper to each other, *"Die meisten Amerikaner sind . . . ,"* German for "Most Americans are . . . ," and we wouldn't have to finish the sentence. Many, if not most of our countrymen whom we saw on the U-Bahn, were variations of the Ugly American—loud, overweight, oblivious to the intelligence of the natives. They would mock the Germans' dark, neat clothes and their harsh-sounding language, not realizing that almost every German on the train could understand every single word that was being said about them. From my father, I learned how to blend in, to disappear in a crowd. He and I spoke German in these situations and never engaged with or acknowledged our fellow citizens.

6

"It is better to fail in originality than to succeed in imitation."
—Herman Melville

Soundtrack: The B-52s, "Roam," 1989

WE FLEW A RED-EYE to Lisbon, picked up a cheap, tiny Le Car, then drove the two hours down the coast to Zambujeira, its bright white stucco houses perched on the red and purple lava cliffs above the rough ocean. At the Café Atlántico, one of the two tavernas on the square, we asked if there were any apartments to rent. For thirty thousand escudos (less than three hundred dollars) we paid up front for two months in a small house behind the home of a couple that ran the town's newsstand. I negotiated in German, he having been a *Gastarbeiter*—a guest worker—in Emden for two years, where he worked on the last German-made original Beetles before production was moved to Mexico. The low, cool house had its own wine cave and a wild, overgrown garden that you had to cross in order to get to the bathroom, which was in its own tiny house. Food and wine cost pennies. We had actualized our dream: We were off the radar.

Freed from the hamster wheel, we slid into the slow rhythm of the Alentejo region, the poorest region of the poorest Western European country. A morning double espresso in the café, then Elissa would start writing, not leaving her desk for eight or ten straight hours. It was as if a switch had been thrown in her. In

New York only a few close friends knew that she was writing fiction on the side. In Zambi, she gave herself permission to commit.

While she wrote, I would bike or run up the coast, then maybe get in some reading, a little bit of writing. The character of Absinthe felt more tangible in Portugal, there in the land of the Green Faerie, but the urgency to write wasn't as pressing as back in New York—time seemed to expand, so that it felt like I had more of it, and why write when you can live? After applying some brushstrokes to *Coffee and Absinthe*, it would be back to the Café Atlántico for cocktail hour, which was more like cocktail three hours, coinciding with the prolonged sunset: infinite shades of lavender against the lava cliffs, out across the water, and up into the late-afternoon clouds. We ate *caramujos*, tiny sea snails cooked in seawater with olive oil, which we pulled from their shells with straight pins, and washed them down with cold pitchers of crisp Sagres beer, then moved on to the local fish soup with bread in the bottom of the bowl, accompanied by bubbly Vinho Verde.

After sunset we headed to a bar run by a glamorous, worldly Lisbonite named Xica (pronounced *Shee-ka*), where we drank absinthe cut with syrupy passion fruit juice and, along with Andreas, Xica's German boyfriend, stayed past what should have been closing time arguing about Gerhard Richter, Rainer Werner Fassbinder, Nick Cave, and Fernando Pessoa, about what makes an authentic artistic life, about creating timely versus lasting work, about whether art should be political, about how your life could and should be art. Andreas favored interiority while Xica advocated for total engagement, both on and off the page. Elissa said we were pretentious blowhards, that there was no right way.

Miraculously, we were doing what we had set out to do. We were Paul Bowles in Tangiers. We were going to go native, write strange novels, and then our artist friends would make pilgrimages to visit us, to get our blessing. My worry about Elissa being able to handle living off the grid shifted to worrying that she was getting *too* into our new life. When not writing, she read Jane Bowles and Virginia Woolf, and would cry over her copies of *Two Serious Ladies* and *Mrs. Dalloway.* She was open and vulnerable to the universe, her emotional highs and lows amplified in our simplified new life. She fixated on Brownie, one of the village's numerous stray dogs, an old female mutt, splotchy brown with distended teats. "How many litters has that poor dog had?" she would ask nearly every time we saw her. "No, we cannot take her in," I would invariably have to say.

The villagers were weathered and gnarled like the coast itself, with its inhospitable red volcanic cliffs, its hard, choppy waves of icy water that masked deadly riptides. They were mostly fishermen and a few farmers, so it had been surprising to come across Xica and Andreas. But they told us that the area had a long history of sheltering artists, drug dealers, and terrorists. "I knew there was a reason we were drawn here," I told Andreas, who acknowledged my humor in the way of his people—dismissively. "Yes, yes," he said, "but in seriousness, if you see a car with a German shepherd outside, stay away. The drug dealers always have German shepherds. And be careful on your bike if you go up into the hills. There are ex-Baader-Meinhof members hiding on some of the farms."

Few tourists stayed along these cliffs, preferring the glitzy Algarve, with its hotel towers, accessible beaches, and smooth, calm waters. German slackers, on the other hand, found it ideal. It was a twenty-four-hour drive from the Ruhr Valley to the

Alentejo region, and we met several young, hippieish Germans who had figured out how to live in Zambi for six months at a stretch. They would team up, and one would work for half the year as a baker or waiter to qualify for unemployment. He would then take off for Zambi and give his job to his friend, who would ship the unemployment money to his partner in Portugal, the two switching off every six months. The one in Zambi would stretch the unemployment money by living in a room on one of the neighboring farms, none of which had electricity or running water, and only buying food from a farm or the weekly markets.

We befriended several of these professional slackers, including Horst, a beatific, emaciated-looking German with a long, wispy blond beard, who told me his life philosophy, after he drained the last of an absinthe-and-passion-fruit cocktail: "Leave no trace."

I envied Horst and his compatriots, to a point. While I, too, loved being off the grid, I viewed Portugal as our Tangiers, as a staging ground, mental preparation for when we reemerged on the world stage of Berlin. I thought of James Baldwin, retreating to Paris in order to catch his breath and be stronger in his fight against oppression back home. I wanted to stomp the earth and leave giant footprints. What is the point of living if you don't leave your mark?

7

"I am not a myth."

—Marlene Dietrich

Soundtrack: Marlene Dietrich, "Where Have All the Flowers Gone?," 1962

BOTH OF MY PARENTS decided they were going to be professional musicians at the age of four. I was not so blessed. Or cursed. Like most sons, I wanted to be like my father. But the desire to be a pianist like him was not met with the desire or discipline to sit down at the piano to bash through countless repetitions of Czerny and Hanon exercises. My father didn't push me, telling me that in time I would find what gave me joy.

My impatience with the piano didn't, however, deter me from being enthralled by the production of the art. I loved to watch it all happen, from practice to dress rehearsal to performance and finally to the payment rituals. In the European classical music world, the link between patron and artist was still direct. "Singing for your supper" was literal. After my father's performances in European concert halls, it was tradition for the patrons to have a dinner for him and the other talent, usually in a grand room backstage. I would sometimes fall asleep during these tedious dinners, but I remember one late night in particular, when I was six, after a performance of Franz Schubert's *Winterreise* by my father and the singer he accompanied, Barry

McDaniel. They were making their name as American masters of the classic German song form—lieder. The patrons, as usual, paid the performers in cash. For the first time I was close enough to see how much they were paid. My father received ten 100 blue-eagle Deutsche Mark notes ($275, or the equivalent of $1,275 today). Barry received forty notes. That night, I was certain I wanted to be a singer.

But more than that, it was the first time I put together that my father and Barry were receiving money for doing what they loved. They felt passionate about these German Romantic poems set to song, and had dedicated themselves to mastering the form, to proving that non-Germans could not only interpret, but inhabit these emotional song cycles. Backstage, it struck me full force—my father was living for art. I couldn't image anything more romantic and ideal. I still can't.

8

"All men dream: but not equally. Those who dream by night in the dusty recesses of their minds wake in the day to find that it was vanity. But the dreamers of the day are dangerous men, for they may act on their dreams with open eyes, to make it possible."

—T. E. Lawrence

Soundtrack: Everly Brothers, "All I Have to Do Is Dream," 1958

BEREA, KENTUCKY, 1939. My three-year-old father is stacking blocks while his mother plonks out a tune on the old family upright piano. Distracted by her two older boys' squabbling, she investigates and when she comes back to the piano and reopens the score she jokingly asks my father, "Where was I?" Without hesitation he gets up and points to the exact note on the page.

Zeigler, Illinois, 1952. Driving on a dusty road back from church, my fifteen-year-old mother asks, "When can I drive?" Her brother, Jerry, age sixteen, has recently been allowed to get behind the wheel of the family car. My grandfather, who runs the town's garage, pulls over, gets out, and says, "You want to drive? Then drive." He orders my mother behind the wheel and gives her no further instructions. Both of her parents are taciturn Scots. Their first pregnancy ended with a stillborn child, which, my mother says, must have hardened their already flinty souls.

They sit by a field of withered corn, my mother shamefacedly jamming the gears and flooring the gas, her brother not daring to offer any help. Her parents, grim and silent, watch her struggle.

My parents rarely spoke of their childhoods, and whenever they let loose some scrap of information, I added it to the other fragments, constructing an incomplete mosaic, the missing tiles as fascinating to me as the filled-in images.

When I was thirteen, my father and I drove to a nursing home in the Tennessee hills to meet his high school piano teacher, Miss Consella. She was tiny up against my bearish father, whom she hugged fiercely on seeing. Though bent and shrunken, she was a whirlwind of energy and insisted that she drive us to her favorite diner, even though she could barely see over the steering wheel of her giant green Oldsmobile. In the diner all the truckers called out, "Howdy, Miss C." It was obvious why she had been such a big influence on my father—besides being a brilliant teacher, she was warm and encouraging and funny. His mother, on the other hand, had been withholding and moody. She was always in slight pain from when a drunk driver crashed into their car when she was pregnant with him (she would ban alcohol in her house from that moment on). At the hospital, everyone was worried she might lose her baby, and she was so grateful to them for saving her son that she named my father for the two doctors who delivered him—Robert Armstrong. Even though he was born healthy, the doctors were worried about his future, since trauma in the womb was thought to sometimes later cause "deviancy."

Still, my grandmother recognized her son's talent and gave him the opportunity to realize it. Miss C., however, guided him, going so far as to bring a Ouija board to his house to determine his fate. In front of his scowling mother, she asked what my father was going to be. The answer came up "Composer." Like me, he was a good kid, the kind who saved all of his allowance and U.S. Savings Bonds so that he could buy the family a real grand piano. At age sixteen, he got a scholarship to the Eastman School of Music in Rochester, New York, and he rarely looked back.

In his senior year at Eastman he met my mother, a freshman from Zeigler, a crumbling town in southern Illinois surrounded by a depressed patchwork of family farms and spent coal mines. She had once more followed her brother, now a junior at Eastman. A musical prodigy, from an early age Jerry was showered with praise and lessons. And then so was my mother, on whom her parents spared no expense getting her lessons and driving her to performances and competitions. When I gave up on the piano, she said it was just as well since if it hadn't come easy, it probably never would. She told me that when she first took it up "I'd walk to my teacher's house, which was only three blocks away, and I could learn the week's lesson while walking and reading the scores."

At their church, the charismatic choir leader fitted my mother and uncle with angel wings and put them in the balcony to sing during funerals. Soon they were performing all over southern Illinois. She won her first singing competition when she was in fifth grade. For the winners' concert, she bought a pretty yellow dress and black patent Mary Janes. She desperately wanted to wear nylons, but her mother insisted on bare legs and frilly yellow anklets. My mother felt exhilarated to be singing "The Wind's in the South" in front of such a huge audience, but also humiliated at being dressed like a five-year-old. At least she got to wear the Mary Janes. For most performances, my grandmother crammed my mother's feet into tight, pointed dress shoes; as an adult she would have to have surgery to correct her crushed, twisted toes.

For my parents, music was a journey and a destination. Music allowed my parents to escape *toward* something. Their stories of determination, drive, and single-minded focus formed the stark background to my opposite childhood of indecision, lethargy, and scattered focus. I didn't know what I wanted to do at age four, or eight, not to mention thirteen or sixteen. My father was on constant alert for signs of a calling. When I played tennis with him and nailed a forehand winner, he arranged for tennis lessons, hoping that this would be like the fateful moment when he'd found the right note in his mother's score. When I started enjoying mini-golf, golf lessons followed. When I started reading, he gave me money for books. If I liked an author, he had ten recommendations for similar ones. While I enjoyed tennis and golf, and especially reading, I felt like I was letting my father down. Where was my spark? Where was my *thing*?

My mother, on the other hand, was dismayed by my meager, unenthusiastic piano-playing, grimacing through each of my mirthless lessons, and had no idea how to handle my easily changeable enthusiasms. She would encourage, but in generalities, like, "You're so smart and quick, you need to get serious." To which I would think, *About what?* Or, "You should apply yourself." *To what?* "You need to have a life that matters." *To whom?*

9

"The truth doesn't have to do with cruelty, the truth has to do with mercy."

—Ken Kesey

Soundtrack: Bob Dylan, "Like a Rolling Stone," 1965

MUCH OF MY CHILDHOOD was spent playing quietly under pianos while my father practiced and accompanied or coached singers. As long as I was invisible and silent, I could stay in the safety of his sonic cocoon, the vibrations of the piano strings rumbling through my chest, a soothing sensation that would sometimes deepen with the rumbling of nearby tanks. The spartan apartment where my father and I lived was across the street from a giant U.S. Army base. At least once a week, piercing sirens would rouse me out of bed and to the window, where my father and I would watch the entire base scramble into full combat readiness, column after column of soldiers marching around the base. On the other side of the Wall, just a mile from us, Russian soldiers were also marching in formation, their movements reported in the morning papers.

Born in 1964, the year of *Dr. Strangelove*, I was a child of the Cold War, living in the epicenter, a city two hundred miles behind the Iron Curtain. During the weekly "duck and cover" drills at the John F. Kennedy School, our teachers would remind us, "Flying glass will rip you to pieces, so make sure you are completely under your desks, curled as low as you can go."

While we played in the gravel yard, B-52s flew low overhead, their huge bombs hanging from the wings like distended water balloons, looking so heavy I wondered how they didn't drag the big planes down. The halls hummed with the constant low-level buzz of the Cold War. Many of my classmates were the sons and daughters of officers. They were exotic to me—neat and tidy like their uniformed parents, most with a mother and father at home, their mothers packing them lunches and picking them up in cars.

For fun at recess we had rock fights in the playground. A group of kids would climb onto a cement shed that was covered with gravel; the kids on the roof were "snipers" and the kids below "civilians." An ex–marine sniper had shot forty-seven people from the University of Texas Tower in 1966, and the memory of this horror still lingered in the military community. In our game, the snipers would rain rocks down on the unsuspecting civilians, who would then try to brave the onslaught and storm the roof, where they would roughly "apprehend" and "subdue" the snipers. Like most of the kids, I loved this daily ritual and threw myself into my role, working myself into an indignant rage while pinging the poor riotous sods below me. The snipers were always greatly outnumbered and doomed. I always chose to be a sniper.

I can recall only one classmate with any clarity, a nice enough kid in my grade whom I played soccer with. But I remember him mainly because of his name—Bobby Fischer. At the time, another Bobby Fischer was the world's greatest chess player, and was engaged in epic Cold War battles with Boris Spassky, a humorless Russian who was the embodiment of Soviet-style communism. My classmate Bobby Fischer didn't play chess. No kid wanted to sit across a chessboard from me, as I would always mercilessly destroy them. My father had taught me how to play when I was five, but stopped playing when I started to beat him. He had only a basic knowledge of the game, and I took it much more seriously, even at that age. I wished that he had kept playing with me, but he practically lived at his piano.

After the school bus dropped me off at home, I played soccer with the Turkish kids at the *Gastarbeiter* complex down the street, then my father would pick me up and we'd go to a rehearsal space or concert hall, where chess became a bridge to his world. I played backstage against singers and stagehands, divas and queens. There were seldom other kids around, but I didn't think much about not having friends my own age.

I also played chess at the American church where, on Sundays, my father played the organ and led the youth choir. Through the church we became friends with a number of soldiers and attended Presbyterian cookouts with GIs, complete with hot dogs and softball. Compared with the flamboyantly dressed artists whom my father worked and hung out with, the soldiers, and Americans in general, were otherworldly and of another time, as if they had stepped out of a Norman Rockwell painting. I found their exaggerated masculinity and reserve comical in comparison to the feminine, emotive men I was used to.

Yet the church and the army base's PX were the closest I came to "real" U.S. culture. After my mom left, we went to the PX to watch movies and eat burgers and fries. The first time I went with my father, as the two of us walked through the middle of the PX's huge dining room, filled with officers and their wives and girlfriends, I was just learning how to whistle, or at least had the hint of a whistle on my lips, and was working on it as we walked to our table. I blew and blew and blew and nothing was coming out, when suddenly I hit it—the culmination of weeks of practice and struggle, a full-on wolf whistle, loud and clear, two notes in succession. There was laughter all around, and a beautiful officer's wife in front of me said, "Thank you," while her husband winked conspiratorially at my father. I didn't understand why everyone was smiling at me, but I basked in the attention.

Whenever the base's sirens signaled the entire brigade into formation, my father and I would lean out the window to see if we could spot our church friend Tommy in the mass of camouflage-clad soldiers. We never could—there were simply too many men, and from a distance they all blended together, unlike when we were up close at the pizza place or at the PX.

The PX movies were meant for soldiers, not children, so I missed the entire Disney oeuvre, and instead saw *Easy Rider, The Graduate,* and *Five Easy Pieces.* At age seven, I was intoxicated by the lush forests of Oregon that saturated *Sometimes a Great Notion,* directed by Paul Newman and based on Ken Kesey's novel, which would become, many years later, one of my favorite books. The walls of green were so unlike Berlin's concrete gray island, and the romantic ruggedness of the central family was captivating in ways I couldn't fully fathom. Near the end of the movie, Henry Fonda's severed arm is mounted on top of the family boat with the middle finger saluting the town. I loudly asked what it meant, and the soldiers around us cracked up. "It's the sign of defiance," my father calmly whispered. I didn't quite get it, but the notion of defiance became wrapped up in Oregon; freedom resided in its dense, wooded river valleys.

Despite the tanks, soldiers, and drills, I felt safe with my father. I was, however, unsettled when we ventured into the East, that oppressively drab landscape scarred with barbed wire and German shepherds and stoic soldiers. I was too young to fully understand exactly how real the danger was, but the menace was palpable.

The adults' fear became much more pronounced during the Prague Spring of 1968, when local newspapers blared headlines warning that Russian troops once again would seal off West Berlin, as had happened at the end of World War II. While my father and his friends talked about what to do if there was a second Berlin Airlift, I only understood that there was an increased urgency in their discussions about "adult" subjects and that they were impatient or worse when Barry blithely declared, "Make mine a double," when everyone else was talking about going to either the airport or the army base. My father later told me that when Russian troops drove into Prague and crushed the protesters, our soldier friend Tommy called him and said, "If I call again, hang up and go to the airport. Don't pack. Just grab Robby and get out." My father quickly and coolly packed a few things, but Tommy didn't call back.

While the Cold War raged, creative Berlin was oblivious. The show must go on. And on. Like previous cultural Meccas, Berlin in the sixties sent out a call like a dog whistle that could be heard only by artists. The spire of the bombed-out *Gedächtniskirche*—the Remembrance Church—beckoned: *Come join us, you gay Brazilian dancers, you French painters, you Spanish composers; bring us your Mexican folksingers, your Turkish guest workers turned sculptors, your Japanese noise artists, your Kentucky pianists—you are all welcome here in Berlin.*

10

"I is another."

—Rimbaud

Soundtrack: Sonic Youth, "Schizophrenia," 1987

ZAMBUJEIRA WITH ELISSA was everything I wanted. We wrote. Elissa much more feverishly than I. But more important, we loved the place and the people, and we loved ourselves as a couple within this culture. For pennies, we bought rounds of hard goat cheese and the crusty bread that we could smell baking in the middle of the night only a few doors down from us. We ate big bowls of soup with potatoes and fennel and fish heads, courtesy of the town's fishermen, who went out to sea at night and then hit the bars at 8 A.M. We explored the coast, the desolate marshes and dunes, the cork and olive farms inland, sometimes spotting shadowy figures who were letting rooms on the nearby farms. There were moments when I felt more alive than I had ever felt before, and never more present than I was with Elissa. This is what life with her could be, should be.

Yet. Yet I was still restless. I was feeling less like Paul Bowles and more like Jack Torrance in *The Shining*. I hadn't done any stringing work. I had left a message on the answering machine of Portuguese marathoner Rosa Mota, who was spending the summer in Lisbon, saying that I would try her in a few days. I did, once, but again no one was home. I told myself I'd call in a week. A big international track meet in Berlin was happening mid-August, six weeks off, but we hadn't made concrete plans about when we would drive there. I hadn't broached the possibility of staying in Berlin longer than the week we had originally talked about.

Zambujeira was scenic, quiet, and cheap, a place to produce Great Art. However, I was beginning to have fears that it was *too* perfect. I couldn't help think about Frank Conroy menacingly writing at the opening of *Stop-Time,* "Life was good, conditions were perfect for my work." I also thought of the king of expat American writers, Hemingway, who once retreated to a quiet, isolated cabin in the mountains of Switzerland and when he got there wrote to a friend, "I have everything I need to write except everything that I need to write."

Once again I distrusted happiness, mistaking it for complacency. This unease was fueled by the barely repressed certainty that the novel I was working on had more intellect than heart. Instead of searching for my heart, I focused on everything that annoyed me. Elissa was the only native English speaker I'd spoken to for weeks. The few tapes we had brought with us were slightly stretched, and I knew every hiss and fuzz of Sonic Youth's *Daydream Nation.* And I was already tired of Andreas and Xica and their perfect little bar overlooking the relentless waves.

But I was not tired of their absinthe, which we downed night after night. I turned to the Green Faerie for answers. Muse to van Gogh, Toulouse-Lautrec, Picasso, Jarry, Wilde, in the late nineteenth century absinthe was as popular as wine in France, especially in Paris, and especially with artists. During the Jazz Age it was outlawed in most countries, because of its addictive properties and because of several high-profile murder cases in which the defendants used the "absinthe defense." In Portugal, however, the Green Faerie had never been banned. Besides its high alcohol content, absinthe gets an added kick from distilled wormwood, the herb that lined the path out of the Garden of Eden. The Russian word for wormwood is *Chernobyl.*

Legend has it that absinthe is what drove van Gogh mad, triggering seizures, although some have speculated that van Gogh might have already had temporal lobe epilepsy, which Elissa has as well, and absinthe has been found to exacerbate seizure tendencies. This we wouldn't find out until much later. For Elissa, each absinthe cocktail packed the neurological bomb a little tighter, but the fuse was long and we'd be in Berlin when it blew.

Xica knew what we wanted, and when we'd walk into her bar she'd pull down the old stone bottle from the top shelf. The very first time she poured us shots of the white bootleg absinthe, we were expecting a flowery anise taste, but we were shocked by the raw ethanol flavor. Xica mixed the absinthe with passion fruit juice, the viscous, pulpy, purple liquid obliterating the burn and masking the harsh aftertaste. Soon, Xica's bright lights were ringed with a yellowy haze. My legs twitched as if they were ready to go for a long run, yet when I stood, my leg muscles fired out of sequence and I had to steady myself on the bar. The absinthe effect is a little like mescaline, speedy and mildly hallucinogenic. Everything glows, warm and iridescent. The whole spectrum subtly shifts to the yellow. The Portuguese moon shimmered as if shining through an ancient lace curtain.

Absinthe could also bring out the maudlin. One late night, as we clung to each other on the way home, I pretentiously mused that if I was, indeed, a modern-day Paul Bowles, where was our Ginsburg, our Burroughs? Then I remembered—Eddie, Pete, and the rest of our crew were still in New York. They had jobs, jobs they needed to keep to be around other artists who were also busy scraping by trying to live in New York. This was precisely the ouroboros that we had fled.

Our friend Hank, however, had no such attachments. A painter living in Cincinnati, he wasn't caught in the New York circular hell of subsistence living, and he had never been to Europe. He planned to join us for a week before he went off on a Eurail Pass. His itinerary included cathedrals and Dresden and Prague, a Formula 1 race in Lisbon, and later a brief overlap with us in Berlin. With Hank due to arrive any day, my Berlin countdown clock clicked on.

We had met Hank in Aspen three summers before, at Pour La France, the restaurant where I was waiting tables. Hard to miss at six foot five inches under a military buzz cut, his caramel Carhartt work jacket flecked with paint, he drank cup after cup of coffee while hunched over *Gravity's Rainbow*. He never looked up when I stopped by his table, silently filling his cup, then asking if he needed anything else. "Nope," he said each time. Artists never passed through Aspen, the home of the rich and shallow, so on the fifth refill, I asked if he had gotten to the harmonica scene yet. That night he showed Elissa and me pictures of his paintings, large, stark canvases of trucks and tools and cups of coffee that contained galaxies, Midwestern realism that was also eerie and enigmatic.

Every night for the next month we had intense coffee-and-alcohol-fueled conversations about art, with amplified emotions you feel only in your twenties, when you are wildly changeable even as your artistic opinions are set in stone—Hank arguing that artists were owed a living wage by society, Elissa that society owed us nothing. Hank was full of absolutes, pronouncements like "Art has no utility" and "Warhol is irrelevant." For him, logic ruled, and he had a mathematical life formula by which happiness was achieved through a perfect balance of comfort and adventure and creation. These could be measured with points, and when one was out of balance, he would say, "I have too many comfort points. I need some adventure points." He and Elissa bonded over knives, both collecting them at thrift stores and flea markets. He had worked for his father in the antiques business, but his dad had died young, and now Hank got by with the odd carpentry or handyman gig.

Here was our Cassady. *Though I wondered, If he's Cassady, which one of us is Kerouac?* But it didn't matter, as everything the three of us did together glowed with importance. Hank said that he was only passing through Aspen, but after meeting us he stayed, finding a preposterous job with Frozen Moments, which made statues out of banal everyday food and drinks—a bottle of beer pouring into a mug, a fork suspended forever in a twirl of spaghetti over a bowl of pasta and meatballs. Like Elissa, Hank attracted the absurd and sublime.

Two weeks after we met, while hiking around the Grottos, a series of ice caves up-valley from Aspen, we came upon a worn black leather boot sitting in the middle of the trail like it was waiting for us. Taped to the inside of the boot was a piece of lined notebook paper wrapped in a clear plastic bag. On the paper three affirmations were written in neat, block letters:

1. I am good with old people
2. I am good at art
3. I am learning

We embraced the second two affirmations. "I am good at art, I am learning" became the final words to any argument, the punch line of any joke, and our collective mantra.

11

"All I can do is be me, whoever that is."

—Bob Dylan

Soundtrack: Bob Dylan, "Blowin' in the Wind," 1963

HANK ARRIVED IN ZAMBUJEIRA exactly when his postcard said he would. Despite all of the writing we were getting done, we were ready to share our new paradise. Hank found a room on a nearby farm for five hundred escudos a day (around $3) and was determined to max out his week with us. At first light, he was perched on the cliffs, sketching. Afternoons, while Elissa wrote, he and I ranged farther and farther up or down the coast, strange new villages emerging out of the rugged lava cliffs. We'd come back at twilight, Elissa still at her desk, surprised that so much time had passed. After snails and beer, then soup and Vinho Verde, the three of us sucked down absinthe after absinthe at Xica's bar, she and Andreas welcoming our opinionated artistic friend. When we talked about our plans for the coming month, I wished that Elissa were more excited about our impending trip up to Berlin. Even as I thought this, I knew that I was projecting my own anxieties. She kept reassuring me that whenever I was ready to get in Dusty, our beat-up, red-sand-encased Le Car, she was game.

She wasn't, however, so sanguine about my still not doing anything to get stringing work. At the end of Hank's fifth day with us, after we'd stumbled back to our cool, cavelike apartment,

Elissa asked, "Have you set up a press pass for the Berlin track meet?"

"I'm on it," I said, but before she could press further I pulled off her Smiths T-shirt. I also hadn't bothered to follow up on the possible interview with Rosa Mota, or looked into getting press passes to the Lisbon Grand Prix. We spent little money, so I felt no urgency. Of course, Berlin would be much more expensive, but I reasoned there were more sporting events to cover, plus the chance to write about the aftermath of the Wall's fall and the pending reunification of the two countries, scheduled for the third of October. After a day of biking along the crumbling cliffs, then swimming in and out of riptides, then luxuriating in our two- or three-hour dinner that blended into blurry bar time, and finally sleeping with Elissa, the very idea of "work" was ridiculous. Finding a means to keep us in Europe I filed in my mental "I'll deal with that mundane crap when I have to" folder. Besides, Hank, with his limited funds, had only two days left with us before he needed to buy his three-week Eurail Pass. Then we'd have to fix a date to meet in Berlin and pray that Dusty could make the two-thousand-mile drive.

12

"Imagination creates reality."

—Richard Wagner

Soundtrack: Igor Stravinsky, *The Rite of Spring*, 1913

THE SUMMER OF 1972, I watched TV for the first time. The Munich Olympics were broadcast around the clock and I loved its opera-worthy spectacle and drama. Before then, I didn't care for German educational programs, nor the news, which was dominated by the Vietnam War, and where I caught glimpses of soldiers crawling on their bellies through the jungle, a naked girl running from her napalmed village, a pile of dead Vietnamese women and children on a dirt road. I didn't completely make the connection between the soldiers at the PX and the soldiers slogging through the rice paddies on TV. The two worlds came together only once, when my father let a GI, his Vietnamese wife, and their half-Vietnamese daughter stay with us for a week while they sorted out army housing. But the girl was two years younger than me and I learned nothing about what it was like being in a war zone. Instead, I taught her how to play Monopoly and she taught me how ketchup made everything, including eggs, taste better.

The war felt like a performance happening far away from the safety of Berlin. Then the Olympic images switched from sprinters to masked Palestinian gunmen with Kalashnikov rifles peering out from the balcony of the Israeli athletes' Olympic

Village apartment. Munich, not Berlin—but still, in my country. The images were everywhere; the standoff stopped the entire nation—we all had to look.

What I didn't know was that the hostage-taking was a global and national convergence of pressures: The Palestinians, calling themselves the Black September group, were given intelligence by local neo-Nazis, and once they had seized the hostages, the gunmen demanded the release of Palestinian prisoners in Israel, as well as the freeing of Andreas Baader and Ulrike Meinhof, the leaders of the Red Army Faction, who the year before had spent time training at a Fatah camp in Jordan, and who had recently been captured and were being held in the heavily fortified Stammheim Prison in Stuttgart.

What I did know was that the entire ordeal, culminating in the failed, fatal rescue attempt during which all eleven of the kidnapped Israelis were killed, was a cause for deep national shame from which every German wanted to hide but couldn't look away. The past generation's sins were supposed to be cleansed by the Olympics, happy Technicolor images of world unity and multiculturalism to replace the iconic black-and-white Aryan fantasia of the 1936 Berlin Olympics as filmed by Leni Riefenstahl. But with the taking of the Israeli athletes, other iconic images of strife and terror replaced the Nazi propaganda, ushering in a new wave of collective guilt. I, too, felt shame, but it wasn't totally mine. I was embarrassed for my German friends, and didn't know what to say to them. But I was also angry and afraid: Could my father stop kidnappers if they came for us?

I was also conflicted and confused. Nearly eight, I saw the world as not black-and-white, but gray, a fluid experience. I didn't think of myself as American or German, but as a little of both. I didn't speak only German or only English, but used

whatever words worked best for the situation. This had exasperated my Teutonic German kindergarten teachers. Aside from
their judgmental glares, this wasn't much of a problem for me,
except when I confused the German words for sink (*Spüle*) and
toilet (*Spülklosett*). I complained to my teacher that my stomach
hurt, and I did as I thought she told me—threw up in the school
sink, instead of the toilet, to loud and embarrassing protests.

My mashing of languages lessened somewhat as I went
through first, second, and third grades at the JFK School. But I
doubted I could ever match my father's command of German,
which he needed to get jobs and also to fully understand lieder.
For him the language was a tool, another means to further his
art, which was his life. He didn't Germanicize like his artistic
partner, Barry, who had bought a big house by the Schlachtensee
and had tacked on a German inflection to his English. My father
did, however, adopt the German love for *Spazierengehen* (literally
"going for a stroll"; yet, like most things German, there is no
such thing as a "stroll" but more like a "walk with purpose that
is supposed to be good for you"). When we visited Barry, we
would *Spazierengehen* around the Schlachtensee on the edge of
the huge, wooded Grunewald. As I struggled to keep up with
their determined strides, I forgot that the forest was part of an
island ringed with concrete and guard towers and gun turrets.

This reality came back into focus whenever my father performed outside of Berlin, which happened a few times a month.
Leaving Berlin, the train stopped at the border of East Germany
and West Berlin, then at the border of East Germany and West
Germany proper. Out the window I'd see kids my own age
and wonder how scary it was to live behind walls and barbed
wire, scowling men with guns everywhere. After the Olympic
massacre, Eastern soldiers terrified me, the Kalashnikovs of

the Palestinians no different from the East German or Russian Kalashnikovs.

On our first train trip after the Olympics, my father tried to reassure me that nothing had changed. I nodded, but held tight to his arm as the East German soldiers entered our train car at the first crossing. As usual, they held back straining German shepherds and blinded us with their long, black flashlights, looking under our seats and above, in the luggage rack, while outside other soldiers swarmed, searching above and below for stowaways. "It's okay," my father kept saying. "They aren't going to hurt us, we've done nothing wrong." Neither had the Israeli athletes. I wasn't worried about them hurting us; I was worried that they'd take my father away.

But the soldiers didn't care about us and the train moved on, through the corridor connecting East to West, past tall metal fences, the tops laced with thick coils of barbed wire. If you tried to escape the East and happened to make it past the machine gunners in the guard towers and over the fence, you would be impaled by six-inch metal spikes welded to metal plates that lined the ground between the fences. Still, every few months an East German would make a suicidal break for the West. As I clung to my father, I wondered what it must be like to feel that desperate.

13

"That's what my life is, writing songs."

—John Cale

Soundtrack: John Cale, "Fear Is a Man's Best Friend," 1974

AGE EIGHT, with my father walking across the border at Checkpoint Charlie, my mouth dry, hands damp, a wad of contraband U.S. dollars hot against the sole of my left foot. It was illegal to bring Western currency into East Berlin, but my father assured me that the border police never searched kids. We walked past the U.S. soldiers on the western side of the small metal bridge, me avoiding eye contact, and then we were in between the double rows of concrete Berliners call No-Man's-Land. On the eastern side we slid our passports and twenty-five West German marks into a drawer that disappeared into a glass-partitioned booth manned by East German soldiers.

To venture from West to East Berlin you had to exchange your West German marks for East German marks, one for one, despite the fact that the East German mark was worth one one-thousandth of a West German mark on the official currency exchange. The minimum exchange was twenty-five marks, the equivalent of only ten or fifteen U.S. dollars, but still a sizable amount for a struggling musician with a kid in tow. But my father loved the adventure, and the smuggled dollars would go far at the Prenzlauer Berg sheet-music shop, which was his reason for this excursion.

The sour-faced East German soldiers glowered at us and
then at our passports. Although we had done this trip many
times, I could still taste the salty butter of my breakfast roll. *What
if the soldiers keep our passports?* A Western passport was worth
insane sums of money on the black market; it was a one-way
ticket out. *What if they search me? Find the money in my sock?
Will they take me away? Separate me from Dad?*

Just when I thought I would faint from not breathing,
the soldiers slid the passports back, along with wrinkled brown
and green East German bills, adorned with harsh-looking hammers and compasses. Through a set of black metal doors that
Easterners were forbidden to exit, we were let out into the drab
world of East Berlin. No matter how many times we had gone
through, I was always shocked by the wall of gray.

Gray is to Berliners what white is to Eskimos and red is
to the Maori. The Maori have names for one hundred different
shades of red; the Eskimos define seventeen distinct shades of
white. Growing up in Berlin, you tuned in to the nearly infinite
gradations of gray—the hard steely gray of the February sky, the
softer, swirlier orange-tinged gray of the low summer clouds, the
light sooty gray of the granite buildings in the West, the darker,
duller gray of the Eastern granite buildings pockmarked with
twenty-five-year-old machine-gun fire, the brownish gray of the
cobblestones, the iron gray of the tram tracks, and of course, the
gray concrete slabs that ringed West Berlin—the Wall, which
closed around the city like a noose.

I resisted the urge to grab my father's hand, afraid to draw
any attention to myself as we walked past official buildings
leached of color. Soon we were on the backstreets of Prenzlauer
Berg, and although there were no uniformed men visible, none

of the ordinary men, women, and even children, all dressed in dull, overwashed pants and shirts, would meet our eyes.

"Why won't they look at us?" I asked.

My father leaned down closer to me. *"Bitte?"* he said.

I repeated myself, and he straightened back up and we kept walking. After a half block he gave me a quick look to check on me, and I guessed that he was gauging how much I needed to know, how truthful he needed to be. After another half block he finally said, "There are secret police everywhere. If anyone talks to us they can be reported to Stasi."

"And what happens to them?"

"They could wind up in jail."

"Are they watching us?" I asked.

My father nodded, and after I grabbed his hand he added, "Don't worry, kiddo. They don't care about us. I won't let anything happen to you."

Down several side streets, my father found the sheet music store, which impressed me, as it didn't have a sign and looked like any other doorway on the old residential block. The window-sills, however, were covered with piles of musical scores. When we went inside, an elderly man with chunky square glasses was startled, then said, *"Yah, yah, yah,"* upon recognizing my father. The white-haired man patted my head as I reached into my sock for the dollars, and he and my father animatedly talked about Shostakovich and Schumann, then laughed as my father counted out the fifteen illicit U.S. dollars for the brown paper bag full of state-subsidized and politically appropriate sheet music. I, too, felt the rush of risk, terrified that Stasi would burst through the door, though I kept my face impassive, acting like any other eight-year-old shopping with his father.

After the owner patted my father on the back, we made our way through the cobbled, narrow streets to the wide-open Alexanderplatz, a vast parade ground ringed with spectacularly ugly Soviet-style office buildings built in the sixties. Looming over the showcase for all of East Germany's power and glory was a huge TV tower, on top of which was a glass ball that caught the sun in two bands of white light, one vertical, one horizontal, forming what appeared to be a solar Christian cross.

"'The Pope's Revenge,'" my father said. "That's what people call it."

I looked around to see if anyone was within earshot.

"They've tried reengineering it to take away the cross, but can't figure it out," my father said.

I suppressed a laugh. I'd thought of God as the infallible, terminally dull do-gooder as presented by the West Berlin Presbyterian Church. But what if God was actually a sick cosmic joker?

In the square, kids a little older than myself were playing soccer, using their brown school bags as goalposts. It seemed impossible in the shadows of these oppressive buildings. But then it didn't—they were kids, doing what kids do.

"You hungry?" my father asked.

"Not really," I said, and stared at the bag of music.

"We need to spend the East German money," my father said, steering me toward the TV tower. Below, wedged between the bureaucratic buildings near what was called a "shopping center," though there wasn't much to shop for, my father led me into a hotel that housed visiting dignitaries and had what passed for a "fancy" restaurant. There were few public restaurants in the East, and they offered stringy meat of suspicious origin, along with withered potatoes, but in the hotel restaurant you were served marginally better meat and a blasted, unidentifiable green vegetable for what was a month's wages for the average Easterner. A meal for me and my father would cost about eight dollars. Even after my father left a big tip, we still had a handful of useless GDR currency.

On our way from Alexanderplatz to the eastern side of Checkpoint Charlie, even though I usually had trouble keeping up with him, I silently urged my father to walk faster, especially as we neared the World War II Soviet monument to "Victims of Fascism and Militarism," an open black granite structure with an eternal flame and two Soviet soldiers posted out front. They were like the Westminster guards in my father's favorite city, London. The Soviet soldiers were frozen at attention, Kalashnikovs with fixed bayonets at the ready. Yet unlike the British guards, with their implacable expressions and fixed stares, the young Russian soldiers were hard-looking teenagers who stared back at us, openly curious and hostile. I sped up as we passed, sure that they could tell that I still had a few U.S. dollars in my sock. I anticipated the cold hand on the back of my neck, positive that they were going to chase and catch me.

Back at our apartment, I lingered in that fear, that furtive thrill. I had cheated a deathly force.

I came to crave this danger, savored it as much as my seemingly inexplicable survival. I never wanted anything more than this feeling of jumping into a dark abyss and not knowing if I would be able to escape—but quietly, the desire so surreptitious you'd never, ever know that about me.

14

"Sometimes I am two people. Johnny is the nice one. Cash causes all the trouble. They fight."

—Johnny Cash

Soundtrack: Johnny Cash, "I Walk the Line," 1956

AFTER A WEEK of steady drinking, I was ready to dry out and get back to the novel in earnest.

"You're good at art, and you're learning," I told Hank over a breakfast of espressos and fish croquettes, "but are you ready for Dresden?"

"Hell yeah," he said. "Billy Pilgrim territory. I can't wait to sketch the cathedrals, you know?"

"As your lawyer, I advise you to let me give you a lift up to Lisbon."

"I'm going to pack things up, finish some of the barn sketches. I'll be ready tomorrow."

"Excellent. I'm picking up Elissa's friend at the airport in ten days, and I don't want to have to make two trips close together."

"Got it, Chief. I'll get it together as fast as possible."

Before dinner, I relayed the news to Elissa, who said, "I'm going to miss our MacGyver. Who's going to fix things around here? Sharpen our knives?"

"And it'll be back to pidgin English until Fiona gets here."

In light of Hank's pending departure, we hit the absinthe hard over the next few days, which brought out a case of the maudlins. We had bonded with Hank over our shared love of history, but increasingly this love of artistic history took over his blood like minerals leaching into a dead tree, and in this ossified state he couldn't picture himself outside of history. It was as if he already existed in sepia. And absinthe tended to bring out the worst of this trait. Toward closing, Hank waxed future historical nostalgic, asking us, "I wonder what the postcards of us will look like?"

"Dogs playing cards," Elissa said.

"Hang in there, kitty," I ventured.

Hank's reluctant smile was absinthe-delayed. He really did believe that he was destined for a postcard, like those famous pictures of Allen Ginsberg, William Burroughs, and Paul Bowles on the beach in Tangiers, the postcards of which we each used as bookmarks.

Apparently we had hit the absinthe harder than ever, and when Xica shuttered her bar, the three of us crawled on our hands and knees out of town, lay down on the pavement, and, level with the road, watched the moonlight dance on the blacktop's shimmering surface.

That crawl-on-fuzzy-blacktop-absinthe night made the sun paralyzingly bright the next day. When I dragged myself over to the farm to check on Hank, he said he couldn't imagine driving up to Lisbon or getting on a train, so we pushed back our travel plans to the next day. I thought about going back to the novel, but I was going to lose the following day and any momentum, so instead Hank and I rode farther down the coast than previously, to a small village where a giant crow tethered to the wall of a café screeched at us until we left.

Windburned and dehydrated, I couldn't wait to stick my head under our kitchen tap, but Elissa was at the little Formica table, a knife with a blob of soft goat cheese hovering over a slice of rough peasant bread. She was staring down at her bare feet.

"What's wrong?"

"Nothing. Why?" Elissa said, not looking up.

"What's wrong?"

"I called *Spy*," she said, still staring at her feet.

"Why?"

I didn't need to ask. Two weeks before we left she'd turned in her last piece, but her editor hadn't read it and it had been eating at her. I wasn't going to say it, but she was too invested in that old life.

I could just see her standing in line, biting her nails, waiting to use the one phone in town.

"My last piece. I had a feeling I should check, in case there were . . . you know, fact-checking."

"And?"

"I'm fucked."

I took the knife out of her hand, poured us both glasses of water, and sat opposite her.

"Screw it. You made your deadline."

"I know. But I'm fucked," she said.

"Bullshit. I can just picture them sweating at their desks: It's ninety-five and humid and the air is full of shit so it feels like they're living inside of a diaper, and they're taking it out on you."

"Don't be stupid. I'm so embarrassed."

"You shouldn't be. It was a great piece. And who cares? It's nothing compared to what you're writing now."

Elissa finally looked at me, searching my face. "What's wrong with you?" she asked with a sadness that stung.

"I'm saying that anyone in New York publishing would hire you if . . . *when* we go back. But I'm also saying that we're here now. If we aren't living now, when will we?"

Elissa looked up at the ceiling and exhaled long and slow. I felt for her, but was impatient. A real artist doesn't need a safety net. This little bit of chaos injected into our routine felt like an opportunity, a possible spur to her real writing; to Elissa, however, this chaos could disrupt her creativity and call into question all the true work she had been doing in Zambi. Her damn parents—I blamed them for her stable upbringing, along with her relentlessly supportive sister. They'd grown up in one big happy house in the safety and comfort and consistency of suburban Delaware. Safety, comfort, and consistency were things you should get over if you wanted to be an artist.

"Absinthe hour will cure what ails you," I told her, and she gave me a sad, fake-brave smile.

Absinthe did and didn't cure us. We felt better for a bit, but then Hank said, "Why so quiet, Sis?" Elissa was staring off at the lavender and green striations above the waves, the sun having just been swallowed up. She told him about *Spy* and he said, "That totally sucks."

That's what I should have said. I was annoyed with myself. I buried this annoyance with another absinthe, but it was still lingering the next morning as I walked over to the farm. Hank was next to the barn, sketching a black cat at attention by his feet. The two of them looked like they were having a staring contest.

"I need a day or two," Hank said, eyes on the cat.

"What's up?"

"I'm on a roll. The cats, the light here . . ."

"But what about the classic cathedrals? You wanted to talk to Proust and Monet."

"I will, I will," Hank said. "But the cat's also worthy."

"Whatever," I said, and walked back home, making a game of kicking rocks as far as I could.

We saw Hank that night, and again the next night. We were developing a routine—a happy one, but it also felt like the routine was digging a rut. I thought of *La Dolce Vita*, where, at a party full of Rome's artists and intelligentsia, Steiner plays back a recording of repartee from what he thinks is earlier in the party, but thunder on the tape signals that it is from a previous party, with the exact same people engaging in the exact same witty banter.

"Let's go to *Évora* tomorrow," I said.

"The Bone Chapel?" Elissa asked.

"I wanted to do one last sketch of—"

"Fuck your cats," I said, cutting off Hank, who laughed, thinking I was joking.

When uncomfortable or when the air needs to be cleared, I avoid conflict. Run. The two-hour drive north to *Évora* would not only get Hank moving toward Berlin, but would hopefully lighten up Elissa, who had been in her writing tunnel.

As soon as we piled into Dusty, a hungover Elissa complained from the backseat, "My leg has withered." She had been reanimated after I suggested Évora, and was even more excited when I told her that I thought the trip would jump-start Hank into heading farther north. While Hank and I slowed and slurred, his artistic dicta making less and less sense, Elissa sharpened with each drink. A new, earnest young German couple had come into the bar late and Elissa had taught them "idiomatic English," telling them, "'The bus' is the new slang for 'the coolest' or 'the

most excellent.'" They carefully repeated each of her phrases—
"the bus," "artichoke poke," "sansabelt spanker."

"Honestly, my leg!" Elissa moaned.

Hank and I laughed, as hungover as Elissa. With no rhyme
or reason, absinthe hangovers seemed to paralyze different parts
of our bodies at different times. One morning it would be a leg,
the next an arm, the next your brain.

"Objects in mirror," Hank said, drawing a giant eye in the
dirty side-view mirror. A long-distance driving junkie, he was
itching to get behind the wheel, even though it would have
cramped his lanky frame. But he got off on that, having fixed up
a series of vintage Volkswagen Beetles and even having nursed
along a Yugo, the disastrous Yugoslavian car his grandparents
had bought him, worried that he was driving old, unreliable cars.

"Handles work," I said, rolling down my window, and
Hank laughed. The Yugos had each fallen off on first use.

"I really want to sketch Prague and Budapest," Hank said
as I kept my eyes forward.

Away from the breezy coast, the temperature spiked, and
by the time we arrived in the sunbaked hill town it was well over
a hundred degrees. We parked near the Roman ruins, then sped
across the scorching plaza to the cathedral, where it took a minute
for our eyes to adjust to the dim light, the stained glass darkened
from hundreds of years of burning prayer candles. Tacked along
the hallway walls leading from the cathedral to the chapel were
what looked like wigs, but were in fact the shorn locks of new
monks who had recently entered the order.

As my eyes adjusted, the chapel's intricate construction
came into focus. The walls were made of a lattice of large bones—
femurs, tibias, pelvises, scapulas, and skulls. The columns, smaller
bones—radiuses and ulnas. The windowsills, clavicles and ribs.

And everywhere the smallest bones—tarsals, metatarsals, vertebrae, and phalanges—were jammed into the gaps. Over the doorway, an old wooden sign proclaimed *"Nós ossos que aqui estamos pelos vossos esperamos,"* meaning, "Our bones are here waiting for your bones."

As soon as I was inside the small room, I felt as if the bones were closing in on me. There was no air and the light was leaking from the room. Having fainted twice before in churches, once with my mother and once with my father, I thought for a second that I might be fainting again. This was beyond spectacle, beyond religion; it went straight to a universal bond of mortality. I pictured skeletons holding hands in chains between Europe's great churches, felt the continent's art history. I wanted to see every church, every painting, every statue, and to be part of this continuum. But first I had to get the hell out of there.

15

"Security is a false God. Begin to make sacrifices to it and you are lost."

—Paul Bowles

Soundtrack: Peter, Paul and Mary, "Leaving on a Jet Plane," 1967

MY CLASSMATES—army, business, and diplomatic kids—were mostly from fixed places: Chicago, Atlanta, Los Angeles. They considered themselves Americans, and more specifically, residents of wherever they were from, and wore uniforms of local sporting teams as outward pledges of allegiance. Even though my parents were U.S. citizens, I considered myself a Berliner. I planned to apply for dual citizenship when I turned eighteen. If I lived anywhere in Germany but Berlin I'd have to serve two years of compulsory military service in the West German army.

At the time, this sounded glamorous. I come from a long line of U.S. Army veterans. My uncle had been a foot soldier under Patton in World War II, had landed at Normandy and then marched on Berlin; my grandfather (on my father's side) had been on the front lines in France during World War I; his father had fought for the Union in Kentucky and Missouri during the Civil War; and, generations before that there were soldiers all the way back to a "Spelman" from Normandy who invaded England in 1066, under the command of William the Conqueror.

A Berliner for certain. A possible soldier. Those were two categories I could live with. This certainty vanished in the spring of 1973, when my father left me for a few days in the care of a female singer who clearly had never had to attend to a child before. She talked loudly to me as if I were a slow three-year-old and mostly let me entertain myself while she read tabloids, and then dragged me from cheap restaurant to cheap restaurant for all the rotisserie chicken I could eat. My father flew to Rochester, New York, to interview at his alma mater, the Eastman School of Music. Rochester was only two or three hours from Chautauqua, New York, where we had been spending our summers, my father teaching at the music festival while I got to be in the operas as an extra or as part of the kids' chorus. He returned with news that he had been hired as a teacher and that we would be heading to Chautauqua in a few weeks for the summer, as usual, but that after that we wouldn't be coming back to Berlin, but would instead be moving to Rochester.

I don't remember my father selling me on leaving Berlin. All I heard was that he was leaving and that I was going with him. I didn't care where. I was somewhat fearful about going to an American public school, but I knew where my loyalty lay: It was with my father. I could imagine that Eastman would be as exciting and as full of passionate, strange musicians as Berlin. My father was part of the artistic tribe that knows no geographical loyalties. The tribe goes where the art is, and that's what I would do as well. As long as I was with my father, I was home.

What he did tell me was that it would be good for me to be closer to my mother, which didn't seem that big of a deal to me. I liked the long solo flights to see my mother during prolonged school holidays. Pan Am, TWA, Icelandic, Laker, Lufthansa. From these solo trips I have a shoebox full of playing cards. Fawning stewardesses would give me wing pins and airline-embossed packs of cards. They taught me how to play rummy, canasta, an infinite variety of solitaires. My classmates would ask me if it was scary flying alone, and I would never admit to the terror of being pinned with an "Unaccompanied Minor" sign and traveling with strangers, trusting them to deliver me from one parent to the other across thousands of miles and through chaotic airports where other travelers were going to hundreds of other cities. What was to keep me from landing in the wrong city? Who could guarantee that one or the other parent was going to be at the airport to pick me up? Instead, I told my classmates that when you are a kid flying alone you are treated like royalty. That the beautiful stewardesses would take me up the spiral stairs of the 747 and into the lounge, where they ignored the first-class businessmen beckoning for drinks and instead entertained me and me alone.

Of course, I also didn't mention that I dreaded landing in Louisiana. I missed my mother, and couldn't understand why she had moved so far away from me. Each time I visited I was afraid to see this person I didn't really know, along with my uncle, cousins, and grandparents, whom I didn't know at all. I felt like a foreign exchange student going off to live with his American family.

I had the same feeling in my new school in Rochester, where I no longer had lingua franca with other kids. TV was the foreign language they spoke. While American schoolwork was ridiculously easy compared with the German curriculum, I could never watch enough reruns or sports to not feel uncultured. So what if I already knew the Pythagorean Theorem? I didn't know squat about *The Mod Squad, The Rockford Files,* or even *Bugs Bunny* and *Scooby-Doo.* After school I wanted to get to the

safety of my father as fast as possible, but before I went to Eastman, I had to watch reruns of *I Love Lucy, The Honeymooners,*
and *Laugh-In,* shows that shaped my classmates' worldviews.

I kept watching, but I was always a step behind. I knew that
no matter how hard I studied, I'd never be a native TV speaker.
No matter how many I watched, these shows appeared to be
about mythological times and places, and I kept wondering,
*Are the people on these shows really like my classmates' families? Is
this American reality?* I found the TV images alluring—nuclear
families, sitting around the table for meals, problems solved
quickly with group hugs. These were the equivalent of another
new cultural experience—cheap Chinese food that we frequently
ate for dinner near Eastman, where my father spent most of
his time. The food was kind of interesting, but left me feeling
empty, and a bit queasy.

Sports was the other subject my classmates talked about,
and I was mostly ignorant about baseball, football, and bas-
ketball. My sport was soccer, and even in 1974, a World Cup
year, just a few of my classmates knew or cared about it. "Only
wetbacks and weirdos play soccer," one of them told me. My
classmates treated me decently or indifferently; I didn't leave
much of a mark on them. It was clear to me and everyone else
that I was not from the same planet.

There were opportunities on my part to connect, like the
day after one of the networks aired a two-hour special about what
went on behind the scenes of the hostage-taking at the Munich
Olympics. I happened to see the TV special, while my father
was at an "adult party" that he assured me would be boring.
He came home after midnight to find me crying in bed. "Why
in the world did you watch that without me?" he asked as he
hugged me. "There's nothing to worry about here." The next

day, at recess, a committee of boys and girls came over to where I was kicking around a soccer ball with the two Hispanic boys. "You see the thing about the Olympics?" a blonde girl asked me.

"Sure."

"Were you there?" she asked, hopeful.

I hesitated, thought about telling them a made-up, heroic story, but the truth was scary enough for me. "No," I said. "I was in Berlin, which was kind of close, sort of like if the Olympics were in New York City and we were here."

"Oh," she said, disappointed. I could have told her I was terrified anyway, told her what it was really like living behind the Wall, but that would've meant exposing myself. Instead, I turned back to kicking around the ball.

After school, I rarely hung out with classmates. Instead I would dash to our sparse apartment for a crash course in TV while I knocked off the easy homework, kept company by Linus and Lucy, the brother-and-sister shelter cats my father let me adopt. While I slept on a single bed, my father slept on a futon on the floor, which I thought was pretty cool for a forty-year-old; I hoped that I could be that cool when I was his age. The futon was an artistic badge of honor, like his indifference to money. One Saturday before rehearsals we went to see a discount matinee of *Harold and Maude,* but arrived late and had to scrounge under the seats of our secondhand, beat-up green AMC Hornet to find enough change to buy regular-priced tickets. To me, this is what you did if you were a true artist.

Most evenings I'd join my father for dinner at a nearby diner or Chinese place. The infamous lake-effect snow, when bitter cold air rushed down from Canada, picked up moisture from Lake Ontario like a massive sponge, then squeezed it all out on Rochester; it started in October and stayed until early

April, the downtown area around Eastman slushy gray, a frozen, dingier echo of winter in Berlin. After a quick meal, we'd trudge through the slush to Eastman, which was worth it because I got to stay up till midnight exploring the massive, creaky old music school. I would sneak into the main theater and sit in the red velvet chairs, work my way up onto the catwalks, and if I got bored go to the main building's basement snack lounge, where I would play chess against the students and faculty. Much to my shock and mild embarrassment, I was good enough to beat most anyone.

My father arrived at Eastman at eight in the morning and stayed until nine or ten or twelve at night. He took breaks only for dinner and to walk the two blocks to the YMCA, where I tried to keep up as he ran on the banked indoor track, but was never fast enough to match his long, loping strides. After a hard run in October, my father saw a sign advertising that a visiting grandmaster was looking for opponents for a simultaneous exhibition, and still thinking that chess might be my thing as piano was his, and with visions of me supporting him in his old age as a chess champion, he signed me up. Most of the other players were adults, but I was one of the last players to be defeated. When I was finally cornered, I made everyone laugh by asking how to spell "resign."

As I adjusted to my new life in Rochester, I wondered what my mother was doing in New Orleans. I received fact-filled letters about how her classes were going and how she was applying for teaching jobs now that she almost had her master's degree. Occasionally we had awkward phone conversations during which she told me how challenging it was for her to be back at school at her age, which I didn't understand and wouldn't appreciate until much, much later.

At Thanksgiving, on my first trip to Louisiana after we moved to Rochester, my family seemed as foreign as the damp, oppressive heat. Compared to cool, gray Berlin and then brutally cold and snowy upstate New York, the lush, teeming world was an assault on my senses, the dense flora lurid, the birds, frogs, and insects disconcertingly loud.

It's hard for me to picture my mother. I'm sure she was happy to see me, but I can't remember her greeting me at the airport. My main memory is of how, when she was near my grandmother, she made herself smaller than she already was. She spoke softly around her mother, a bitter, sullen woman who lived in the huge yellow recliner from which she watched Lawrence Welk on a bulging, green-tinged TV. Occasionally I would notice her lizard stare fixed on me and I would attempt a smile, and her eyes would go back to the dancing bubbles on the screen. How tough must my mother have been to have forged a strong self under that judgmental glare?

By contrast my grandfather, as soon as I arrived, took me out to their junglelike backyard, and when he spotted a black snake sneaking through the strawberries toward the porch, he moved with surprising speed for a big man and chopped the snake's head off with a hoe and laughed as the headless body writhed around my retreating feet. My two cousins also thought my fear was hilarious, and one handed me his BB gun and offered me a shot at the cluster of small songbirds in the bough of the nearby willow. I sighted a blurry-winged brown bird, but shot wide, on purpose. At night, the strange world became stranger in the dark, with a cacophony of insects and frogs, and when I stepped out of my grandfather's big green Cadillac, huge, scurrying water bugs crunched underfoot. Small green lizards, the quick ones that stuck to the bathroom windows at night, dashed across the crushed white seashell driveway.

After two nights I felt more relaxed, but when my mother brought out a tray of lemonade I said, "Thanks, Dad," and my strong, in-control mom flinched, then covered it with a tight smile. I was once again reminded that she never talked about him, never asked me what life was like with him. When I returned to my father, it would be the same thing—as if they didn't exist to each other.

I was more relaxed and comfortable with my two cousins, with whom I had no baggage. As long as my two cousins were doing something physical—swimming, climbing trees, picking strawberries—I could play along with the concept that we were related and should therefore be close. When they started rehashing the last episode of *Charlie's Angels*, I nodded politely as they broke down Farrah's latest close brush with death and whether or not she did her own stunts. The subject exhausted, I told them about playing soccer with the Turkish kids in the *Gastarbeiter* complex next door in Berlin and what it's like having tanks roll down the street in the middle of the night, and then one of them asked, "But don't you live in Rochester now?"

I paused. I nodded. But I thought, *No. I am a Berliner. And I'll always be a Berliner.*

16

"Honor thy error as hidden intention."

—Brian Eno

Soundtrack: Brian Eno, "Baby's on Fire," 1973

ELISSA LINGERED in the chapel while Hank and I waited outside in the shade, the sun now baking the red hills, vendors putting up umbrellas to cover themselves and their brightly painted clay plates. When Elissa came out, she glided over to our shaded area. "More, more, more," she said, wide-eyed. "I want to see every ossuary and every crypt from here to Berlin."

Hank raised his hand. "Second that."

"Well, we'd better motor if we want to make that funeral," Elissa said, and headed for the car.

"Guess I picked a bad day to stop drinking absinthe," Hank said.

I, too, was now fired up to drive to Berlin. First, we were due to join up with Elissa's childhood friend Fiona in Lisbon and were going to take her around Lisbon for the weekend and then over to Madrid. Our plan was to recover in Zambi for a week, then drive to Berlin where we would overlap with Hank for a few days. If Hank left within a day or two, he'd have two weeks to see cathedrals on the way to Berlin. If.

Yet after our day in Évora, he did not pack. Nor the next. Nor the day after that. I couldn't explain his reluctance to myself.

Or to Elissa. I avoided him and wrote in the café while Elissa barricaded herself in our place and wrote and slept and glowered at me when I came in to check on her.

"What're you doing?" I asked him at Xica's on the third night back from Évora.

"Change of plan. Condensed trip. Too good here."

"Seriously?" I said, with not a trace of the usual lightness of tone we had between us.

"Seriously," he said, willfully ignoring my urgency.

"Don't you think you've racked up enough comfort points?"

"Still plenty of adventure points to be found here," Hank said.

"You should go," Andreas said from behind the bar. "You must see the magnificent *Kölner Dom*."

"I will, I will."

Elissa was sitting at one of the small tables with Xica, their heads together.

On our walk home I pointed out the waning moon over the dunes.

"Why doesn't he leave?" Elissa asked, looking at me, not the moon.

"I don't know," I said, still pointing.

"Have you asked him to?" Elissa said as we entered the long alley behind the bakery.

"You know I have."

"Like you've asked about getting stringing work?"

"That was shitty," I said.

"If the shit fits . . ."

"I've tried," I said, and held open our garden gate.

"Well, you need to do *something*," Elissa said, pausing on the threshold.

"I have. I don't know what else I can do beside throw him in the car."

"That's not what I'm talking about," Elissa said, and marched ahead.

"What?" I asked, but she went inside without answering.

After two more tense days, Hank was still sketching dunes and the Zambi locals, human and animal. Elissa and I left him behind when we drove up to Lisbon to meet Fiona, who hadn't traveled that much and was either going to marry or break up with a former rugby player back home, and so gave herself over to our giddy tour of Lisbon and the smaller towns down the coast and back to Zambujeira. Elissa and I remembered how well we traveled together and were a great team as tour guides, me handling the logistics, Elissa doing the hand-holding. We mostly forgot about Hank. Yet four days later he was still in Zambi as the three of us drove off toward Madrid.

"Send a card and let us know when you'll be in Berlin and hopefully we can meet up there," I said as I got in Dusty.

"Definitely. I'll write as soon as I hit Dresden," Hank said, his hands jammed into his paint-flecked Carhartt cutoffs. I nodded and looked to Elissa, who rolled her eyes, and I wordlessly reiterated my old argument that we have to trust our friend when he says he is going to do something and this time he really does have to leave because he has reached his financial limit and has to buy his Eurail pass now.

The drive from Zambi to Madrid was eight hours across Spain's "frying pan" of scorching sunflower fields, the July sun pushing the temperature up to 43 Celsius (109 Fahrenheit).

Dusty, alas, had no air-conditioning, so Elissa poured water over a bandanna I had wrapped around my head. We were burned clean and ready for Madrid's sensuous beauty, a louche contrast to southern Portugal's rough purity. For three days we rambled through beautiful parks and around ancient fountains and statues, and reveled in the magnificent Prado, where, as Louis MacNeice wrote at the beginning of World War II, "half-wit princes looked from the/Canvas they had paid for/(Goya had the laugh)."

La Movida, the post-fifty-years-of-Franco exuberance, was infectious, dizzying, the country moving at twice the speed of Portugal. At cafés we sipped espressos and watched women with long dark hair and short sundresses scooting by on their Vespas; at bars we squeezed past couples making out at the brass rails, then ate dinners outside in the plazas surrounded by sprawling Spanish families, eating at midnight at the earliest; and then we would dance past dawn.

After we dropped Fiona off at the airport, we decided to stay an extra two nights and found a cheap hotel room whose windows rattled when the trams passed right below. I have a clear memory of the moment I realized I had the thirty pesetas in my front pocket stolen; it was after dinner at an open-air café in an ancient square packed with late-night revelers. Yet even having our last pesetas pickpocketed couldn't dampen my joy; it was a small tax to pay for being in such an alive city.

"Why don't we live here?" I asked Elissa as we stumbled around the bustling postmidnight streets. This is how you are supposed to live—exuberantly. I pictured us on our own Vespas, going native. This was her kind of city—warm, vibrant, where people's emotions were wild and uninhibited.

"It *is* fabulous," Elissa said, veering us toward a fountain of nymphs.

"*We* could be fabulous," I said, squeezing her hand.

"What's this 'we,' white man?"

"Okay, *you* could be fabulous."

"And you would make money so that I could be fabulous?"

"We'd take turns."

"Deal," she said, then sat on the edge of the fountain, took off her shoes, and swung around to dip her feet into the cool water.

"But first Berlin," I said.

"Berlin," Elissa said, as if she could love my city as much as she loved Madrid. The way she held open that possibility . . . that is why I loved her.

17

"Experience is what you get when you're looking for something else."

—Federico Fellini

Soundtrack: Giacomo Puccini, "Vissi d'arte," from *Tosca*, 1899

AT THE END of the school year in Rochester my father and I drove the three hours to Lake Chautauqua, where he was the director of musical preparation for the opera program at the 130-year-old music festival, which, he said, hadn't changed in that time, certainly not since he was sixteen, when he first attended as a student. In the passenger seat of the Hornet, I stared down at the hole between my feet, watching the road blur below, my mind drifting to the past winter when we had driven to Lansing, Michigan, through Ontario, in a subzero squall, a blue-checked blanket over the rusted-out hole, me reaching my left foot over onto the gas pedal so that my father could stomp his numb foot.

This was my favorite time with my father, just the two of us in the car, mostly quiet (he never listened to music in the car or at home, getting his fill at work), sometimes playing word games, both of us pointing out trees, barns, and other aspects of a landscape that were fixed, permanent, and timeless, markers of our transience. "Nice willow tree." Nod. "Pretty lake. Let's build our cabin there, Pa." Nod.

I loved Chautauqua, but was in no rush to get to the creaky gates of the "compound," as the natives called the private, fenced-in community. Once we were there, my father would be back to work and I would have to share him with the young musicians and faculty, who grumbled about having to "go off the reservation" for a drink, the more effeminate men feeling like they had to rein in their flash, and most everyone believing that Chatauqua's permanent residents lived in a McCarthyite's dream of how Victorian America should have been.

With its ancient wooden houses and laws prohibiting noise, cars, and alcohol, which were strictly enforced by private security, Chautauqua felt frozen in the 1920s, or even the 1890s. The natives were ancient and cartoonishly stodgy, and could be overheard earnestly saying "Things must be done in the proper fashion" when talking about how the Welch's Grape Pavilion should dispense hot grape sundaes (the hot grape syrup should be spooned on lovingly from a dignified tureen versus ignominiously splashed out from a spigot).

Yet for me, Chautauqua was a sanctuary. Once you passed through the gates, the "real world" was barred. Vietnam, the Cold War, OPEC, Watergate—things I didn't understand but knew were scary from overhearing their threats repeated on the nightly news my father watched—didn't have IDs to get in. Opera seemed to thrive in this ahistorical vacuum. I had grown up behind and on the Chautauqua opera stage. When I could barely walk, I was an extra in *Aida*. If there was a kids' chorus, I was in it. I could sing on key and follow instructions, not to mention that I was always around. I loved being part of the giant spectacles. I loved the big, messy operas, like *Tosca*. When the bad guy, Scarpia, comes into the church during the Te Deum, singing about how he's going to kill the revolutionary and steal his girlfriend, I got the hell out of the way, one time scraping my knees bloody on the stage's hard pine planks, not acting at all but genuinely scared that Scarpia was going to kick me if I was in his path.

The whole opera scared me: Tosca and her lover, a painter, try to help an escaped political prisoner. The painter is caught by the Roman chief of police, Scarpia. Tosca tells Scarpia that she will sleep with him if he frees her lover. After Scarpia tells Tosca that she has arranged for the painter's mock execution and safe passage from the fortress for herself and the painter, Tosca stabs Scarpia to death. But he double-crosses her from the grave—in front of Tosca the police really shoot and kill the painter, and she jumps off a turret and kills herself. The end.

As a kid, I was always destroyed by the melodramas no matter how many times I saw them. I was repeatedly heartbroken when Madame Butterfly was abandoned by her American sailor lover, and was crushed by *La Bohème*, the Paris garret full of starving artists who pool their resources, the writer burning his manuscript to keep them warm on a cold night. The poet falls in love with the housekeeper, Mimi, who is, of course, consumptive: There is nothing he can do; his love for her isn't enough to save her, and she dies.

I loved these operas in a distant, safe way, the way I loved seafaring novels and Westerns, with their lone, manly heroes and their rugged landscapes, onto which I could project an idealized version of my future self. Still, though I embraced conflict and emotional messiness onstage, in real life I did everything I could to avoid it. But now, at age ten, I wondered for the first time how opera fit in with the frightening present. Before, I had been swept up in the romantically tragic plotlines and had let myself get lost in the spectacle of the elaborate productions, happily transforming myself into a nineteenth-century Roman choirboy.

Now I couldn't fully let go of myself, and found this semi-alienated self staring out past the footlights to the comfortable audience watching an opera about doomed nineteenth-century Italian revolutionaries.

Self-awareness in a ten-year-old can only mean sadness. How I wished I were less self-conscious, both onstage and at the Chautauqua Boys and Girls Club, the hokey old summer camp that I had always loved. Past summers I'd paddled in long Indian war canoes, made ceramics from the gray lake clay, and wrung out my bathing suit between the same pitted wooden rollers that kids had been using for a hundred years. I looked like them in my shorts and Charlie Brown striped shirt as I rode to the camp on my purple banana-seat Sting-Ray and briefly stood out during interclass competitions, where I excelled in chess, and then quickly and happily blended back in.

That summer started with me losing myself in communal activities, but one day the counselors announced that the campers would have a tug-of-war against each other. Overcoming the older and stronger campers a year ahead of us was daunting, but I liked playing the doomed hero. That is, until I learned that the losers would face a "spanking machine," a crawl through a tunnel of the winners' legs, each boy smacking the asses of the losers. My peers laughed and whooped, but I was all business, pulling on the thick, dingy white rope so hard I yanked one of my own classmates off his feet, stalling the inevitable for a few seconds. Afterward my classmates dutifully marched into formation for the spanking machine. I couldn't believe they were letting themselves get spanked—that, in fact, they seemed to be enjoying the prospect.

I took off in a dead sprint. After a hundred yards I looked back at the three surprised, swearing counselors, but they were far behind. I squeezed through the wooden fence separating us from the neighboring public beach, dashed across the sand to the entrance where I parked my bike, then pedaled madly across the compound toward a smaller, rockier beach, which was rarely used, especially early in the day. I glanced back, but the counselors didn't have bikes and so they had stopped chasing me. Yet I kept riding as fast as I could until I was on the empty beach, alone except for the bored teenage lifeguard, my pulse pounding in my head, loud and fast, then slowing until it was in sync with the lazy waves.

Freedom. I didn't care if I ever saw the counselors or my fellow campers again. I was dizzy with the realization that not only could I flee, but that I had acted upon this possibility, turning fantasy to reality. I had vanished. It was a moment of sweet perfection. I threw off my T-shirt and ran into the chilly water, dove down under the waves, and felt the murky green darkness envelop me. Pure nothingness. Bliss.

I lost myself. I would chase this feeling for years, running thousands of miles, year after year. I got good at catching and holding on to this nothingness for hours on end, but here, this first time, my bubble was easily burst. As Proust wrote, "The anesthetizing influence of habit having ceased, I would begin to have thoughts, and feelings, and they are such sad things."

The specific sad thought that brought me back from nirvana was that my father was going to kill, or worse, banish me. I could remember only one time ever when my father had been truly angry and disappointed with me. It was almost two years before, in late October, when Berlin briefly sheds its gray coat, the sun shines, and orange, red, and green leaves fill the clear air. With two friends I'd skipped religion class and gone to the neighboring park, where we spent the afternoon jumping in piles of leaves. We would have gotten away with it, but the grounds-keeper was upset that his neat piles of leaves were scattered by us hooligans. The principal told us that we each had to write a confession and have it signed by a parent.

The thought of disappointing my father was crushing to me. Instead, I came up with a scheme: I told my father that we were working on a writing assignment and that I needed his signature. This was believable, since they were always having us work on our handwriting, and in addition I transposed my German and English words, and mixed up English words like "their," "there," and "they're."

I couldn't find a clean piece of paper, so I grabbed the cardboard backing that was at the end of one of my father's used yellow notepads. He signed the cardboard without question, and I wrote my confession. The principal scoffed at the cardboard and said that it needed to be on real paper. I went back to my dad, and when he guessed that I had done something wrong, I told him the awful truth. After a terrifying silent minute, he said that he was very unhappy with me, not for skipping some stupid religion class, but for trying to trick him. He looked sad and wounded. And confused.

"I'm going to have to really punish you," he said.

"It's okay, Dad, I understand," I reassured him.

"I'm afraid that I'm going to have to spank you, like I was spanked when I did something seriously wrong," he said.

"Okay."

I lay across his lap and he gave the back of my jeans a few halfhearted whacks with a spatula. There was no pain, just humiliation for me, embarrassment for him. As soon as my father put down the spatula, he cheerily said, "Let's go downtown to the international food fair."

I blinked away the start of tears and nodded; my father looked blurry, but I could clearly make out his wounded, disappointed look—the worst punishment possible. It burned right through me. On the U-Bahn, walking through the food-laden isles of the massive International Green Week pavilions, I was sick with regret. I vowed never to elicit that disappointed look from him again. In the U.S. pavilion there were huge pink grapefruits from Texas. The bittersweet pink flesh was the most exotic and flavorful thing I'd ever tasted. But even now, when I smell grapefruit, it triggers a memory of pure anxiety.

That day I ran away from camp, I swam back to shore, then stared out at the waves for I don't know how long. I didn't try to run when a counselor finally tracked me down. He was seventeen or eighteen and kept brushing back his shaggy blond hair. I was surprised that instead of displaying anger, he showed fear. While I was horrified that my father would be disappointed with me, I was also thrilled with the new knowledge that I could cause fear in an adult.

At the end of that long, long afternoon, when my father came to pick me up, the counselor took him aside and explained what had happened that morning. As we walked back toward the house, my father looking serious, thinking hard, I thought I was going to faint or vomit or both. A minute of silence stretched into two, then five. "Sounds like you've outgrown camp," he finally said.

18

"Art is the highest form of hope."

—Gerhard Richter

Soundtrack: Sonic Youth, "Spirit Desire," 1988

AFTER MADRID, we decided to tilt at one more expat fantasy: the running of the bulls at the Festival of San Fermín. Pamplona! What could be more romantically clichéd? On the hot, gritty drive into the Basque hills, I pictured Pamplona to be like an opera set, as if Hemingway had just exited and now it was our turn on the stage. And I wasn't that far off base—the inner, old city was very much as it was when Hemingway was slinging his wineskin through the narrow, cobbled streets.

We parked Dusty on the outskirts and hiked into the old city, where we came upon six or seven black-clad older men gathered in a semicircle around a hefty, middle-aged German or Dutch man who was passed out in the middle of the street. A young Spanish woman was slowly sliding a fat wallet from the tourist's back pocket. The old men silently watched her skill and nodded their approval when she succeeded. The collective wisdom appeared to be that if you were stupid enough to pass out in the street, you got what you deserved.

The town was coming to life with the fast-approaching five o'clock bullfight, the daily centerpiece of the weeklong festival that honors Saint Fermín, martyred by being dragged by bulls through the city streets. This is reenacted each morning, when all the local men—in white pants and white shirts, with a red kerchief fastened around their necks with a pin denoting the particular Basque region they are from—gather in the quarter-mile corridor leading from a pen on the outskirts of town where the bulls are released to the bullfighting arena in the center of town. Before the bulls are released, the men casually stand around, engrossed by the pink-tinted morning paper, which features, on the front page, pictures of the previous afternoon's action in the ring, and on the back page, photos of those gored or trampled the previous morning.

At exactly 8 A.M. a priest comes out onto his balcony and blesses those about to honor San Fermín. Bells signal the release of the bulls, and as the enraged, terrified animals clatter through the narrow, twisty corridor, the men roll up their newspapers into wands and start sprinting. To be blessed, you need to run up close to the passing bulls and tap one with your wand while avoiding flying hooves and well-aimed horns. This frenzy usually lasts all of two minutes. Those foolish enough to follow the bulls into the arena are doused at the gateway with leftover sangria and flour, and then quickly dragged away before the bulls can get to them.

After the running of the bulls, everyone disperses and collapses wherever they can find a comfortable bit of ground. There are very few hotels in Pamplona, which are mainly filled with foreign tourists, and the faithful sleep on anything horizontal and relatively clean; no one bothers the visiting Basques, the true pilgrims. In the afternoon, when the sun begins to bake the cobbles, the city stirs back to life and the eating and drinking begin again.

After the five o'clock bullfights, the stadium emptied out into the already packed streets and all of the Basques danced behind small bands of musicians. We jumped into a group trailing two tubas, a snare, and a smattering of horns, and marched and danced and drank sangria with them until we joined up with another band, forming a larger band which shifted from a danceable tune to a traditional Basque nationalist song that everyone around us sang full throat. This would go on and on until shortly before eight in the morning, when the running of the bulls happened yet again. Seven straight days.

All night we danced and drank dirt-cheap sangria from bottles that street vendors refilled, eating egg sandwiches on crusty bread when we got hungry. But at five in the morning I couldn't march another step. I nodded toward a bar and Elissa and I ducked in off the crazy, raucous street as the Basque marching band continued on without us.

The long, brightly lit bar was packed with Basques, half of them drinking at the brass rail, the other half on the dance floor. Elissa and I squeezed up to the bar and I ordered beers.

"How can they keep dancing like this?" I asked as we watched the whirling, elegant dancers.

"We're so JV," Elissa said as she plopped down on a vacated bar stool.

"We're not doing too badly."

"I can't believe we're really here."

She had pressed *The Sun Also Rises* on me shortly after we met. I had ripped through it, Elissa hovering. We pressed books on each other as tests, me dropping *Naked Lunch* on her to see if she could be shocked (and her instead processing it more fully than I had). She asked what I thought of Hemingway's ending, and I said I thought it was kind of lame. It turned out that the cheap paperback she had given me was missing the last page, so I never got to the gut punch of "Isn't it pretty to think so."

In one gulp I drank half my tall glass of cold beer, and as I put it back on the bar, a broad-shouldered Basque scowled down at me, then at my beer.

"Excuse me," the man said in English. "I do believe you are drinking my beer."

I looked at the half-empty glass, then at the man. With his taut muscles and weathered face, I had a gut feeling that he was the kind of guy who knew how to cause maximum damage with one punch. At the thought, I imagined my ribs cracking. I'd never been in a fight, so hadn't experienced what it was like to be hit, and as much as I sought out extreme sensations, I had no desire to get punched by anyone, much less this big Basque dude who was in his bar during his holy festival. Still, I was pretty damn sure I was drinking my own beer.

"I'm sorry," I said. "I believe this is my beer." I felt Elissa's protective, or warning, hand on my forearm. "However," I quickly added, "just in case I am mistaken, let me buy you a beer." I called the bartender over and ordered two more. The Basque solemnly clinked glasses with me, his expression unchanged, then drank down his entire beer. I followed suit, and as I was draining the last few drops, the man grabbed the brass bar rail with both of his huge hands and swung himself over the bar, then refilled our glasses as the old bartender looked on with a bemused smile. The man jumped back over and clinked glasses with me once more. No wonder Hemingway liked the Basques so much. Beers finished, he gave me a very serious look and said, "May I have the honor of dancing with your wife?"

Elissa's nails dug into my forearm and I couldn't help but think of the scene in *Animal House*—"Do you mind if we dance with your dates?" I saw no graceful escape. "That would be an honor," I said, wondering what choice we had as Elissa's nails went deeper. But I was ripped free, dragged onto the dance floor by *his* wife, a perfectly postured black-haired woman with eyes so dark I wondered if it was possible to have black irises. I spun and whirled to the fast, brassy music, clueless as to what I was supposed to be doing, but trying to follow the blue, spinning skirt of my elegant partner. "Spin, spin, spin, just give in," I thought. Elissa was dancing a few yards away, shooting me a look of "How did you get us into this?"

I couldn't gauge how long the song would last and hoped that I could maintain and wouldn't vomit, but then the song built to a crescendo and crashed to a halt. I focused on my partner, who bowed. I looked for Elissa and spotted her a few yards away. She glanced at me and then back at the Basque, then signaled to the center of the dance floor like she wanted to keep going, the man smiling awkwardly. I looked to his wife, who frowned and led us over to them, where she clamped onto her husband's arm.

Off the dance floor the man said, "I am Carlos. This is my wife, Margarita."

I introduced us with as much grace as I could muster and Carlos said, "It has been an honor to meet you."

"I am honored to meet you, and to be here at your festival," I said, the music starting up. Carlos bowed again and Margarita spun him away.

"Don't sell me out like that," Elissa hissed.

"Wait. I thought you liked—"

"I would have *liked* to have choice."

"But we didn't have one," I said.

"Bullshit. I went from thinking he might deck you and I would rip his eyes out, to all of sudden you're giving me away and he's whirling me around the dance floor."

I stared at my wife, wondering how I had miscalculated the situation.

"You could've asked me," Elissa said, taking my hand.

"Right. Sorry," I said, squeezing her hand, willing us to be at our best as a couple, to go with the flow. But I was blindsided by self-consciousness. I had been part of the crowd, had given myself over to the collective celebration, and then, in an instant, I felt like a coward and a fraud, exposed as the play-actor I was. The heat, the sangria, the beer, the lack of sleep—none of that explained why I was feeling flat, two-dimensional in a three-dimensional world. I had seen our whole adventure in Portugal and Pamplona as if everyone we encountered were on a large stage set, performing for us. But I was the fake. I was putting on a show. Carlos and Margarita were real people, and the festival meant something to them. Their city, their friends, their family, their faith, their heritage, their present existence were all meaningful to them.

Was there any meaning to me being in Pamplona? Other than being with Elissa? Approximating Hemingway? And what was taking me so long to get to Berlin, my home?

19

"I decided as a kid I wanted to be a baseball player. Then I wanted to paint pictures and from there I decided I wanted to sing."

—Jonathan Richman

Soundtrack: Jonathan Richman and the Modern Lovers, "Modern World," 1976

THE REST OF JULY until the very end of August was my first extended experience of freedom. My father freed me from camp and Chautauqua became my own gated playground. The festival provided us with a cabin, the former servants' quarters to a grander house next door, where the head of the opera program, Mr. Treach, lived with his wife. I loved the little three-room cabin, only a half block from the lake, with a cedar smell and an ancient claw-foot bathtub that was so long and deep I could almost do laps in it. Once a week, Australian bats—big, brown, and fuzzy—flew into our cabin, and we had to guide them out the open doors and windows with tennis rackets and brooms. The lake had once had a mosquito problem, and legend had it that around the turn of the century someone had the brilliant idea of importing a mosquito predator—the Australian bat. Now the lake was overrun with nonindigenous bats.

After breakfast at the music festival canteen, my father went to rehearsals and I'd head back to our place to see if the cats had caught anything. Most mornings a half of a mole or mouse or sometimes a bat would be waiting for me on the threshold, Lucy's work, no doubt, Linus being too lazy to chase anything down. I would then grab my bike and spin by the rock beach and the dock by the clock tower, where I sometimes fished with slimy worms, catching small sunfish, sometimes bass, and once a fierce-looking pike. Under the docks there were crayfish to collect, and along the creek leading into the lake there were salamanders and tadpoles. I rode past the docks and clock tower, past the hundred-foot-long scale replica of the Holy Land, with each hill town and topological feature marked—Jericho, Jerusalem, the Red Sea. I cruised round and round the grounds, grabbed a quick lunch at the sub shop, and pedaled up to the great Norton Hall, where, as at Eastman, I tried to find all of its secret spaces.

One day toward the end of the summer, I dropped in on the barnlike shop house adjacent to the opera house, where carpenters were painting a scrim to look like the skyline of early nineteenth-century Rome. The schedule for the set builders was crazy—full sets for nine operas in nine weeks. But Vince, the lead builder, with his golden hoop earrings and red, watery eyes, appeared unflappable and never minded having me around, putting me to work doing nondetailed painting and carting away wood scraps. Vince and his crew were a lot more down-to-earth than most of the singers. They didn't baby-talk me, and with each other they talked about nonopera things like cars and sports and Saigon. I liked that the carpenters were making actual things; there was a finished product to their labor. With singers, after dozens of hours of rehearsals, then a two- or three-hour performance, it was over. The sets could be used again and again.

That afternoon I became so consumed painting a sky-blue scrim, I looked up and it was almost five o'clock, the time the day's last rehearsal was due to finish. I had to race across the street from the compound to an old garage that was now used for blocking rehearsals, but not before I stopped near the gate to pick wildflowers and cottontails. When I arrived, the rehearsal had just ended and I was able to catch a few of the chorus girls, whom I gave my bouquets to, and one of them, a student of my father's at Eastman, mussed up my hair. I joined her and the other singers heading for the Main Gate.

"Wait, Robby," my father said as he gathered up his scores from the piano. "Let's take the East Gate. We need to talk."

I wondered why he looked so serious. I hadn't done anything. At least not that I knew of. "What's wrong, Dad?"

"Nothing's wrong," he said while getting out his ID to show the security guard, who talked to my father about the unusually rainy summer we'd had. We walked on and I waited for whatever bad news was coming, worry escalating with each step across the soggy lawn by the small practice cabins. Finally he said, "Your mother and I think it's time that you lived with her for a while."

I tried to keep pace, my body numb.

"Why?" I managed to say. "What did I do?"

"You haven't done anything wrong," my father said, staring straight ahead, marching forward. "We feel that you need both of your parents. You've had a chance to live with me, so now you'll get a chance to live with your mom." My father spoke as if he were delivering a speech against his will. The practice cabins were mostly deserted, though a stray oboe was working a scale up and down, up and down. It took me three strides to match his two.

20

"A man lives not only his personal life, as an individual, but also, consciously or unconsciously, the life of his epoch and his contemporaries."

—Thomas Mann

Soundtrack: Kraftwerk, "Autobahn," 1974

SUNSHINE LEAKED THROUGH the bar windows, driving the Basques outside, and we followed them to a corridor already full of white-shirted men, the sides five or six deep with spectators. Elissa tugged on the tail of my T-shirt and pulled me back from pushing through, then pointed to a drainpipe that led up to a window caged in black iron bars. "Seriously?" I said, doubting her inebriated logic and climbing abilities. We'd have to dangle off the ledge, then shimmy up the drainpipe to get to the bars, where we would then have to hold on fifteen or twenty feet above the stampeding bulls.

But as the bells rung out, Elissa deftly scampered up. *Damn her ex-gymnastic dexterity*, I thought as I followed, not nearly as easily, but with enhanced motivation, as everyone was now whistling and yelling, the men below running with their pink newspapers. "Hang on," Elissa yelled as the roar grew, and then the frantic black and brown bulls, their hooves sliding across the worn cobbles, careened below us, carrying with them a musky funk of rage as they ran through and over and around the sprinting Basques, who swatted them with their wands even as they were knocked to the unforgiving stones.

Fifty feet past us the bulls and men somehow funneled themselves around a narrow bend and out of sight, and a roar followed. Before I could exhale, another wave of bells and cries came from the other direction. I pulled up and hooked my arm through the bars, my feet fighting for traction on the granite wall. "Hold on," Elissa yelled as the din grew louder. I twisted around in time to see a dozen calves galumphing into view. Bells tied to their tails, they were being chased by children, and the massive crowd cheered and whistled for the future bull-chasers. The children jangled below us and I heard Elissa say, "You okay?" as I skidded down the wall.

As we looked around for someplace to lie down, I wondered where I was on the drunk–hangover continuum. There was a strong probability that I was very drunk and very hungover at the same time, and I thought about lying down in a shady spot on a side street, but then I remembered the passed-out tourist we had seen on our way into the old city. Instead, we hiked back to Dusty, then drove away from town and along a dirt road, where we found a grove of what looked like cottonwoods and collapsed under them. We slept the sleep of the dead, awakening in the broiling mid-afternoon sun to red ants biting our legs and arms.

"Once more into the brink?" Elissa asked as she brushed ants off my back.

"Really?" I said, wondering how she could be so cherry when I felt like death.

"What's the matter, Scarecrow, scared of a little fire?"

"If you want to," I said. But as we drove toward the city, Elissa said, "We did it, didn't we?"

"We did," I said. "Papa would be proud."

"I guess," Elissa said.

Had we lived up to Hemingway? Certainly with the drinking. But had we engaged? Or were we just tourists? I kicked this around my tired brain, then turned to Elissa to ask her, but she was peacefully asleep against the passenger door. Instead, I grabbed the cassette of *Daydream Nation*, an intentionally brilliant album, its ambition announced in the title and with its cover art, Gerhard Richter's painting *Candle*. I wanted to live like Hemingway, yes, but I also wanted to risk and create like Sonic Youth. I popped in the tape and listened for clues as I focused on the narrow road ahead, which wound through the hot hills and through the cooler, greener Portuguese valleys, and once more into the heat along the coast and sixteen hours later we were in Zambujeira.

There was no iconic postcard from Hank, so I guessed that he had simply left, which was a relief as I collapsed into my own bed. But in the morning, I was surprised and not surprised to see Hank at the Café Atlantico, a double espresso comically small in his big hand, his other a blur as he sketched the black café cat curling around his long legs.

Elissa unlatched her hand from mine and gave me a quick look that said, "You had better deal with this," then turned around, all of the good vibes from Spain gone in an instant.

"Hank, man, I don't get it," I said, fighting the urge to flip his little iron table.

"I wanted to sketch the town some more," he said. His half frown, half smirk contained contrition but also a challenge. Why the hell was he challenging me?

"What about Budapest, Prague, Dresden?"

"The light here's just as good," Hank said, and nodded over my shoulder. *The light in the kitchen?* I wondered, but then saw that he was nodding to Constança, the morning waitress, who was bringing me my espresso.

"Obrigado," I said, and the teenager hesitated, as I was still standing, but I nodded and took the cup and saucer from her.

"But there's no history here," I said to Hank. "You said you wanted to be in conversation with the French and German greats."

"So?"

"Berlin?"

"Still on the table," Hank said, and I laughed. "Seriously. I've got enough for a round-trip train ticket."

I downed my shot. "We're out of here."

"What do you mean?" Hank said. I wanted to slap his little smirk. He didn't believe me.

"I have zero faith that you'll be there, but I'll look for you starting exactly one week from today at noon or eight at night, in Berlin, on the stairs of the *Gedächtniskirche.* Got it?"

Hank's smirk slowly faded as he realized I had called his bluff. "Sure, Chief. I'll be there. I promise." Hank said it like he meant it, but I was betting he'd stay in Zambi until he had to take the Lisbon bus to his flight home.

"Seriously?" Elissa said when I relayed my plan.

"Just us," I said.

"But I'm so fucking tired."

"You're the all-time transportation sleeper champion," I said.

While Elissa repacked, I went to tell our landlords that we would be gone for two or three weeks, though I was hoping for longer.

As we pulled out of Zambi, dirt turning to pavement, I was hit with the realization that we were about to drive two thousand miles of European roads. *What the hell is wrong with me?* I thought. But then I looked over at Elissa, who gave me a tired smile. *At least I've done one thing right.* I vowed to slow down, to make this journey last, to be in it. And I was, as we car-camped outside of Biarritz, then meandered through the south of France, pissing away money on wine and cheese and cute hotels that looked out over lavender fields. And then to Rouen, resisting Paris's pull (she would have taken all of our dollars), where we bathed in the warm light pouring through the walls of spectacular stained glass, and where I thought about Hank, missing the cathedrals where Proust met his gods.

At sunset, bobbing in the chilly waves off a rocky Norman beach, I thought, *There but for the grace of God go I.* My uncle might well have landed on this very beach, only while I dog-paddled, he had stormed out of an amphibious assault vehicle as shells exploded around him. From Normandy he'd marched all the way to Berlin, and was decorated with a Medal of Valor for his bravery during the Battle of the Bulge. J. D. Salinger was in his unit, and they both went through the "meat grinder" of close infantry combat following D-day. Would Salinger have been the writer we know without having gone through slaughter? Is that what I needed—atrocity?

In Amsterdam, after eating "space cakes," Elissa and I walked in circles along a looped canal, laughing at the endless, all-vowel Dutch street names. We would have kept walking till dawn if we weren't pulled into a Mexican bar/restaurant by Dutch sailors who were scaring away customers. The squeaky-clean, if slightly drunk, sailors bought us dinner.

"This is the most perfect place in the world," I told Elissa over burritos so bland and flavorless that I thought they were works of genius and perfection, and could never be duplicated in a million years.

"Hoogenboogenstrasse!" Elissa repeated, swatting away my stoner sentimentality.

The next morning, cotton-mouthed and fuzzy-eyed, I put on my prized Joy Division *Unknown Pleasures* T-shirt, suitable for the final push into Berlin.

"What if we don't stop?" I asked as we crossed the German border.

"What do you mean?"

"Like in *On the Road* where Dean drives from Berkeley to New York to say hi to his friend, and does just that—walks up the stairs to his friend's apartment, says hello—then drives right back to Berkeley. It's the journey, not the destination. Keep moving, keep moving, keep moving."

"It's going to be okay," Elissa said.

I wasn't so sure. Hanover, Magdeburg, Potsdam—the signs sped by. German signs. Was I really doing this? And then, in the gloaming, signs for *Zoo Berlin*, *Berliner Weisse*, and *Tiergarten* blurred by.

"What are you thinking?" Elissa asked.

I was thinking that it had taken me seventeen years to get back home. But instead of feeling a rush of relief, I felt the panicky sensations of no relief from myself. I was both the skittish eight-year-old and the restless twenty-five-year-old.

"You okay?" Elissa asked.

"Hard rolls with butter for breakfast. Soldiers marching in the street in front of our apartment. That's what I'm thinking," I said, wanting to feel more. I wanted to feel embraced, to be welcomed as the prodigal son. Instead I felt like an American tourist.

"Do you remember any of this?" Elissa asked, waving at the broad avenue in front of us.

"Sort of. But everything is cleaner than I remember. Everyone looks cleaner and neater."

"It's okay to feel weird. Do you want to pull over?"

"No. Thanks. I'm good," I said, desperately craving a beer, but keeping the car moving. I drove up and down the Kurfürstendamm, willing some kind of emotion from the familiar sight of the Sunday afternoon window-shoppers; but it didn't elicit strong feelings. I avoided the Wall—not yet ready. Elissa, I could tell, was giving me space, not saying anything, nodding as I occasionally pointed out a landmark.

After we had cruised around for an hour, maybe two, streetlights popped to life, and Elissa asked, "Think Hank made it?"

"No way," I said.

"We should check," Elissa said. "Where's the church?"

"We've driven by it already a couple of times. The half-bombed-out church with all the people in front. Supposed to be a living reminder of the horrors of the war, the civilian toll. They call it 'the Remembrance Church—the *Gedächtniskirche*."

"Gesundheit."

"You're funny," I said, and swung back onto the Kurfürstendamm. In front of the church, before I had completely stopped, I spotted Hank jogging down the stairs past a swarm of tourists.

"I don't believe it," I said.

"No way," Elissa said, her expression at once puzzled, angry, and excited at the same time, mirroring what I was feeling and thinking, which was that I was happy our friend had rallied, but that I was still pissed at him and that we once again were going to have to navigate as a trio.

Hank was ashen and wide-eyed, his jeans and black T-shirt streaked with dirt. "You look like shit," I said when he reached the car. "What happened?"

"I got here yesterday morning," Hank said. "I spent the night in the bushes over there, curled up with my knife."

"Stupid, but serious adventure points," I said, impressed by the needless Rambo act.

"Why didn't you stay in a hostel?" Elissa asked.

"Too many junkie kids," Hank said, his eyes darting around to the innocuous-looking punk teens clustered on the steps.

"I'm glad you made it," Elissa said, giving him a hug. "Let's find a place to crash and get you cleaned up."

"Yeah, that would be great," Hank said.

"Hell no," I said, and they both turned to me, surprised by my vehemence. "I haven't waited all these years and driven all this way to go find a shower. Get in. Let's go to the Wall."

"But Hank—"

"It's okay," Hank interrupted. "Your rodeo, partner."

Yes it is, I thought, *and you're not holding me back.*

At the sign for Checkpoint Charlie, my stomach tightened as it had when I was a child. But terror slipped to confusion—it seemed that everything had shrunk. The giant guardhouse on the Western side now looked like a British phone booth; the quarter-mile-long metal bridge to the East was just a hundred feet long. I looked around for the looming guard towers, which I remembered as being a hundred feet tall, then spotted one of them, only twenty feet high, but now toppled, its windows, through which soldiers had fired on anyone approaching from the East, smashed.

And what of the Wall itself, that massive, impassable mono-lith? It was still imposing and awe-inspiring. The twelve-foot-tall

ribbon of concrete stretched to the horizon left and right. The
only difference was that now both the eastern and western Walls
were missing four-foot sections. The Wall now looked like an
old prizefighter's smile.

So this is the monster in my closet? I couldn't believe I was
driving right through it. "I'm going *under* the Wall," I sang out,
my T-shirt sticking to the seat as I leaned forward.

"Woo-hoo," Elissa cheered, and Hank leaned out the window like a dog wanting to get its first breath of ex-Communist
air. Over my shoulder, I was surprised to see the pristine eastern
side of the Wall, still graffiti-free. I was thirsty and hot, but I also
had goose bumps, just like when I was with my father. A few
blocks in, there were no Westerners, but plenty of Easterners,
peering curiously into our car.

"Jesus, their clothes are grim," Elissa said.

"Exactly like I remember," I said. "Except for that," I added,
driving around yet another pile of cobblestones that had been
ripped from the streets.

"Why the roadblocks?" Hank asked.

"Beats me," I said.

"Isn't the West now helping out the East?" Elissa asked.

"Not until reunification in October," I said, "and until then
we're in legal limbo."

"At the church, I heard that Westerners are getting rolled
in the East," Hank said, "and that Western cars are being stolen
by a Russian mafia ring and then caravanned to Moscow. And
skinheads have been coming in from the north to attack Westerners and the anarchist squatters."

Drama queen, I thought, but said, "I haven't seen any
Westerners."

I vaguely remembered my father's walking route and drove into Prenzlauer Berg. I couldn't understand why, but with each block that I was farther away from West Berlin I felt happier. "I can't believe this. This is so damn cool."

"Easy, Chief, eyes on the road," Hank said.

"My father and I walked through here," I said, pointing to a little park.

"I'm so happy to finally see this," Elissa said.

"Let's walk around a little," I said, and pulled over. "I want to see if I can find the old music shop we used to go to."

"Think it's safe?" Hank asked, his hand on the car door.

"Absolutely," I said, giddy. I tapped my chest, feeling for my money belt and my passport, with its "Get out of jail free" stamp—a German place of birth.

"If it doesn't look safe, we'll turn back." As soon as I said this, I realized I was lying.

Hank got out, grim but determined, and cuffed his jeans up slightly higher so that he would have quicker access to his knife. I guided Elissa down the block, now noticing that most of the streetlights had been smashed out. There were no people visible and the street was strewn with glass, much more glass than could have come from the lights. I hurried us along to the next block, which was better lit, but which was also spookily unpopulated.

"You know where you're going?" Elissa asked with mustered optimism.

"I think so," I said, though by now all of the streets looked the same, including the one we were on, which dipped downhill and dead-ended in a small green park. Dark, thick with trees, the park was dotted with islands of heroic statues of old warriors, and in the center a Teutonic figure on horseback leaning down to run his sword through a Hun.

And there were cops. Or soldiers. How could I not have seen them? Next to the pith-helmeted Hun, a handful of men in modern military gear. Now that we were closer, I saw sixty, eighty, perhaps a hundred helmeted soldiers casually leaning on their clear plastic shields, black batons at their sides. Four German shepherds sat at attention in front of an armored personnel carrier, its bed filled with coils of barbed wire, the top of the cab fixed with a water cannon. Many of the men were smoking, no one in a hurry to do anything.

"What the . . ." Hank said, several steps behind me.

"Soldiers," I said, stating the obvious. "C'mon, guys." I kept walking.

"What do you mean, 'c'mon'?" Hank asked. I turned and he looked at me as if I were deranged.

"We're not doing anything wrong," I said. "And we're not skinheads or anarchists. We might as well stay in Kansas if we're not going to see what's really going on."

Would Joseph Conrad, George Orwell, Jack Kerouac, or Ken Kesey turn back? I don't think so. Would Johnny Cash or John Lydon flinch? No chance. Would Hunter S. Thompson not walk right into the fucking breach? Hell yes.

"But, Rob, man, this is . . ." I didn't hear the rest, because I was already marching down the hill, Elissa at my side. I nodded to her and she nodded back. I could see that she was exhilarated but also frightened. And trusting. I would like to say that I was thinking about her, about her safety. I wasn't. I was thinking about me. I hadn't felt this alive in years, not since I was in a spinning car waiting for the extreme sensation that the onrushing brick wall would deliver me.

A few of the soldiers looked our way, but none of them moved. I headed for the path leading to the side of the armored personnel carrier. As we neared, more and more heads tracked our progress. Their green uniforms were crisp. Elissa squeezed my hand tighter. A hundred eyes watched us from under their upturned visors. Elissa's pulse raced ahead of mine. Then they were right in front of us, shields down, batons dangling.

"Abend," I said, hoping to sound casual, but not too casual.

"Abend," several voices called back.

I kept walking. Elissa relaxed her grip, then squeezed twice. That signal—to me it meant that yes, we had walked through the fire. Together. This was the moment I had been living for.

But I had to go on.

At the edge of the park I turned around, and Hank was still at the top of the hill, by the corner, a good hundred meters away. Shoulders hunched, he was trying to shrink, to disappear on himself like a black hole. I waved to him, aware that the soldiers were watching our pantomime. I knew I was publically humiliating and emasculating Hank, and I didn't care. If he wanted to be part of the show, he had to come along. After a few seconds, Hank rocked off his heels, then hesitantly shuffled forward, eyes down.

"C'mon, c'mon," I urged, impatient, punishing, but also not wanting the soldiers to have any excuse to detain us. *Nothing to look at here. Just us chickens, on a harmless stroll.* When he finally caught up, I led us away from the soldiers and out of the park. *This is my fucking city.*

"What was that?" Hank hissed.

"Nothing. Just soldiers." Glass crunched under my hightops. I could've taken them off and sprinted over the shards without getting a scratch.

21

"You can't copy anybody and end up with anything. If you copy, it means you're working without any real feeling."
—Billie Holiday

Soundtrack: Billie Holiday, "Don't Explain," 1944

WHEN THE CHAUTAUQUA FESTIVAL ENDED, my father and I didn't go home to Rochester, but instead drove our trusty old Hornet south, to my new home without him. After two days of driving we passed the Georgia-Florida border, the humid, late-August air thick with bugs. I put a plastic bag over my hand and stuck it out the window to see how many I could catch. The bugs—some big and black, others smaller, yellow, black, and red, a few bottle-green—stung my hand as their bodies smashed into my plastic-covered palm. My father flicked on the windshield wipers to smear away the dead insects, not wanting to miss the turnoff for Disney World. This detour was his way of distracting me into forgetting what was coming, or maybe to make up for the upcoming drive back north to my mother's house in Lynchburg, Virginia, where she'd moved to teach after getting her master's degree. I kept thinking, *First my mother leaves, now my father's leaving. I don't even know my mother.* I hadn't seen her since Easter. At least in New Orleans I would have had my cousins. In Lynchburg I would know no one except my mother, who didn't know anyone there either.

My father tried to be cheery, in his manner, playing our usual word games, pulling over for strange foods, signaling funny signs and strange town names—Jane Lew, Mink Shoals, Hurricane. It could have been like any of our other drives, except that Linus and Lucy kept yowling at the heat and uncertainty, panting in their carrier. I tried to smile through the misery, never thinking about how excruciating the experience must be for him.

At Disney World, we parked in a massive parking lot. I wondered how we'd ever find the car again, and hoped that, at the end of our day of fun, we wouldn't. We tromped around the squeaky-clean grounds till we reached the line for Space Mountain, surrounded by fat Americans in bright colors. I had plenty of time to study the warning sign: "IF YOU HAVE A HEART CONDITION, DO NOT RIDE SPACE MOUNTAIN. PUT YOUR GLASSES IN YOUR SOCK. ENJOY THE RIDE."

When my father stopped in front of my mother's nondescript brick apartment complex, I think he said, "Love you, kiddo." I don't remember my father and mother talking, though they must have. He must have handed her my suitcase, my cat carrier; he didn't just dump me and my possessions on the curb. I do remember him getting back into his green Hornet. *His*. It used to be *ours*. Now there I was, in my new home, with my mother. With a reassuring smile, she showed me around an apartment that was twice as big as my father's, and ten times more orderly and clean, though a hundred times more bland. While the cats hid under the big, clean white sofa in the living room, I went to my new room and sobbed. I cried and cried and cried, all the while trying not to. Even though I didn't really know my mother, I didn't want her to think I hated her. After collecting myself, I went to the bathroom and doused my face with a cold washcloth.

But she could tell.

"It's okay to be sad," my mother said, her hand on my back. "You've been with your father for years. Of course you're going to miss him. But it's going to be okay."

I nodded. Why did she want me there? Did she think of me as a feral child? A reclamation project?

"No!" my mother suddenly yelled, and ran toward the sofa. Lucy stopped peeing and dashed past us into my room.

"I'm so sorry," I said, the three-inch yellow circle slowly spreading. "What can we do?"

My mother ran into the kitchen and came back with paper towels, a bottle of seltzer, baking soda. "Here, blot it as best you can," she said, handing me the roll of paper towels. I pressed down on the warm liquid, and then my mother carefully covered the spot with baking soda and slowly poured seltzer over the fizzing, bubbling mixture. As she wiped up the mess, she said, "See. It's going to be okay."

I guessed it would be, and was impressed that only an hour later the spot was gone. It wasn't until months later that I noticed that my mother had flipped the cushion, the stain almost gone, but still noticeable if you were looking.

Lynchburg was a different kind of green than New Orleans, more woodsy and controlled, and in the heart of the town was the school where my mom had taken a tenure-track job as an assistant professor: Randolph-Macon Woman's College, down the road from Jerry Falwell's Liberty University. At the public school I attended, all of my classmates had lived in Lynchburg their entire lives. They were more welcoming and genuinely friendly than my Rochester classmates, but I didn't know what to do with this collective kindness.

However, I had to learn, and quickly. I wouldn't be going to my mother's job with her, as I had with my father. I was supposed to play with other kids. Marbles, Fort, Pretend—I didn't know how to play, or how to do most anything that other eleven-year-olds seemed to do naturally. I had a bedtime. I ate regular meals. I chafed at any routine; I was bored by the regularity, the predictability of every aspect of my new life. At home, I tried not to show my unhappiness, but I can imagine what a sullen picture I made, what a miserable job my mother had as a parent as she tried to integrate me back into the world of "normal" kids. She signed me up for piano lessons, which were tedious for both me and my teacher.

I tried to be a good son, a decent citizen. At Halloween, my mother, an expert with needle and thread, fashioned a bear costume out of an old fur coat. A couple of my new friendly class-mates walked with me through our development and I knocked on the door of a nice older woman I'd seen out working in her garden. The door opened, the lady's arm in a cast, her left eye red, the area around it purple, green, and black. "I'm sorry," she said, "I fell down the stairs a few days ago and couldn't get candy. Here's a quarter."

"Thank you, ma'am," I said, the tears starting. Such was my fragile state that while I craved disruption from the rou-tine, if that disruption was sad, my normal-happy-kid façade instantly shattered. I walked past my classmates, mumbling something about needing to get another bag from home and that I'd catch up. But seeing that banged-up lady took away what little manufactured joy I had mustered for the evening. I didn't go back out. I told my mother that yes, I had had a great time.

I read and read and read. To escape, yes, but also to find myself. In the real world, no one was like me. But in the pages of *The Chronicles of Narnia, Lord of the Rings,* and *The Prince of Central Park,* there I was. Or at least there was who I wanted to be. Unlikely hero Bilbo Baggins, dogged and quietly enterprising. Unflappable Susan Pevensie, with her badass bow and arrows. Or the kid who runs away to Central Park and lives in the trees and scrounges for coins in the Met fountains, invisible to the adult world.

Outside of books, I saw the future as a predictable morass. Though my parents hadn't said anything to me, it was apparent that I would be spending the next seven years, until I graduated high school, with my mother in Lynchburg. The overwhelming reality of my confinement gripped me in church one day as I was sitting by myself in a pew, fanning myself with the program. My mother was the principle soloist, something I thought she would be proud of, or take joy in, but she treated it like just another gig, professionally singing hymns right out of her dour Southern Illinois childhood. We had a deal—I would go to church and behave while she sang, then we got to go to Friendly's, where I could have any kind of sundae, with four flavors, the whole works. I would have behaved even without the bribe, but I liked the bribe. As she sang, I considered watermelon, cherry, black raspberry, and chocolate—mixed together. Or maybe peppermint and lemon. Seven more years of sweating the big decisions like cherry versus peppermint. But first stand up, sing, sit down, stand up, sing, sit down.

The next thing I knew there was light on the other side of my closed eyelids. I was lying down. When I opened my eyes, I was in the church's vestibule, my mother kneeling over me in her black robes. I watched her lips move. "Are you okay?" I nodded. Then she said, "Is this the best way to get attention?" I couldn't tell if she was joking.

22

"We make the oldest stories new when we succeed, and we are trapped by the old stories when we fail."

—Greil Marcus

Soundtrack: Elvis Presley, "Any Way You Want Me (That's How I Will Be)," 1956

WE ZIGZAGGED FARTHER into the heart of Prenzlauer Berg, the old bohemian section of East Berlin, along light and dark blocks, then down a narrow street which terminated in another city park, this one bigger and brighter, and instead of a heroic Teuton, a statue of the martyred German socialist artist Käthe Kollwitz. A few blocks later we hit another park, across from which a dozen or so young men and women were standing in soft yellow light spilling out of an open doorway. Smoking and laughing, most holding beer bottles, these people were the first we'd seen since the soldiers.

"PTA meeting?" Elissa ventured.

"If they're skinheads . . ." Hank said.

"They're not skinheads!"

"I see hair," Elissa said. "Definitely hair."

"Anarchists?" Hank asked.

"Who cares? Let's go," I said.

"Great. Let's go get killed," Elissa said. "After you."

I nodded to the young men and women as we passed through the doorway, and they nodded back, each of us feigning indifference.

Inside, the large square room was filled with more young Easterners sprawled on mismatched furniture: tattered leather armchairs, a black-and-white Bauhaus-print love seat, a three-legged kitchen chair. Many of them wore altered military clothing, the hammer-and-compass cut out of the East German flag insignias, black and red anarchist "A" patches in their place; others had tied on swatches of pink cloth ribbon. Spacemen 3's "Revolution," coming from unseen speakers, set a fuzzy, feed-backy musical vibe that felt like a sonic handshake meant for me. Through the haze of pungent Eastern cigarette smoke, I saw beers sliding out of a slot in the back wall, a foot high and three feet wide, what might once have been a receptionist's window.

"Open to the public?" Elissa asked, gesturing to the bar.

"Let's find out," I said.

"Dreimal, bitte," I requested, tentative.

A raspy female voice politely responded, *"Eins, bitte,"* and I slid her a mark.

"Danke sehr," I said as she slid me back three dark bottles.

"Three beers for a mark, about a buck fifty," I told Hank and Elissa, handing over the bottles with what I'm sure was a shit-eating grin. I pointed out that everyone in the room was an Easterner. "Look at the clothes, like faded copies of Western clothes. And the eyes. They won't look at you directly—in the Stasi years you'd get reported for simply making eye contact with a Westerner. You'd go to jail if the Westerner turned out to be undercover Stasi."

"No wonder it was such a destination vacation," Elissa quipped.

We stayed close to the makeshift bar, near a long corridor lined with small rooms. Out of the corner of my eye I noticed a sparking Cuban cigarette, made with foul tobacco and wrapped in sugarcane-soaked rolling papers which set off tiny sparks when burned. I had forgotten about those, and wondered what else was going to show up from my past.

The cold beer took the edge off the cultural time warp. My body felt like it was still speeding forward, like after an overnight drive when you are exhausted yet still buzzing, the body saying, *We can still go, go, go.* I ordered myself, *Settle. Be here; don't run.*

After we ordered a second round of beers, a tall, serious man asked me if I was *"Engländer?"*

"Nein."

"Amerikaner?" he ventured, wary but curious.

"Ja, aber ich bin in Stuttgart geboren," I told him, quickly adding that my friends didn't speak German. I held my breath as the man scrutinized us.

"I am so glad you are here," the man said, effortlessly switching to English. I exhaled along with the rest of the room; everyone had been waiting for one person to be bold enough to approach us. Ralf, who was slightly older than the others, turned out to be a world-renowned particle physicist, but had been denied his own computer because he was a member of the New Forum. "We advocated more tolerance," Ralf told us, "but within the socialist movement. And for this we were all marked by Stasi."

"Was this a New Forum meeting place?" I asked.

"Yes, yes," Ralf said. "We used to meet here. It was a secret alcohol-rehabilitation clinic. It was shut down two years ago, and one of our members had the key. Now it is the Café Westphalia, but everyone calls it the CV."

"Who runs it?" I asked.

Ralf looked puzzled. "Runs?"

"Owns?" I asked.

"Owns?"

"Yes, whose place is this?"

"Everyone's. We all give Ringo over there money," Ralf said, nodding toward a ponytailed guy with a quarter-sized silver hoop through each ear. "He is a carpenter's apprentice, but fixes other things. He goes to the West with his truck to buy beer and we then have an inexpensive place to drink and gather."

"But who owns the space?" I pressed.

"No one. Everyone," Ralf said with a shrug.

As we talked, others approached, and Ralf introduced us to Margaret, Dieter, and Liesl, who worked in the Bat Theater Studio around the corner, which had been state-funded but was now in reunification-pending limbo. Soon we were surrounded, the Germans pressing in with their six-inches-too-close for me sense of personal space, and I was assaulted by an onrush of sesquipedalian German nouns, Teutonic mash-ups of four, five, or six small noun-ideas that formed one mega-noun-idea. I hadn't really spoken the language since I was ten, and then the deepest concept had been arguing about soccer, specifically the merits of Beckenbauer's rugged national team versus the elegance of Pelé's Brazil squad (I took the politically incorrect stance of favoring Brazil's free-flowing "beautiful game" versus the brutal and controlled style of the Germans). Now everyone wanted to talk Art and Politics and Reunification.

Voices were rushing at me, and I felt like I was in a Hong Kong action flick where the hero is being attacked by a dozen thugs at once—*Look out, he's got an axe! Behind you, a cudgel!* To the left, a guy with a mini-Mohawk was asking me about the secret East German funding of the Baader-Meinhof Gang. But this was no joke to them. They wanted real, deep conversation. The guy with the Mohawk looked earnestly through his smudged oval glasses and asked me, "When does the universal struggle for freedom cross the line to terrorism and oppression? And can you justify revolutionary acts if they are being supported by government forces fighting proxy wars?" What led their elders in the East and West to join Baader-Meinhof-influenced Revolutionary Cells, to kidnap bankers and then work with the Popular Front for the Liberation of Palestine to commit two very high-profile hijackings in the late seventies, ending in bloody rescue missions in Entebbe and Mogadishu? I understand the impulse in the face of oppression and fascism, and said, "My revolution is your revolution."

He nodded and said, "Or, as your Martin Luther King proclaimed, 'Until all people are free, no people are free.' But what would you have done here?"

I took a deep breath and said, "I would have joined the fight against fascism in the Spanish Civil War, and, if I had been a young German in the seventies I could see kidnapping bankers like the Baader-Meinhof Gang did, but, like MLK, I am opposed to violence and terrorism, especially against civilians."

"Then you do not have the moral fiber for revolution and would have lived in fear under the East or West governments, which were equally oppressive at the time," my new friend said without a trace of humor.

"Perhaps," I said, his true words stinging, "but I would have fought peacefully, with words and art." By the look of the young East German's condescending smile, I realized how naive and ridiculous I sounded.

But before I could form a more thought-out response, a woman who had been listening to us interjected a question about whether I would now join the resistance against resurging fascism, skinheads blaming Muslim immigrants for the lack of jobs, brazenly attacking them in the streets, their ire stoked by factories shutting down across East Germany? "However we can help," I said, which felt weak and nebulous. I was over my head. The man and woman looked at me expectantly, and in the uncomfortable silence I tried to collect myself. I fumbled on for a few more minutes until Hank's head swiveled violently and I followed his gaze down the hall, where three women were emerging from a back room. One of the women was black, the other two Hispanic.

"Looks like we're not the first Westerners in here," Hank said.

"Alas, Livingston, we tried," Elissa said.

"No, no," Ralf said. "They are not from the West. Those two are Cuban, and she is from the Belgian Congo. They were here to study at the university, which may or may not reopen in October. Now they are trapped here. Their governments are not able to bring them back."

For hours I tried to engage with these descendants of Dietrich, Kollwitz, and Brecht, to rise to their intellect and sense of urgency, but their words and ideas were beginning to run together, and my brain muddled like a kid's watercolor set after too much use—all of the colors had a puddle of brown on the top. Over or under the din of conversations I tuned back in to the music, which I now noticed was coming from four small, white speakers mounted in the top corners of the room. Spacemen 3 had given way to a tape loop of The Residents covering Elvis Presley songs, a hallucinatory Elvis-from-hell sound. Weirdly, we had seen The Residents performing these exact same songs a few months before in New York, which felt as likely as having seen Marlene Dietrich's cabaret show the previous week.

We'd been at the CV for what felt like a long time, but I couldn't tell if it had been one hour or eight. I was reoriented when Ralf said that it was 2 A.M. and he needed to get some sleep before he went to work in the morning, but not before he led me to Ringo, who introduced himself to me with "I find you a flat, for mostly nothing."

"How much?" I asked.

"Fifteen marks for the month," Ringo said, his dark eyes bright with anticipation, his neat ponytail bobbing as he rocked on his heels. Fifteen marks? Roughly twenty dollars for an apartment? For that, we could stay in Berlin almost indefinitely.

"Yes, for fifteen marks," Ringo repeated. "Across the park, a little down Dunckerstrasse. I take you now, so that we do not disturb the neighbors later. I have key. I walk you there, then we come back and if you like, you give me money and I give you key."

"Legal?" I asked.

"Legal?" Ringo laughed. "There is no 'legal' here."

"My kind of place," I told him, though I wasn't sure why— my words and decisions seemed out of my control. "Let me check with my friends," I said.

"Is it safe?" Hank asked.

"Safer than sleeping in the car."

"Like with a lock and key?" Hank asked.

"Lock, yes, but I don't know the neighborhood."

"Is this crazy?" Elissa asked, slightly unsteady, and I wondered if I was as drunk as she was. Somewhere down in my drunk reptilian brain her question registered as a valid concern, but I wasn't letting on. Both Hank and Elissa were deferring to me. They were now less partners than sidekicks.

"Maybe," I said, "but let's check it out. If it doesn't look safe in the morning, we'll go find someplace in the West." I said this, but like when I walked through the soldiers, I had no intention of honoring the safe and the secure. I was positive Ringo's flat was going to work out. It was meant to be.

23

"My loathings are simple: stupidity, oppression, crime, cruelty, soft music."

—Vladimir Nabokov

Soundtrack: Elton John Band, "Philadelphia Freedom," 1975

AT THE END of the school year in Lynchburg, I was nervous about my father picking me up. Would he be different? Was I? Would our car time no longer be sacred? But only a few miles along Route 29 my father pointed out the first Stuckey's and I knew that we were safe. As we drove to Chautauqua, now via an unfamiliar southern route, we settled back into our driving rhythm, the entire tense year dissolving behind the Hornet.

That summer I was finally old enough for a substantial opera part, in a production I was genuinely excited about. Most operatic plotlines were safely far-fetched, but *Albert Herring* hit home. The small, intimate comic opera has only thirteen roles and a thirteen-piece orchestra. Albert is a young man who is so good and kind and unworldly that he is elected King of the May because the village maidens are corrupted and couldn't possibly be elected Queen of the May. His friends, the couple Sid and Nancy (really), can see that poor Albert's soul is dying from all the goodness. They spike his lemonade and he goes on a bender, finds himself having sinful and worldly desires, and then gets up the courage to be who he wants to be, which is not a teetotaling churchmouse who does what he is told but someone who will question authority and leave his tiny village to engage the great, big messy world. At age eleven, I was a pre-bender Albert Herring—always well behaved, always blending in, never getting in trouble, and always on the verge of exploding. I wanted nothing more than to be post-bender Albert Herring.

The second act began with me, alone in the middle of the stage, bouncing a pink ball off a door, singing in rhythm to the bouncing ball: "Bounce me high, bounce me low, bounce me up to Jer-i-cho." I thrived on the pressure of performing, basked in the attention, and couldn't believe I was being paid. Union scale for a principal role was $110 a night, minus ten bucks because I was only eleven and the festival was fined for violating New York State Labor Laws, a cost they passed on to me. Still, a hundred bucks a night buys a lot of grape soda and a lot of rounds of mini-golf.

I spent my days either at the opera house or playing mini-golf. The course was across the parking lot from the rehearsal garage, and hour after hour disappeared as I whacked around red, yellow, blue, and green golf balls. I got good enough to switch to a more "professional" white ball and play tournaments. The Sumners, the nice, white-haired couple who owned the place, let most of the regular kids spend the afternoons hanging out, not charging us for more than a couple of games even though we played ten, twenty rounds a day. We pros drank Welch's grape soda and looked down on the "civilians" who were there for the fun of it. Thirty-plus years later I can tell you the layout of each of the thirty-six holes, from the loop-de-loop to the windmill. I loved the logic and control of the game, all anxiety vanishing as I focused on one simple problem—how to get the ball from point A to point B. I played so much that summer that I won the Junior

Putt-Putt Championship and got a big, shiny trophy and a snazzy Liberty Bell–shaped putter. Overhead, against the backdrop of the hazy sunset, mosquitoes and moths popped and sparked in the bug zappers hanging next to the tinny speakers that played a rotation of two songs: "Afternoon Delight" and "Philadelphia Freedom."

Midsummer, my mother wrote to tell me that we were moving to Baltimore. I was surprised, but I shouldn't have been. The previous December my mother had started calling in sick to the church gig, me missing Friendly's in order for us to drive to Baltimore to see David Fetter, a college classmate of my parents. David's roommate at Eastman, a tuba player named Roger Bobo, had briefly dated my mother right before she and my father started going out. Now the principal trombone player in the Baltimore Symphony, David and my mother had run into each other at a concert in Washington, D.C. Recently divorced, he also had a son, a few years younger than me. Most winter and spring weekends we either drove to Baltimore or David came to us.

Mom, always deft with her sewing machine, now made copies of designer dresses, wore more makeup, and had her hair done more often. I did want my mother to be happy, and it helped that I liked David. He gave me plenty of space, didn't try to throw a baseball with me and replace my father. David reminded me of a George Booth cartoon character from *The New Yorker*, which my mother subscribed to, and which I looked through for the cartoons, loving the very un-Lynchburg-like Booth eccentrics sitting on porches with their wild hair and cats and plants and musical instruments. David lived on the edge of Hampden, a grimy working-class neighborhood of narrow Baltimore row houses. The second or third time David came to Lynchburg, he brought me two old blue-cloth hardback novels by Joseph Conrad. I was stunned. How did he know?

I liked having David in my life, but it made me miss my father even more. When I went to Rochester at Christmas, I was expecting Dad to be as lonely and miserable as I was. Yet, while he was happy to have me there, nothing had changed—he lived to play, consume, and teach music. The one thing that had changed was that he no longer needed to be near a suburban elementary school, so he had moved closer to Eastman, into a smaller, sparer apartment. Holding down two positions—one in the piano department, one in the opera department—he would wake up and grab a coffee cup, go to work, refill his mug fourteen times, then go home at midnight. He told me that he knew it was fourteen because his doctor asked him to count. When he tried to quit cold turkey, he had heart palpitations and severe headaches. His doctor asked him, "Why the hell did you quit?"

Toward the end of summer, my mother wrote again, this time to tell me that she and David had married. "A small, private wedding," my mother told me. It was so exclusive, in fact, that I wasn't invited. I was happy for my mother, truly, and happy that she had found David, but I didn't understand why I wasn't included. It made me feel that I was some kind of reclamation project, a ward of her state, not a member of her family. I felt like I was going to be a boarder in their garret—visions of *La Bohème*.

Two weeks later, as my father and I drove through Hampden, I said, *"Die meisten Amerikaner . . ."*—German for "Most Americans are . . ." This was the old game from our Berlin years, where we filled in the blank with words like "fat" and "lazy" and "stupid."

"Ja, ja," my father said, trying to force a smile.

I remember little of the exchange, the handoff from one parent to the other.

But I was determined to make the best of my latest hometown; no crying in the closet this year. I would start by exploring on my new bike. I guessed this was my mother's welcome-to-Baltimore present, or a gift to distract me from noticing that we'd moved in with David and I was attending my fourth school in four years (in two countries, and in three different states). *Let's see what this sucker can do,* I thought as I jumped on my shiny silver Schwinn ten-speed.

The air was thick and dirty, the streets filled with people trying not to die from heatstroke. Fire hydrants were open, kids running through them, no one noticing me riding by. I skirted around the Johns Hopkins campus, headed up Twenty-eighth Street, but it had too many cars, so I zigzagged into the thirties, crossed St. Paul, Calvert, the row houses getting smaller and smaller. Past Greenwood, then round a corner and headed down a smaller side street in the middle of which a dozen black teenagers—bare-chested, their tattoos glistening with sweat—were playing football. I pedaled toward them, and the game stopped.

Every single kid stared at me as if I were a three-headed mermaid. *What's so weird about a kid on a bike?* I smiled at them, and this was met by a wall of incredulity. No one moved. I was halfway through their stalled football game when a tall guy with gold caps over his incisors yelled out, "Let me hold your bike." Suddenly all the teenagers were laughing, laughing like it was the funniest thing they'd ever heard or seen. Another kid yelled out, "Nah, man, let him go—he's from Oklahoma." He said "Oklahoma" long and slow, enunciating each syllable— *Ohh-klaa-hoh-maaa*—like I was brain-damaged.

I sped away round the corner and sprinted to my new home. At the back door I gathered myself, slowed my breathing. I didn't want my mother to worry about me. I never said a word to her about that first ride.

24

"Everyone chases after happiness, not noticing that happiness is right at their heels."

—Bertolt Brecht

Soundtrack: Bertolt Brecht and Kurt Weill, "Lied von der Unzulänglichkeit Menschlichen Strebens (Song of the Insufficiency of Human Struggling)," from *The Threepenny Opera*, 1928

WE FOLLOWED RINGO out of the CV and across the park, then a half block down Dunckerstrasse, through a tall, white marble archway that was riddled with bullet marks, unrepaired since the Russians had fought through there on their way to the Reichstag thirty-five summers before. "Let me go first," Ringo said, and crossed the dark cobbled courtyard to an unmarked door. "There is no light." He wasn't joking—it was utterly black in the hallway. We stumbled behind, up one flight, regrouping on the landing, which was barely illuminated by diffuse moonlight peeking through the window. Up two more flights, Ringo unlocked a large, square, empty room, maybe twenty by twenty feet, with four arched windows along the southern wall, facing the central courtyard.

"I will help you with furniture and lights," Ringo declared.

"No lights in here either?" Elissa asked.

"There is electricity, that I know," Ringo said. "And tomorrow morning we will find chairs, tables, lamps, whatever you want. All of it free."

"Where?" I asked, wondering what Ringo's scam was.

"Everywhere. The streets are filled with thrown-away treasure."

"Come on," I protested.

"No. I am serious. My people are throwing away all things old. They now go over to the West to buy your new plastic furniture. Our streets are filled with excellent old things. I show you tomorrow."

"If you say so."

"So do we have a deal?" Ringo asked, handing me the key like he already knew the answer.

I looked to Elissa, who was sitting on the granite windowsill. "I'm tired." And to Hank, who was lying down on the floor, his arms crisscrossed over his face.

"Yes," I said. "We'll take it."

25

"My claim is to live to the full contradiction of my time, which can make sarcasm the condition of truth."
—Roland Barthes

Soundtrack: Bee Gees, "Stayin' Alive," 1977

MY NEW SCHOOL in Baltimore was private, white, preppy. I adapted. I blended in. I hunkered down. I existed in order to make it to summer. I made it.

I'm unscathed and unchanged, I thought as I breathed in the familiar plastic smell of the fake-grass putting greens at the Chautauqua Putt-Putt. Everything was the same, including the Top 40 coming out of the tinny speakers that hung from poles scattered around the two courses. But immediately I felt that something had changed. The same cheery songs now bugged the crap out of me, and I was playing like shit. The problem with my game started with thinking. Before, I never thought—I just played. Now, when I flubbed an easy shot, I overthought the next shot, which I would then also flub, which led me to swear that if I heard the Bee Gees's "Stayin' Alive" one more time, I'd use my Liberty-Bell-shaped champion's putter to club the speakers into submission.

To bring myself around, I'd go to the overgrown field behind the water hazard on the seventh hole and tee up some balls, sending them over the cattails and into the woods. This usually calmed me down, but one day, after teeing a few into the woods, I returned to the windmill and nailed the slowly spinning blade twice in a row. I tossed my club over my shoulder and nearly hit a civilian. The offended father turned in my Liberty Bell putter to the Sumners, who had no choice but to ban me for a week.

"What triggered this?" my father asked when I told him.

Where do I begin? I thought, but said, "Guess I felt the pressure of being the defending champion. I need a break anyway."

My father hesitated, needing to leave for a rehearsal, and I almost said more, but I didn't.

I spent much of my Putt-Putt banishment week down the street from our cabin, in a grand, lakefront Victorian owned by Senator Charles Goodell, a hero of my father's. Even though Goodell was a Republican, he had been appointed to the Senate after the assassination of Robert Kennedy, had fought publicly against Nixon over Vietnam, and had even tried to impeach Nixon in 1970, four years before Watergate would finally bring him down. Senator Goodell always welcomed me into his house. His five sons, the youngest a year older than me, enjoyed having yet another boy around to beat at games, particularly pool and Ping-Pong. Food was always out, and friends constantly dropped by for organized activities like football (one of the sons, Roger, would become the commissioner of the National Football League), fishing, and sailing, and sometimes we'd sail over to Midway, the ancient amusement park on the other side of the lake, where we'd play skeeball for hours.

I felt like an honorary member of their family and fantasized about stowing away with them at the end of the summer. I envied the raucous, sprawling solidarity of the Goodells and wondered if they'd notice or care about the addition of an extra boy, or if my mother would notice or care about the subtraction of one.

Since Chautauqua was dry, the cast parties were held off the reservation, near a river and cold springs that kept the kegs and watermelons chilled. After my Putt-Putt-free week, there was a cast party for *Tosca*, which had been a trying but ultimately powerful production. It was early August, the summer company now a cohesive unit, inhibitions shed, drunk singers swaying in the grass, Al Green singing about Love and Happiness. I didn't know what to do. How did you dance this slow? I was fine when we were dancing to James Brown, but now what?

A sweaty hand grabbed mine. Julie. The choreographer for the opera. Julie was lithe and graceful, and I found it hard to form words when she was around. *Help me*, I tried via telepathy. "Forget your legs," Julie said, and wrapped her free arm around my lower back. "There—sway with me." She shifted my weight with the palm of her hand. "That's it. Slow," she said into my ear, dampening my skin with her breath. "Forget your feet. It's all in your center of gravity, what you're doing with your upper body, how you're expressing yourself through the movement in concert with the music." I tried to listen and obey, my mind attempting to override my body, which wanted to run far, far away.

I gave in and swayed, lost but ecstatic. I could have stayed on the side of that river forever, but after a few more songs it was time to pack up the van with the empty kegs. "Ride shotgun, kid," Radar, the big baritone who played Scarpia, called over to me.

I looked to my father, and he said, "Fine by me," his small Hornet quickly filling with singers.

As we pulled through the gates, a whirling red light appeared behind us, and Radar pulled over. "Fucking Supercop," he said, and jumped out of the van. "Supercop the Rent-a-Cop" is what everyone called the head of the private security company that served as Chautauqua's police. From my mirror I could see Supercop in his cruiser, reaching for his bullhorn. "What? What is it?" Radar yelled. Radar was huge—six foot four and barrel-chested. Supercop stayed in his cruiser. At the beginning of the summer Supercop had given me a summons for riding a moped, because all "loud motors" were forbidden on the grounds.

"What's your name?" Supercop said through his bullhorn.

"Radar Sampson."

"And your passenger?"

"Robby Spillman. Now what do you want?"

"Have you been drinking?"

"No. I'm the fucking designated driver," Radar yelled.

"What's in the van?"

"Empty kegs that we're returning tomorrow."

"All of them empty?"

"Of course. We know the fucking laws," Radar yelled.

Supercop tossed his bullhorn into the passenger seat, backed up, then yanked the wheel violently to the left and peeled out.

A month later, on the way to my trial (apparently Supercop had filed charges after he left us), I should have been nervous, but my father and Radar were nearly in tears cracking each other up about the absurdity of me being charged with drunk and disorderly conduct.

"Robby the Rebel," Radar joked from the passenger seat of the Hornet. "You need some tattoos."

"We should have drawn some on him," my father said. "I remember when he was three and he stopped a dress rehearsal of *Die Fledermaus*."

"I don't remember that," I said, wondering what I could have possibly done.

"You climbed to the top of a hundred-foot ladder that led to one of the spotlight towers, terrifying everyone."

"What did you do?" Radar asked.

"I wasn't scared. Robby always listened. I asked him to come down and he did. The idea that Robby would be drunk and disorderly . . ."

Well, maybe I could be like Albert in Albert Herring, I thought. But the "disorderly" part scared me, seemed so public and exposed.

When the bailiff walked Radar, me, and my father up to the bench, Supercop was already there.

"Robby Spillman?" the judge asked my father.

"No, sir," my father said.

"I am, sir," I said.

The judge looked over at Supercop, and our miniature Clark Kent turned red.

"It . . . it . . . was dark, Your Honor," Supercop said, and everyone in the courtroom started laughing. I almost felt sorry for the stooge. Almost. But mostly I was exhilarated. My father had no time for authority, as it had no artistic function. But I was thrilled about going up against raw, stupid power.

That summer I had some small parts, but nothing as good as *Albert Herring.* For the season's last opera, *The Barber of Seville,* I was put to work as the unofficial assistant stage manager, and on the day of the first dress rehearsal I found myself carrying a window box full of fake flowers that needed to be hung on the plywood lip by the "window" painted on the scrim at stage right.

The Barber of Seville was a frothy, frivolous opera, with intricate, multipart singing which required elaborate but precise staging. Before the start of the dress rehearsal, the director had the set builder, Vince, out onstage to look at the fountain, around which revolved the first-act finale, a large ensemble song-and-dance number. Richard's directorial tendencies tended toward the obvious, the big, easy gestures and sight gags. Even though all of the singers were onstage in full costume, Richard was delaying the start of the rehearsal because for the first act finale, he thought that the fountain was being wasted. Sure, the singers danced upon and proclaimed their love from its two circular tiers, but the painted plywood fish sticking out of the cartoon waves should be made to dance. But how?

"Not with strings—they'll be seen," he told Vince. "What if someone goes under the fountain and waves the stick?"

"No one's small enough to get under the fountain," Vince said.

Richard looked around and saw me, hands full of fake red tulips.

"What about Robby? He could crawl under the fountain and at the end of the act, move the fish back and forth to the music?" I looked at Richard. Was he serious? I looked over at my father, sitting at the upright piano on the edge of the stage. He shrugged, as if to say, *Up to you, kiddo.*

"Sure," I said, "I'll do it."

My father gave me a big smile and Richard said, "That a boy." The entire cast was onstage, smiling at me, and I felt like the most important and useful kid in the world.

I put down the window box and the stagehands lifted up the side of the big black fountain so that I could crawl under. When they dropped the fountain over me, I couldn't see my

fingers in front of my face. I also couldn't breathe. *Don't panic,*
I thought, fighting back a scream.

"How is it?" Vince's muffled voice asked.

"Okay, but I don't think I can breathe under here," I said.

The lip of the fountain rose up and I scrambled out. "It's
really dark," I said, trying to sound calm.

"Damn it," Richard said, and I felt like a gutless loser.

"I can do it," I said. "Let me try again."

"You sure?" my father asked.

"Wait," Vince said. "I can cut a hole in the back."

He walked around the fountain twice, checking the sight
lines. "Yeah. The audience won't see it."

Vince got his hacksaw and cut a square hole in the back of the
fountain, just large enough for me to crawl through. Inside, I could
see my hands and the stick I was supposed to move back and forth.

Every night for a week I crawled under the fake fountain
and waited for my cue. Every night was the same fight against
panic. Every night the curtain would go up and I would have
to wait almost an hour for my cue. I would hear the curtain
whoosh open and the singers moving around me, the audience
settling in, putting their programs down. I had a flashlight pen,
but worried that I'd use up the batteries as I followed along in
the score. I waited until the tenor jumped onto the fountain
right over my head, which meant I had four pages to go. Every
night I fought the urge to scramble out and dive under the back
curtain. No one would see me, but if they did, the whole opera
would be ruined and I would disappoint everyone, especially
my father. I breathed steady, shallow, not too loud, and focused
on the stick in front of me, barely visible in the dim light, with
a small weight duct-taped to its end so that it remained fixed
until I was supposed to make it dance.

At least I didn't have to stay in character. Ever since *Albert Herring*, even with the minor parts, I found it harder and harder to be who I was supposed to be. My mind kept drifting and I would find myself thinking, *I'm not a nineteenth-century Roman altar boy, but a twelve-and-a-half-year-old American*. Unlike the characters of the books I was reading, I couldn't identify with these operatic constructions. I found it easier to imagine being a hobbit or a Narnian than Italian nobility. I also couldn't project identities onto fellow performers. I would look across the stage and see that Tosca wasn't really a lovely revolutionary, but Susan, a homely, two-hundred-pound soprano from Des Moines who was a whiny diva, and that her lover wasn't really her rebel lover but Michael, who wore a lot of leather and hung out with other men.

I also started focusing in on the audience, the same cranky old blue-hairs week after week. Sometimes, when I wasn't onstage, I would sit among them while they kibitzed and compared the current performance with all of the other versions of the same opera they had seen over the years, the opera itself—the story and the present performance, the *thisness*, the emotional core of music and libretto that once, a hundred, a hundred and fifty years ago, was immediate and vital—now an afterthought.

Under the fountain, as my breathing became more and more shallow, as the fear gripped me tighter and tighter, I had time to nurse a deeper worry: that I had no soul. Opera was no longer reaching me. Everyone around me, especially my father, was moved by this music, but I found it as emotionally disconnecting as an electrical manual. Worse than disconnecting—oppressive. For so long I had wanted to be part of this creative process, but this wasn't creative—it was a hundred-year-old pantomime performed for the rich and comfortable. I wanted to explode, to make noise, to throw bombs at the audience.

And then—*bam!*—James would jump up onto the fountain. He was an inch from my head, the wood sagging down toward my scalp as he jigged and squawked above me. *How sturdy is this plywood?* I would wonder as I switched on the penlight. Following the bouncing notes, there came the chorus, and then—cue the dancing fish to join in the joy of the ogre fooled and of true love triumphing. I'd wave the stick back and forth in tempo and hear the audience laughing. Relief. I could hear them, but I wished I could see them. I wished that they could all see me. They were all laughing at my fake fish. I wondered what they'd say if they knew it was me in there, a twelve-year-old kid waving a stick in the dark.

26

"If you don't know where you are going, any road will get you there."

—Lewis Carroll

Soundtrack: Jefferson Airplane, "White Rabbit," 1967

SOMEONE WAS CALLING my name from the bottom of a well. I didn't recognize the voice, nor the dark, dirty hardwood I was sleeping on. I sat up, head throbbing. The acrid smell of burning tires lingered. So it wasn't a dream that we had been awakened in the early morning by the smack of a Molotov cocktail and the screams and taunts of street-fighting skinheads and anarchists brawling their way up Dunckerstrasse.

I wound the evening back farther, to paying Ringo fifteen marks for a month's rent, then hiking ten blocks to where we had left Dusty, finding the flat in the dark and in our drunken state, then hauling our duffel bags up four flights. My memory loop skipped backward, to the CV and the incredible information dump we had received: about how in the year before the government's collapse the New Forum had bravely and publically pushed for reforms, about the closing of the obsolete Eastern factories and the East's looming unemployment crisis. But the dozen or more people also told us about how they loved and created amidst the confines of such thorough and systemic repression, how they found or made space for themselves. Jesus, did I envy them. And, as I held my head, I cringed as I thought about how much I wanted them to like me. I wanted everyone I met to be my best friend. The dancer, what was her name? The one who had told me that Pina Bausch was her church.

I looked over at Elissa, hoping she wouldn't see my shame, but she was asleep, peacefully so, curled in the fetal position atop a towel. She had seen my naked need when I was talking to Liesl, who was standing uncomfortably and arousingly close as she told me about her theatre's agitprop productions. I'd nodded earnestly but was fantasizing about living with her and Elissa as a revolutionary threesome. And then I'd started in about my own time onstage and how much I wanted to get back to performing, about the immediacy of the experience and how you can reach right into the audience with your words and feelings. I had looked over at Elissa, who had heard this bullshit, and she gave me a quizzical, amused look before turning back to her own conversation.

"Rob!" the voice called out again, from the courtyard.

I pulled myself up, hoping for another chance. I can do better. Be better. *Be myself,* I thought as I shuffled over to one of three giant Western-facing windows with massive gray granite ledges, something else I hadn't noticed the night before.

"Ringo?"

"Hello, Rob," Ringo said with a wave.

"Morning?" I said.

"Come, let's get furniture."

Right. I guess he wasn't joking. "We'll be right down," I yelled.

Hank and Elissa stirred, barely, Hank clutching a ball of jeans like it was a life jacket.

"He better damn well be bringing us coffee," Elissa said, but after a little cojoling I managed to get her and Hank downstairs.

"How far?" I asked Ringo.

"One or two blocks. You will see."

"Coffee?" Elissa pleaded from the backseat.

"Yes, yes, we can get that," Ringo said.

"All this broken glass," I said as I drove around a smoldering Trabant.

"The *autonomen*, the anarchist squatters," Ringo said, "from the fights with the skinheads."

"We heard them early this morning," I said. "Ralf warned us about the skinheads. Where do they come from?"

"North of the city where the old factories have shut down. They come in simply to mix it up with the anarchists. The Nazis have no jobs, so this is what they do instead. And our police have deserted because they do not get paid. The riot soldiers are paid, and they will crush anyone they find on the streets."

"Really?" Hank interjected, giving me the "you're an ass-hat" look.

"Yes, yes. The Western authorities cannot cross the border until reunification in October. Our riot soldiers are the only order. And they are a hard order."

Elissa and Hank's collective glare burned the back of my neck. How stupid had I been to march through those soldiers. We could have had our heads smashed in. We could have all vanished. No one knew we were in the East.

"Stop!" Ringo ordered.

"What?"

"There," Ringo said, pointing at a spread of furniture across the street.

Hank was already out of the car. I parked and we were right behind him. "Damn. Look at that inlay," Hank said, examining a set of ornately carved dark wood dining-room chairs set around a matching table. The chairs were placed as if someone expected us to join them, but there wasn't another soul on the street. Elissa waved me over to a half dozen open cardboard boxes.

"Check these out," she said, holding up a handful of red textbooks.

Next to the box was a hulking black tube radio with faded names along the dials—Dresden, Prague, Warsaw, Leningrad.

"Titov," Hank said, holding up a framed picture of the famous cosmonaut. "What are we going to do with all this?"

"Look at these textbooks and maps from the fifties and sixties," Elissa said.

"Elissa! You've got to come here," Hank ordered, holding up an enameled hairbrush set with combs.

"Dibs!" Elissa called out.

"Negatory. I saw them first," Hank said.

"No, not the things," Elissa said. "The story. I got dibs on the story." Soon she was spinning scenarios about whom these brushes had belonged to.

"Is okay?" Ringo asked.

"We've hit the mother lode," I told Ringo.

"Okay. This is okay. But every block is like this," Ringo said. "You will see. My countrymen are putting all things of the old order out by the curb."

27

"When words become unclear, I shall focus with photographs. When images become inadequate, I shall be content with silence."

—Ansel Adams

Soundtrack: The Clash, "Lost in the Supermarket," 1979

MY SECOND YEAR IN BALTIMORE was much like the first—forgettable. I lived in my fifth house in five years, but there was some continuity: I stayed in the same city and the same school for the first time since I was eight. At the beginning of the school year my mother and David had moved, from David's small Hampden row house to a bigger, nicer row house in Charles Village, a mile and a socioeconomic class away. It was a fixer-upper, and I helped strip the dozens of layers of wallpaper, peeling down through years and years of previous owners' tastes. Though it was a step up in class, it was still well below the suburban mansions most of my classmates lived in. I took the city bus to school, where I camouflaged myself to appear like any other preppy Baltimore eighth-grader.

After I'd spent another school year blending in and counting the minutes until summer escape, my father and I headed west to the mountains, where my father had been hired as co-director for the operas at the Aspen Music Festival. It was just in time: I'm sure I would have gotten into serious trouble as a teenager in Chautauqua. My father's green Hornet, more rust than iron, had finally fallen apart, and he replaced it with an equally hideous orange Pacer, which looked like a glass casserole dish and handled like one as well. The summer of '78 we started a ritual that would continue for the next nine years: The minute my last class ended, my father would pick me up and we would drive across the country, each year taking a different route, around a different theme. One year it was how many Major League Baseball games we could fit into ten days, which meant Baltimore to Cincinnati to Chicago (Cubs) to Milwaukee to Chicago (White Sox) to St. Louis to San Francisco to L.A. Another year it was national parks—Yellowstone, Glacier, Yosemite, Bryce, and Zion. Another year it was the World's Fair in New Orleans. And as I became more serious about running, my father planned the routes so that I could run twice a day.

Inside the car, hours could pass silently, my father Buddha-like as the West flowed by. He was absorbing it all, refreshing his soul for his art. Everything in his life was pointed toward his art. These two weeks in the car were his downtime for the year, a restorative break so that he could once again give everything to his music. How I envied this calm, this focus, this purpose to being.

I loved the long, close hours with my father, stopping at Stuckey's restaurants for pecan shakes, the windy miles ticking off, windows down, my right arm reddening in the sun, the country flattening, the horizon expanding into nothingness. And then, past Goodland, Kansas, and the Colorado border, the watch for Mount Evans began. We would stare straight ahead, due west, to where the clouds looked like mountains, and then, when Route 70 bent northwest near Limon, the white-tipped peak would begin to take shape through the haze, solidifying with each westward mile, and soon thereafter the entire front range materialized, the gateway to my new jagged playground.

On our way we always stopped for a few days in Kentucky. When he first told me that we were going to Aspen, my father said, "And we'll need to check in on home." *What, head back to Rochester?* I thought, but then realized that he meant his first home, to see his brother, parents, niece, and nephews. I had spent time with them sporadically, mainly at Christmas, but now we were locking into a summer-visit ritual, starting with the segue from rural western Maryland into hilly West Virginia, and then along Kentucky's rolling roads and white fences running through the bluegrass, past the grand horse farms outside of Lexington, to Paris and my uncle's flower farm, the greenhouses filled with multicolored carnations visible from the road.

As we drove up the long driveway, I felt like we were entering a negative time warp and that my blood was slowing down. In Paris, the pace was glacial. My three cousins, my aunt Tula, and my uncle Don did everything deliberately—not slowly, but with a determined earnestness. My uncle, thirteen years older than my father, was a career army man, and now that he was retired, the flower business supplemented his pension.

When he was seventeen he had lied about his age in order to enter the army. This was in 1940. He would become a platoon leader under Patton and march, on foot, from Normandy to Berlin, through the bloody Battle of the Bulge. He earned a Purple Heart and Medal of Valor for leading his men out of a booby-trapped village. Uncle Don had brought a Brownie camera with him, and when his unit liberated a concentration camp, he was pressed into service as an official photographer. His grim photos were used at the Nuremberg trials and were now locked in a trunk in his basement. He never spoke about the war, not even to his children. When I was little, he would speak to me in German, describing various German cities and the countryside he had seen, but nothing about the war.

My aunt Tula matched his calm and quiet with her loud Irish dervish, spinning through the kitchen as she barked orders about the multiple dishes she was always preparing. "What ya got for me, sweetie?" she would patiently ask when I came in. She had a simple rule—if you picked it, she'd cook it. So if I went out and picked a bushel of strawberries, she'd make ice cream and pie. "Thank you so much for picking those berries," she would say, pausing amidst the chaos to make sure that I felt at home, even though I was essentially making more work for her.

That night, my father and I riffed on any and all commercials, twisting them and jousting with each other over who could come up with the best wordplay—"What do you *mean*, I'm soaking in it?" Even as a spastic, hormonal teenager, I could tell by the blank stares that our riffing on Madge and Palmolive was coming off as glib and superior. Yet I couldn't stop, hoping to impress my family. But my father could—after I repeated the "soaking in it" joke, my father gave me a slight nod, as if to say, "Enough," then turned to his brother and asked, "Whatever happened to Lou?" *Where did he get that slight southern accent?* I wondered, before hearing his brother's matching lilt in response.

I was now on an island, stranded, but during a long and awkward *Love Boat* intermission, my cousin Chuck threw me a lifeline and took me up to his room to show off his huge collection of rock records. "Check this new one out," Chuck said, and handed me the jacket of Bob Seger's album *Night Moves* as he put the vinyl on the turntable. "I really admire Seger's work." I tried to focus on the music—plodding, earnest—but was hung up by Chuck's use of the word "work." I'd never heard

the word associated with rock 'n' roll or any other kind of popular
entertainment. You mean this is "work," as in it takes craft and
artistic intent and passion like classical music? You mean this
isn't cynically tossed off?

I had grown up with pop music being tolerated at best.
Back in Baltimore I had joined the Columbia Record Club. I
picked safe choices—The Beatles, Simon and Garfunkel, Jim
Croce, Roberta Flack. But for my first choice for my record of
the month—the self-titled debut album by Kansas—I thought
I was being daring. I snuck it up to my room and played it at
the lowest possible volume on my Tandy all-in-one eight-track/
record player, terrified that my mother might hear it.

"Work" implied that you didn't need to go to music school
or art school. It also implied that non-turtleneck-wearing in-
tellectuals and non-blue-hairs could seriously appreciate this
"work." I know it sounds ridiculous now, but at the time I existed
in such a rarefied world that hearing my cousin pair "Bob Seger"
and "work" unlocked future possibilities for me. Or at least
pointed me toward the doorway to possibilities.

After the initial day's awkwardness, I slowed down, and
that second afternoon, after stuffing myself with my aunt's
strawberry-rhubarb pie, I had the sudden romantic notion that
I wanted to live on the farm, that I could live with my Kentucky
family and be identified with a real, singular place. Besides, I
liked them—they were funny and kind and smart. The men were
unabashedly masculine, sincere, sure of themselves, unlike the
more entertaining but sometimes bitchy men who were in my
father's orbit. I could get used to the unhurried, serious life. But
the next day I came around to the reality that despite the blood
ties, and my aunt's grace, I never felt that I was truly a part of the
family. And even if I lived with them for twenty years, I doubt

that I would have ever truly fit in, or let myself fit in. This was my father's place and his people. He had chosen to leave, but he could choose to return, I imagined. For me, this would never be my place. These would never be my people.

This was reinforced when we went to see my grandparents, who lived twenty minutes away in Lexington, in a small, dreary, clapboard house that had none of the warmth of my uncle's farmhouse. As my grandmother opened the door, I was hit with the smell of mothballs and liniment oil. I had been around many older, active musicians—including the legendary Madame Mauz in Berlin, blind and unsteady and in her eighties, but still teaching voice to the best young singers, who flocked to her—but my grandparents weren't like Mauz or the other older people who lived their art until the day they died. My grandparents were ancient to me from as far back as I could remember them, and acted as if they were on call for a visit from death. My grandfather was a small, frail man who spoke so infrequently it was startling to hear his soft, southern tenor. And if you had met my grandmother, you'd know why—she was judgmental and mean, her worldview narrowed to only a handful of acceptable possibilities.

"So, you've come from the farm?" she asked me with a little sneer. "Your cousin Diana make you any of that 'sperimental cooking? Like that awful Quick Lorraine?"

I glanced toward my father, who stepped in. "We've had a nice time out there, Mother."

"Couldn't pay me enough to go out there," my grandmother said. "All them niggers on the way just as soon slit your throat as let you pass." My jaw must have been on the floor as my father gave me a complicit nod, as if to say, "Yup, your grandmother is a stone-cold racist."

We'd barely arrived when my grandmother said, "Let's go visit Tom"—my uncle Tom, the charismatic ladies' man, her beloved middle son. My father had told me that growing up, Tom had wanted to be like all the men in the family—a combat vet. Tom had enlisted in the army during the Korean War and sent home spectacular letters about his theater of action, with detailed, vivid accounts of heroism amidst horrific battles.

Only he'd never made it out of Washington State, where he was stationed. He had sent the letters to a friend stationed in Korea, who then mailed the letters, complete with war stamps, back to the U.S. My grandmother never knew. After the war, Tom ran a small canning company in Louisville, and somehow quickly parlayed this into being the president of a large export-import business in New York City, with a Gatsbyesque mansion on Long Island. His brothers would later find out that the company was a mob front. Always looking for a better angle, Tom skimmed off the top.

When he was caught, he was given the Roman option—kill himself or subject his wife and two sons to the greater horror of watching him get gunned down. He took the first option, locking himself in his garage and letting his BMW run until he was blue and dead. My father and my uncle Don told my grandmother that Tom died of a sudden brain tumor. At his grave, my grandmother wept over her "one true good son."

"Mother, Robby is going to stay here and keep his grandfather company," my father told his mother with none of the southern accent I had heard on my uncle's farm. I was surprised by my father's stern tone, as was my grandmother, who gave a stiff nod. I was relieved to be away from her, even though this meant that I would have to spend two or three hours with my grandfather, who hardly moved or spoke.

After the Pacer pulled away I sat on the sofa opposite my grandfather, who was sitting in his faded pea-green easy chair. With his equally well-worn green cardigan, it appeared as if he was melding with the upholstery. I didn't know what I should do or say. *Does he even know I'm here? Does he care?* But he was watching me, and in his eyes there was a spark of life. I didn't know that much about my grandfather except that he was really old—eighty-three, born the previous century, in 1895, the last of eleven children. I thought about asking him about his siblings, but instead reached for more reliable family-story fodder—combat.

"Where were you during the war?" I ventured.

My grandfather smiled and slowly sat up. It was like he'd been buried alive and I had yanked him into the light. "I was a truck driver," he said. "I drove supplies to the front. I was in Verdun when the Germans used mustard gas on our boys. I drove through clouds of the stuff. I drove with water-soaked rags over my face."

My grandfather's skeletal hands fluttered as he spoke of his many perilous trips to the front. "That was my *hardest* adventure," he said, leaning forward. "My *greatest* adventure was when I spent two years in India."

"You were in India?" I asked, stunned. My grandmother, who wouldn't go fifteen miles down the road to visit her son, had lived in South Asia?

"Incredible—the people, the food, the land. After I retired from the university in 1960, I joined a State Department–sponsored program to help third-world countries help themselves. I chose to work in Goa, which is in the southern part of India. At the time they were in the middle of a very bad drought and many people were starving."

"What did you do there?" I asked.

"I taught basic crop management and crop rotation, which was hard, but very gratifying when it worked. And it was beautiful. A beautiful, beautiful place with lovely people."

"How did Grandma like it?" I asked, trying to imagine her anywhere foreign, much less India.

My grandfather chuckled and shook his head. "She didn't. She didn't go. She stayed in Lexington," he said with a wistful smile. He didn't need to say that those two years were the happiest of his life.

Though he flagged a few times, my grandfather was animated for the two full hours that my grandmother and my father were gone, shutting down when the Pacer pulled into the driveway, apparently not wanting to be noticed by his wife. Later, driving back to my uncle's farm, I told my father about our conversation.

"Wow, that's terrific," my father said. "I haven't seen him come to life in years."

"I feel bad for him," I said.

"If I ever get like that, please shoot me," my father said without a hint of humor.

"What did he tell you about India?" I asked, not wanting to even go near my father's mortality.

"What he told me," my father said, "is that my mother said she would never live among 'Indian niggers,' and instead moved by herself from Berea to Lexington to be near Uncle Don, even though the family has to come to her. After he returned from Goa, your grandmother insisted that your grandfather's stomach had been ruined by the spicy food, so that's why she makes 'the meal' every day."

We had just suffered through the meal—a beef roast surrounded by carrots and green beans, which she put in the oven at
noon and didn't take out until 6 P.M., by which point the meat
and vegetables were desiccated. Twice on that trip, including the
last afternoon of our visit, we managed to take my grandfather
out to my uncle's farm. We sat him at the dining room table,
where he was surrounded by his grandchildren, who peppered
him with questions. My uncle brought him a snifter of Scotch
and my grandfather accepted it in silence, his eyes teary. He
lifted the snifter slow and steady, then took the smallest of tastes.

28

"If you want to know all about Andy Warhol, just look at the surface of my paintings and films and me, and there I am. There's nothing behind it."

—Andy Warhol

Soundtrack: Velvet Underground, "Beginning to See the Light," 1968

I LACED UP MY BATTERED ASICS, the same shoes I had worn when I injured myself while running in the mountains four years before. If I took it easy, didn't run too far or too hard, my left knee would hold up. After a week in our Prenzlauer Berg apartment, I needed to stretch my legs, get away from people, even the ones I loved. Hank was off sketching the Wall, like he did every afternoon, and Elissa was fast asleep, having gone on a six-hour writing jag where she didn't move from the little desk we had found. Every morning we had scavenged, decorating our new flat with refuse, constructing our lives out of the detritus of other lives. Now our bare, cold-water flat had been transformed into a cluttered home, filled with a half-dozen working lamps, two sofas, eleven chairs, stacks of books and framed pictures of spacemen and generals, piles of Communist trinkets, and two tube radios that pulled in a strange stew of music along with a cacophony of unknown tongues.

I jogged past the brand-new, impromptu wine bar on our corner, wondering if it would be open again that night, then crossed into the park, overruling muscle memory, my body's former ability to churn out six-minute miles ad infinitum, and instead focused on running slow and steady. I passed the CV, where we would no doubt start off our night like we had every night in the East. I focused on my breathing, slowly pushing out my abdomen as I inhaled, then forcefully exhaling. Cadence and breath synced with the first song on *Daydream Nation*, "Teenage Riot," and my internal soundtrack pushed me forward toward the Wall.

As I cut through backstreets, the chaos of the week sorted itself out. How ignorant had I been; I had thought that the Easterners had been in the dark, deprived of Western music and books. But they loved Sonic Youth, had passed around paperbacks of Kerouac and Ginsberg. It was a game they played with the Stasi. American and British and French radio stations were blocked and jammed, but everyone in the East shared smuggled tapes and books. We met Ralf every night at the CV, and he, in his scientific manner, answered any and all questions for us, from the mechanics of Stasi to his yearly springtime visits to Lake Baikal, where he was part of a research team looking for the neutrino, the elusive subatomic particle.

With music and literature, Ralf explained, "We would make copies; Stasi would take them and put them in our files. But we could always make them faster than they could take them." The game was much more serious when it involved creative acts by Easterners, which, if not state-approved, could be deemed subversive. "Last year a friend wrote a novel," Ralf told us, "and it was not so political—a fairy tale about Chernobyl—and she made six copies and gave them to her friends. Stasi tracked down all six. They took my copy from my apartment while I was at work."

Out of Prenzlauer Berg and into a blasted and blighted industrial area, I ran under dead traffic lights and past crumbling warehouses to the Wall, then along it until I reached a collapsed brick building that blocked the path. I thought about scrambling over the piles of bricks, but I had already been out for a half hour, so I turned back toward home. In August 1945, Berlin had an estimated forty million tons of rubble. Forty million. It took thousands of workers, mostly women, two-and-a-half years to clear the ruins. How long would it take Berliners to replace forty-five years of Communist rubble?

Not long, I imagined, as this was the self-reinventing Berlin of Marlene Dietrich, the polite schoolgirl born Marie Magdalene who reimagined herself as an androgynous chanteuse, who was the belle of the drag balls in the twenties, who toughened herself up for stage and screen auditions with boxing lessons from the "Terrible Turk," Sabri Mahir. Mahir himself was a reinvention. He was born Sally Mayer in Cologne, and picked up boxing, and his Turkishness, in Berlin. Then there was Berlin ballet star Helene Bertha Amalie, who reinvented herself as the filmmaker and intentional or unintentional (depending on if you believe her denials) Nazi propagandist Leni Riefenstahl. Or going back another hundred years, Hegel, who said, "Nothing great in this world has ever been accomplished without passion." He had been studious and thought within proscribed norms in his birthplace of Stuttgart, but reinvented himself as a revolutionary idealist philosopher here in Berlin.

Now, everyone in the East was going to have to reinvent themselves once again. Every time we went to the CV we heard new tales of re-creation. Craftsmen from the neighborhood were volunteering at the Rykestrasse Synagogue, a grand house of worship that had survived the Nazis and the neglect of the GDR, and which was now being refurbished. Everywhere, doors were being knocked down, secrets spilling out, the frenetic energy stoked by most everyone's lack of money. Apartments were cheap, but what would happen when the free market invaded in October? Same with food, clothes, alcohol. Cheap is expensive if you have nothing. The theater people had subsisted on government subsidies. Now there were no subsidies and theater patrons (aka theater people's friends) didn't have money for tickets, so writers, directors, actors, and anyone else involved were basically putting on their shows for free, with no admission price and no pay.

There was no work on the Western side of the Wall for Easterners, who were considered lazy and untrained. Instead, we kept hearing crazy stories of how people were surviving, like the previous night's wine-bar experiment. Others we met were being paid to give away "West Brand" cigarettes at bars, employed by a West German tobacco company hungry for the huge new market of smokers raised on crappy East German cigarettes. And then there were all of the shadier dealings that were going on. Ringo was always darting in and out of the CV, fetching things for anyone with money. Where he found these "things," I don't know, but he had connections everywhere. In a few weeks the Rolling Stones would be playing Radrennbahn Weissensee, the huge cycling stadium in the north of East Berlin, and Ringo was going to work the lights.

"Is there anything you can't find?" I asked him in a rare moment of stasis.

"No," Ringo said with a mischievous smile. "Let me tell you, I have this friend, who, I am not joking, said that he can get me old GDR tanks."

"C'mon, Ringo."

"No, no, I swear. He says they are the real Soviet T-55s and T-72s."

I should write about the new rebuilding, this new transition, I thought, not for the first time, and again felt sick about the idea of being a mercenary journalist. I wanted to protect my new friends, not exploit them. I had sporadically written in my diary, but nothing more. When I looked at *Coffee and Absinthe,* I was horrified by the frothy intellectual nonsense. As I ran back through Prenzlauer Berg, I knew there wasn't a single genuine thought or emotion in that book.

I slowed down, our corner in view, my knee achy but bearable. *Screw it,* I decided—I would reinvent myself, here in this secret interstitial zone that raided both East and West, Communist and capitalist. It was a well-used slate, pockmarked and cracked, but it was ready to be written over. East Berlin was about to cease to exist. In October it would become part of a new city, a new state. I could be at the rebirth of Berlin. I could live here. Not just for a few weeks. This could be *the* place. This could be the cultural moment I'd been waiting for my entire adult life. I was at the epicenter of post-Wall life, a petri dish of creation and foment, a rubble field in which to create a new world and life with the woman I loved.

I took the stairs two at a time, stiff and sore, but exhilarated. I wondered if this was how my parents felt when they'd settled in Berlin. Did they believe they had found their own perfect space, completely removed from their parents' cold, narrow, judgmental worlds? Or was Berlin just a way station, just another city but with better gigs than the last city? Did they believe there would always be other cities, other gigs? "Leave your mark, make your music, make the town remember you, but put down no roots."

As I banged into our apartment, startling Elissa awake, I thought that I wanted nothing but roots. I wanted to be ivy. I wanted to be a strangler fig. I wanted to dig down into the concrete and wrap myself around the cobbles and never let go.

29

"The only important elements in any society are the artistic and the criminal, because they alone, by questioning the society's values, can force it to change."

—Samuel Delany

Soundtrack: Joy Division, "Disorder," 1979

THE TRANSITION FROM Chautauqua in 1977 to Aspen in 1978 felt like a leap from 1877 to 1978, from a near-parody of Victorian correctness to jet-set cocaine-fueled disco fever. Aspen was just starting to become the playground of the filthy rich, fueled in part by moneyed Texans wallowing in expendable cash from the post-OPEC-crisis years. The drugs and decadence spilled over into the relatively sheltered summer classical music festival. Only thirteen, I was mostly on the outside, literally. I spent my days riding my bike, hiking, fishing, playing in the Roaring Fork River, and rafting the Colorado River forty miles down-valley.

I started the summer thinking that I would take part in the operas, like I had in Chautauqua—especially since the first production was *Albert Herring* and I could reprise my role of Harry. But I was not eleven, and I couldn't get into inhabiting the persona. The festival had a coach who worked with kids, and she had advice for me about how to lose myself in the small details of the clothes, the set, the lyrics, and I felt like saying, *I was born on the damn stage.* But I should have listened to her. My performances were okay, but just okay, going through the motions. I felt nothing except uncomfortable. Even while I was singing, I knew that this would be the last opera I'd ever perform in.

I still, however, loved being around the production and the spectacle. And was very curious about the nightlife and these strange new party animals.

"What're they doing, Dad?" I asked my father at the first big Aspen cast party. I gave a meaningful glance toward Gary, a tenor wearing black leather hot pants and a leather-and-chain bondage top. The party was in a sprawling ski condo on the edge of Aspen, overlooking a burbling river, snowcapped mountains cutting through a wall of fir trees. The festival faculty and performers were housed in ski condos, and Max, a composer and teacher at the festival, had lucked into this huge, secluded house, which was now filled with young musicians letting loose. I had grown up going to rowdy cast parties and had been around many a "scandalous" outfit, so Gary's leather getup was not the source of my confusion. What I couldn't figure out was why Gary had a straw sticking out of his left nostril. Katie, a quiet soprano in a plum-colored peasant dress, was holding up a square-foot mirror like a serving dish and Gary was bending down toward it.

"Coke. Cocaine," my father said matter-of-factly as I watched a thin line of white powder disappear, Gary sweeping the straw along the mirror like some kind of a leather-clad anteater.

"Isn't that . . . dangerous?" I asked as we kept walking toward the bar. I'd seen plenty of people smoking pot, and had even tried it once with a fellow faculty brat, resulting in something resembling a high that was no doubt due to a lack of oxygen to the brain caused by uncontrollable coughing. But I thought that cocaine was like heroin and LSD, things that either killed you or made you crazy, and seeing a professional singer doing this scared me. But I also didn't want to let this fear show.

My father slowed and looked at me. I could tell he was measuring his words, deciding how much I needed to know. But he said nothing and kept walking. I followed him out of the den, where I had recently finished a game of chess with our host, a somewhat decent player. We squeezed into the crowded common room but got stuck behind Sarah, the cute redheaded violinist from Eastman, who was kissing Mary, the surly blonde violinist from Juilliard. There were women in men's laps, and men in men's laps. I could usually tell which of the guys liked other guys and which of the girls liked other girls, but I missed Sarah's queerness, and I was bummed that she wasn't kissing me.

My father and I maneuvered around the intertwined couple, then through other groups of musicians tossing back glasses of wine and vodka, toasting each other and themselves. The whole packed place buzzed with happiness and relief after two tense weeks of rehearsals and three demanding performances of the Francis Poulenc opera *Dialogues of the Carmelites*, a grim little tale about pious French nuns who end up being guillotined.

As we moved through the crowd, singers reached out to take my father's hand or pat him on the shoulder. "Great job, Bob," I heard. "You really pulled it off." My father humbly said, "Thanks," and "You were great." I was proud to be his kid and wished that I could accept praise like he did, instead of mumbling into my shoes, my hair in my face.

In the living room people were gathered around the grand piano, listening to Karen, a beautiful brunette soprano, playing and singing Joni Mitchell's "Chelsea Morning." Her voice was similar to Mitchell's—light and sweet, but with ragged edges, a soft smile

hiding some private hurt. Hearing her, my stomach tightened. I
didn't feel this way when I saw Karen on the stage. But now, up
close, I was in love. I wanted her to put her arm around me and
whisper in my ear all the secrets of the world. The last notes fell
from Karen's lips, and she smiled at me. Not a cursory smile, but
a smile that said she was full of joy because I was in front of her.

Her lips moved again, and it was as if I were underwater,
the sounds moving slowly toward me. "Hey, Robby, having fun?"

"Sure, yeah," I said, trying to sound adult. "Going to get
a drink."

"Okay, kid, come back and I'll sing you something."

I nodded, trying to look casual, like I belonged at this
adult party.

My father made his way through the knot of singers and
I followed in his wake. Ahead, stagehand Dean, looking like a
townie in his jeans and embroidered western shirt, passed a joint
to two teenage Korean violinists who were crashing the party.
We stepped out onto the deck, to the table with the booze and
mixers. I breathed in the cold, clear night air, the high-altitude
sky bright and sharp, then filled a red plastic beer cup with
Orangina, which I loved as a kid in Berlin.

"Well," my father said, "everything in excess is dangerous." I
stared at him, wondering if this was one of his absentminded-artist
outbursts. But then it came to me that he was finally responding
to my earlier question. "Alcohol, for example," he said, lifting his
Stoli and cranberry. He'd drink one, at most two drinks over the
course of a party. I'd never seen him tipsy, much less out of control.

"But cocaine—isn't it addictive?" I asked.

My father looked at me, blinked, blinked again, measuring
his response. Two years before, we'd had a talk about smoking.
In Berlin everyone smoked, but my father had told me flat out,

"I never want you to smoke. Period. It will kill you. So tell me what it'll take for you not to smoke. Would you like me to set aside some money and when you are twenty-one you can have it if you don't smoke?"

I didn't have to think. I said, "No," and I meant it. It didn't ever occur to me to refuse him anything. If he didn't want me to smoke, I wouldn't.

I was ready for him to make me the same offer now—but this time I would think about it. I was curious about the white powder, and maybe I wouldn't mind going a little crazy.

"You're a smart, curious boy, and you're probably going to experiment with drugs."

"But . . ." I protested, not wanting him to think that I could ever be bad. Yet part of me was curious. And I wondered if I needed drugs to be creative, to feel things, the way most everyone around me seemed to.

"You might," my father continued. "But you should know what you're getting into. Cocaine is, yes, addictive. It's a powder that you snort, and it can do incredible damage to your nasal passages and deviate your septum."

"What's that?"

"The connective tissue between your nostrils. And if you're a singer and get a hole in your septum, your career is over."

I nodded, imagining my nose collapsing like a pug's.

"Cocaine is a stimulant, and it can make you feel power-ful," my father added.

"Okay," I said, wondering how he knew this, whether he had done it himself.

"Do you know about marijuana?"

"Sort of," I mumbled, not wanting to confess my unsat-isfying cough-fest.

"It's smoked like a cigarette or in a pipe, but is even worse for your lungs than tobacco. It makes you mellow and slow, and dumb. Everything is funny. Imagine a mellow drunk."

So that was what was supposed to happen. Not just dizziness and nausea. "Is it addictive?" I asked.

"Mildly. Not like cocaine. Or heroin. Heroin can be smoked, but is usually injected into your veins with a needle. It's highly, highly addictive and can kill you instantly if you get too strong of a mixture. I don't want you ever experimenting with heroin."

"Right," I said, staring at my father as if he had been replaced by a stranger, some dangerous deviant who shoots up, snorts coke, and gets high. Was my dad a closet junkie?

"LSD," my father said—and this hit me harder than if he had said, *I'm a flesh-eating zombie*—"LSD makes you go crazy and is only for hippie freaks, right? Please make this book knowledge, not personal knowledge.

"Acid," my father continued, even though I wished he'd stop, "is a psychoactive drug, meaning that it plays tricks with your brain. You see things that aren't there, hear things that aren't being said. It's called tripping, and some people go crazy from doing it."

"How?" I asked, and made a silent prayer that my father— or worse, my mother—hadn't lost it on acid.

"They don't stop tripping. Same with PCP or angel dust, which also can make people violent."

"Sounds great," I joked.

"Well, you shouldn't go into the world blind. Knowledge is power," my father said. I nodded.

"Any questions?"

I had only two—*Why did Mom leave?* and *Will you always be here?*

A couple of singers hovered, waiting to corner my father, but he had created a mental force field around the two of us, his focus on me alone.

"Robby, you sure don't have any questions?" my father asked, serious; he had all the time in the world.

I shook my head. "No, Dad, I'm cool."

30

"I have found that words that are loaded with pathos and create a seductive euphoria are apt to promote nonsense."
—Günter Grass

Soundtrack: Can, "Halleluhwah," 1971

"I HAVE NOT SEEN my station in fifteen years," Ralf said as he squeezed into the backseat with Elissa, Hank riding shotgun as we set out to find the sector of the Wall where Ralf had served his two years of compulsory military service. Ralf directed me through Prenzlauer Berg and onto a broad avenue, past a row of officious federal buildings where Ralf said, "Look up," and pointed to the blank circles in the tympanums. "That is where the socialist hammer and compass had been pulled off, and before that the Nazi swastika, and before that the Prussian eagle."

"What's next?" Hank asked.

"McDonald's," Ralf said. I looked over at his straight face to see if he was joking, as he never joked, but I could detect the slightest upturn in the corners of his mouth, and then we all cracked up.

Ralf had me turn off the avenue, back into an urban area where old stone houses pressed right up against the eastern side of the Wall. From these houses people had lowered themselves or relatives down and over the Wall in baskets, and then sprinted across No-Man's-Land (Germans called it the *Todesstreifen*—"the death zone"), to the Western side of the Wall, almost invariably getting shot between the two sections of concrete, though a few did manage to make it.

There were two adjoining four-foot sections of the Wall missing, and I drove through the gap into No-Man's-Land. I cruised along between the two halves of the Wall for a few hundred yards, then ducked through another gap back onto the Eastern side. After less than a mile the concrete panels joined together to form one long, impenetrable ribbon, and the apartment buildings gave way to stand-alone houses and then fields of wild grass dotted with purple and yellow flowers. The missing sections of the Wall became fewer and farther between, with longer and longer stretches completely intact like impossibly long Richard Serra sculptures.

Up ahead we spotted a small village with a few modest old houses, a church, some stables. It looked like it hadn't changed in a hundred years, except, of course, for the twelve-foot-tall Wall running through the three backyards on the edge of the village.

"Look at the kid," Elissa said, her hand shooting past my right ear. "He's chipping at the Wall."

"What? Where?" I asked, and she pointed over my shoulder at a boy, perhaps eight or nine, by the Wall in the backyard of the first house.

"How'd I miss that? And what's he using?"

"Hammer," Hank said. I stopped the car a hundred meters away so as to not spook the kid, but as soon as I opened the door, he turned around and bolted across his yard.

"Wait," I called, sending him dashing into a small house a mere twenty feet from the Wall. No one else was around, but as we walked up to where the kid had been, I felt like we were being watched.

"He's chipped out a good fifteen inches," Hank said, measuring the hole with his large hands.

"Every day this is what he looked at," Elissa said. "This was the limit to his world. This was going to be his life, right here."

"I wonder if there was a certain comfort in knowing that," I said, "a certain resignation to knowing the parameters of your confinement."

"I think," Ralf said, "that the hammer answers your question."

"True, true, but wasn't there some comfort in knowing that you all were going through this together?"

"Are you high?" Elissa said.

Ralf laughed, but continued his polite humoring of me. "In some ways," he said. "We have our families, our friends, yes. The boy would not have suffered alone."

When I was the boy's age I thought there were no confines. "You can do anything you put your mind to," my parents told me. The world was wide open. Roots didn't matter. Family didn't matter. What mattered was passion and a devotion to your chosen craft. You lived for your craft, and this life could be lived anywhere.

"Should we . . ." Ralf politely suggested. I was hoping the kid would return. I thought we would have a lot to talk about. I slowly worked my way to the car. I walked around Dusty a couple of times, pretending to look at the tires. But the kid stayed hidden.

"We are close now," Ralf said as I drove away from the boy's village. After passing one more cluster of houses, Ralf pointed ahead to a ghostly guard tower— intact, graffiti-free, as if waiting for the next shift of snipers to take up their stations.

I parked a respectful distance away and let Ralf go ahead. After a few minutes of pacing and a quick trip up to the observation tower, Ralf waved us over. "I would march back and forth, here to there, my gun ready," Ralf said, pointing to the next tower, about a half mile off.

"It must have been quiet out here?" Elissa said.

Ralf looked around, took a deep breath, then shut his eyes, placing himself fifteen years into the past. He opened his eyes and said, "Yes, but it was always dangerous. The sergeant was in the tower, with his gun pointed at us below."

"Why?"

"In case we tried to run to the West," Ralf said matter-of-factly. "This happened. And sometimes the soldiers would shoot each other, and the sergeant, then escape."

"How horrible," Elissa said. "How did you deal?"

"We drank whenever we could, and I would work formulas in my head."

"Would civilians try to escape?" I asked.

"No. Too easily seen here," Ralf said with a shudder. "They and the others in my unit were not a worry. What was most dangerous was Russian soldiers. They would go crazy and shoot anyone in their way. It never happened here, but close to here. Some of the sections were secretly made to be easily knocked down from this side."

"Why?" I asked.

"So that tanks could attack the West faster. Only the senior commanders knew which sections were weakened, but one time when I was on duty a Russian stole a tank and tried to flee right here and we had to blow it up."

Later, at the CV, as I went to grab a round of beers, I overheard Ralf talking about our trip to his station, telling a young woman, "I went right back into the feeling of those Death-Strip Years."

"'Death-Strip Years'?" I asked as I slid Ralf his beer, and he gave me a rare smile.

"It is funny, yes," Ralf said, "how one can reduce such a meaningful time that contained infinities into a dismissive phrase."

"Exactly," I said, slapping the table. "With me it's the 'Car-Crash Years.'"

"How do you mean?" Ralf asked.

"I call the ages sixteen to twenty-one my 'Car-Crash Years,' a drunken, womanizing haze of five years punctuated by three moments of extreme clarity while in the teeth of three near-fatal car crashes."

"My goodness," Ralf said, and looked over to Elissa with concern, but she shrugged.

"She's sick of my reductionist stories," I explained. Ralf half-smiled and sipped from his beer, not knowing what he was in the middle of.

"'Wah, wah, wah, I'm *so* sensitive,'" Elissa said, and squeezed my right earlobe, a pebble of embedded safety glass rolling between her fingers. "You need some new material."

31

"Anybody singing the blues is in a deep pit yelling for help."
—Mahalia Jackson

Soundtrack: David Bowie, "Sound and Vision," 1977

OUR POSH SKI CONDO was right in the center of town, at the
base of Ajax Mountain. Four stories below, on East Durant
Avenue, everyone passed by sooner or later. When my father
returned from the afternoon concerts at the music tent, he'd
crank up the blender, which called friends, students, and friends
of friends to come join the Sunset Society. Jan DeGaetani, my
father's best friend, musical soul mate, and Eastman colleague,
lived down the hall, and she frequently joined us, as did her son
Mark, who was slightly older than me, and much more worldly
and wise. The balcony was filled with lawn chairs, and latecomers
had to drag out the chunky walnut bar stools if they wanted to
sit. The mountain sunsets were a two- or three-hour extrava-
ganza. Each hot, clear day gradual evaporation from lakes and
rivers would build until there were enough gathered clouds for
a brief late-afternoon shower, the tall, billowing clouds lingering
to give the setting sun a canvas. The sky would explode in garish
reds and purples, streaks of color stretching across the Woody
Creek Valley, where my new hero, Hunter S. Thompson, lived.
When his part of the sky was at its most fiery red, I'd surrepti-
tiously raise a glass of cranberry and orange juice in his honor.

Despite the infusion of oil and ski money, 1978 Aspen was still Thompson territory. From our balcony I could look across the street onto a cluster of tepees where you could buy tie-dyed T-shirts and pot pipes. The cops wore shorts and bright blue Hawaiian shirts. Nine years before, Thompson had run for county sheriff and put up a biker friend for mayor on the Freak Power ticket, the campaign poster a double-thumbed fist clutching a peyote button. Their platform included renaming Aspen "Fat City" and violently discouraging tourists and investors. Legend has it that they lost by a single vote.

The day after the cast party where my father told me all about drugs, he gave me two books, Thompson's *Fear and Loathing in Las Vegas* and Tom Wolfe's *Electric Kool-Aid Acid Test*. He told me that these were the two scariest books about drugs he had ever read. Well, sure, Neal Cassady's speed overdose on the Mexican train tracks was harrowing, but what resonated with me most about both books was not the drugs, but the improvised families of Kesey and Thompson. Kesey's Merry Pranksters were an ad hoc family held together by their rejection of the square world, and Thompson had a fiercely loyal friendship with his lawyer. "When the going gets weird, the weird turn pro" became my new motto. The world split before me into two kinds of rebellion, embodied by Kesey and Thompson, and it was hard to decide which one attracted me more. On the one hand there was Kesey's communal celebration of creativity, on the other Thompson's bold, riotous rage. The two paths were equally inviting, and equally scary. Both would involve risk, especially emotional risk, something I was averse to. My father clearly fell into the Kesey camp, of transcendence through art.

The previous year, I was startled to come upon my father sitting in a chair quietly crying. He was reading a book, and I asked if he was all right.

"Oh, yes, I'm fine," he said, still reading.

"Then why are you crying?"

My father looked up, blinking, and said, "It's just so beautiful."

He showed me the cover—*Gravity's Rainbow*, by Thomas Pynchon. I was stunned by the idea of a book moving someone so deeply. I always associate this memory with my favorite line about art: "He forces you to use the word 'beautiful.' What more do you want?" Robert Motherwell said this about Joseph Cornell.

Gravity's Rainbow must truly be amazing, I thought, because the only other time I saw my father cry was when he sat down at the piano, and then he swayed and smiled and sometimes cried. I worried that I would never find something that moved me like this, and that even if I found something I loved, I wouldn't let myself express my true feelings.

A few days after finishing *Fear and Loathing*, while up on the balcony, I secretly acknowledged that my heart leaned more toward Thompson, and that if I went toward Kesey, I would live off the grid in the Oregon woods, happy but unengaged with the world. Like most teenagers, I thought didactically, that I had to choose one or the other, and not combine the best parts of both to form a third way that would suit myself.

I struggled with this dialectic as I sat in my favorite orange lawn chair, feet up, enjoying the pre-party peace with Mark, the two of us scoping out the girls passing below. When the Pacer cruised by, about to pull into our building, I could see my father talking to Peter, his favorite grad student, in the passenger seat. Peter had flown out from Rochester for the last two weeks of the festival and had mixed right into the Sunset Society, even though he was intimidatingly tall, almost like a German with his clear, square glasses and the fastidious way he buttered his toast—he would take a rock-hard pat of butter and slowly, evenly spread it over the bread without disturbing the surface.

Peter and my father banged into the kitchen and I could hear them opening the chips and salsa. Soon other students and faculty materialized around the blender, my father pouring out slushy red drinks. We stayed on the balcony, waiting for the party to come to us.

"Robby, man," Mark said, his usual smile sliding into a quizzical, serious frown.

"What's up?"

"Dude, Peter just went into your dad's room," Mark said.

"Yeah, he's staying with us."

"Man, I didn't know your father was switch-hitting," Mark said, and I stared at him blankly.

"Batting from both sides . . . AC/DC," Mark followed.

"What do you mean?" I asked, clueless.

Mark looked at me to see if I really meant it, then flatly stated, "Your dad's gay."

Imagine a long, awkward silence. Multiply "long" by a thousand. Multiply "awkward" by ten thousand. I was a cartoon cat hanging off the edge of a cliff, my legs pinwheeling. I wondered how long I could hang out there before I plunged into the abyss.

"Oh. Yeah, sure," I eventually said, casually, like, *Of course my dad is gay. It's obvious that my dad is queer. How could anyone not know that my father is a homo, especially his own son?*

I couldn't look at Mark. I wanted to say something, but I had no words.

To myself, I said, *My father is gay*, testing the words out. I'd known this at some level, but before now the thought had never made it to the clear surface. *Is that why my mother left? Has he always been gay? Was he gay when he married her? Does this mean that I'm gay? Am I going to want to make out with Mark?*

"You okay with this?" Mark asked, and I nodded. Mark nodded. We went back to watching the sunset and were joined by the first wave of sunset partiers, though Mark kept glancing at me.

Surrounded by gay people all of my life, how could I *not* know? It wasn't like my father was hiding Peter. They were sleeping in the same bedroom. And when I'd visited my father the previous Christmas, Peter was always around. The first morning, when I woke on the sofa to the sounds of my father's making coffee, he motioned for me to be quiet, and I looked over into the bedroom and saw why—Peter was asleep on the futon. I dressed quietly and we slipped out to have breakfast at a diner before my father started work.

"Just, you know," my father had said over his eggs, "keep this quiet."

"Sure, Dad, but why?" I'd wondered what the big deal was.

"People might get the wrong impression," my father said, not meeting my eyes. I nodded, but didn't understand what this "wrong impression" might be. It never crossed my mind that he was going out with Peter, who was fifteen or twenty years younger than my father, closer to my age than his. Plus, faculty didn't sleep with students, right?

But now that he was out of school, I guess it was okay. Was I okay? The shock was fading, and anger and self-loathing were taking over. I wanted to jump off the porch. How could I have been so blind? And why did this have to happen now? "Dad and sex" was the last thing I wanted to be thinking about. I had much bigger worries: my own sexuality—or, more accurately, my lack of sexuality. I was surrounded by beautiful young women, high school and college musicians from all over the world, none of whom acknowledged me the way I wanted to be acknowledged. Sexually, that is.

"Betty at four o'clock," I said, nodding toward the townie on roller skates, her button-up shirt tied Dallas Cowboys–style, showing just the right amount of cleavage.

Mark gave me a thumbs-up.

32

"Words can be very powerful. I find them very difficult."
—Bryan Ferry

Soundtrack: Bryan Ferry, "The 'In' Crowd," 1974

ON OUR TENTH DAY in Berlin, Elissa and I got up early and washed as best we could in our cold-water flat, which meant splashing our faces in freezing water in the ancient sink down the hall. We never saw other people in the building, though we could hear muffled voices somewhere behind the walls. It had been another late night at the CV. Word had gotten out that we'd taken an apartment in the neighborhood and were staying indefinitely. Conversations were still earnest, but were now more measured and less fraught, there being an expectation that they would continue the next day. We no longer had to go through the strange ritual of people telling us about their trips to old concentration camps and their feelings of collective guilt, which almost all of the young East Germans felt compelled to lay on us. We also weren't getting the suspicious looks from those who thought we might be speculators, scoping out future real estate. I, too, was more comfortable, trying less hard, letting the conversations come to me. Hank had also become emboldened. He went out on his own, walking off to sketch at the Wall at dawn. And on this morning he was already long gone.

Downstairs, we peered through the arches of our courtyard, making sure there were no lingering skinheads, then hopped in Dusty. Our tires crunched over broken glass for two blocks and then we were on the wide-open Prenzlauer Allee, which shot us out of our tightly packed neighborhood and across Alexanderplatz, as massive and soulless as I remembered it, and past the Wall, where tourists were chipping away for souvenirs, hucksters renting out chisels and hammers and selling prime chunks to those too lazy to chisel their own history. We were less than two miles from our apartment, but had yet to see a single one of these tourists in our neighborhood.

Across the Spree River, the avenue broadened, turned into Unter Den Linden, passed Checkpoint Charlie, and led to the Brandenburg Gate, isolated and surrounded by barbed wire during the Cold War, now awash with tourists gawking up at Victory driving her chariot. We skirted the massive city gate, passed the Reichstag and went into the Tiergarten, Dusty shabby next to all of the shiny new West German cars. We made our way from the city center to the edge of the Grunewald park, skirting past the Schlachtensee, where I remembered long walks by the water with my father. I found Schopenhauerstrasse and then 31 Kronprinzessenweg, Barry McDaniel's big, blocky house hidden behind a wall of bushes and trees. Miraculously, I had been able to connect with my father's old musical partner from a pay phone in the West and he had insisted that we come to his house for tea. "I must meet your new bride," he said. Though only thirty minutes from our flat, we could've been in suburban Kansas, where Barry was originally from. He appeared as I remembered him from almost twenty years before—the same square seventies glasses, a blue turtleneck.

"Robby, I can't believe it is you, yes?" Barry said, his Mid-western English heavily inflected from thirty years of living in Berlin. "And with your lovely wife," he said, turning to Elissa and shaking her hand. "When he was a boy, he used to spend hours in my garden," Barry said, and waved us through the elegant, plush living room and out into the backyard, where the tiers of flowers triggered a memory of playing with his long-haired collie.

"Amazing," Elissa said, taking in the hundreds of different flowering plants.

"I collect varieties of fuchsia."

"Remarkable," Elissa said as Barry began guiding her to the far end of the garden, weaving along a path decorated by basket after basket of red and purple flowering plants whose vines spilled over the sides of the pots, their frilly, complicated blooms varying in size from plant to plant.

Over tea in the garden's pagoda, Barry told us that Albert Speer had built the house in 1935 and had lived there until 1941 and afterward it sat idle and in legal limbo until Barry was able to buy it for "a song" in 1962. It seemed that no German wanted to live in the former house of the Nazi's chief architect.

Barry had preceded my parents to Germany by four years, one of the first Fulbright scholars to come to the country, in 1958, also to Stuttgart, and then shortly after that to Berlin, where he had been singing in the Berlin Opera since 1961. "But it was with your father, singing lieder, that I truly made my name, truly became accepted by the Germans."

Here was someone who had left a former life and reinvented himself, creating an existence fully integrated into his art. Sitting in the strangely familiar garden, I envied Barry, and at the same time felt shoddy, half-assed. What was I doing here? Besides

being? But being what? I wanted to be Hunter S. Thompson, Ken
Kesey, Jean-Luc Godard, Thurston Moore, Patti Smith, Nick
Cave, James Baldwin, John Lydon, and anybody who wasn't me.
Barry had gone to Berlin to become himself, not anyone else.

My father had walked away from this, I thought. He could
have had something like Barry's expat life. I wondered if I had
held him back. Barry told us that he was winding down his opera
career, retiring after doing "one more *Magic Flute,* my favorite."
But he would keep performing songs until he wasn't satisfied
with the quality of his voice. He asked after my father—how
he liked teaching, whether he was able to perform as much as
he would like. I said that I thought he was.

"And how is your mother?" Barry asked. My brain seized
on hearing about one parent right after the other. I had forgotten that Barry had known my mother when my parents were
still married. I wasn't only confused, but angry to hear Barry
ask about her, as he had been instrumental in her breakup with
my father. I looked over to Elissa, who betrayed nothing as she
sipped her tea.

My mother had revealed to Elissa, with the full knowledge
that she would then tell me, that my father had never come out
to her. Barry had summoned my mother to his house. At the
time he was married with two children. In a veiled way, Barry
told my mother that he was like my father, and that he was
"making it work and so could she." Even though Paragraph 175
of the Reich Criminal Code, instituted in 1871, criminalized
homosexuality, and it was still the law of the land, my mother
had no intention of "making it work." My mother told Elissa that
the entire doomed relationship suddenly made sense. They were
each fulfilling family-driven expectations—to marry a suitable
partner from a similar background and have children. This was

their bulwark against the chaos and uncertainty of the nomadic, artistic life.

Somehow they had stayed together while my father was sublimating in the army and my mother was on the road, singing as a soloist with Fred Waring's enormously popular big band, traveling four or five hundred miles a day by bus, singing in front of thousands of people a night. After Barry's revelation, she could have gone back to Waring, or found opera gigs around Europe, but she now had a child. So she stayed in the marriage—that's what good Midwestern wives did. My father also stayed. He was having brief affairs, but my mother, feeling alone and frustrated by her hamstrung career, entered into a more sustained affair. In the summer of 1969, when I was four and a half years old, my father went to Chautauqua while my mother remained behind to work in Berlin, and I stayed with her. When my father returned, I called him "John." I don't remember this at all. Now there was no pretending that the marriage was healthy, so my mother left. I don't remember this, either.

Thirty years old, and the financial trapdoor opens. No steady income, a child, thousands of miles and an ocean and a culture between you and your family. But she was tough, and logical. She stuck it out in Berlin for nearly two years, scrambling to make a sustainable career for herself: singing any and all opera roles, running a large piano class, singing background vocals for German pop stars like the albino-white singer Heino and the terrifyingly Aryan duo Adam and Eve (I tracked down their records, and they are comically awful—oompah meets disco). Much later, in a rare tipsy moment, she revealed that she did some voice-over for German porn.

This patchwork life was no way to support a child. She resolved to go back to school and earn a master's degree so that she could get a stable teaching position. This meant leaving the country—and me, temporarily. At the time I knew nothing of the sacrifice and risk her decision involved. I thought that she had simply disappeared. Of course, "simply" isn't that simple. The shadow of her disappearance hung over me my entire childhood.

"My mother is doing quite well, thank you," I said, and poured out more tea from the flowery Bavarian pot. I wasn't going to give Barry anything about her. While I wanted to know more about my parents' dissolution, I didn't really know the person in front of me. Or if I had the guts to go there. Instead, I let sleeping dogs lie and asked him if he ever missed Kansas.

"He's fabulous," Elissa said as we got back into Dusty.

I nodded, and realized that she was expecting a verbal reply, but pushing even one word out felt like a great effort. "Absolutely," I managed to say.

"You okay?"

"A little weirded out. I don't recognize myself."

"I can imagine. But you're not eight, remember?"

"I'll try to remember that."

"You have a wife—hello."

"Oh, I thought we were just friends."

"Let's go see some art, asshole," Elissa said.

"Sorry. Good idea."

I pointed us to the Gemäldegalerie, the home of the masters. As I drove, I tried to sort out the collision of past and present, Barry bridging both. It hit me that I was driving away from the place where my parents had ceased to be man and wife. The actual place where my mother had learned the truth about her husband. For years after Mark had finally made me see that my father was gay, I'd assumed that my mother had been so shocked when she found out that my father was a homosexual that she'd had a nervous breakdown and fled Berlin. Why else would she have left?

When I told my father that I was engaged, I asked him what he thought of marriage. We were in Boulder, where he had moved to teach after Eastman, and he was driving his solid, staid Buick Skylark, silly little AMC cars in his past. "I was a disaster as a husband," my father said. But he didn't pin the reason on his sexual orientation; rather, it was his single-minded dedication to his craft and career. He was determined to have a major concert or win a major competition by the time he was thirty, and to achieve this goal my parents had to move from Stuttgart to Berlin, even though my mother was under contract with the Stuttgart opera house.

And now, twenty-five, married less than two years, I looked over at my own wife, and was terrified. We could fail. Just like them. Our own bullshit getting in the way of us. As we walked toward the museum, I grabbed onto Elissa's upper arm, both to steady myself and as a public show of affection. We were partners in crime, full partners, and this was not my parents' city, but ours. Or at least we were going to claim it as ours. Surprised and off balance, Elissa leaned into me and steadied herself.

I wanted to fully be with Elissa, to see the paintings through her eyes. She could always unpack the hidden narratives. Titian, Dürer, Rubens, Rembrandt—I let them wash over me, but wasn't able to settle before any of our old friends. I stepped back as Elissa lost herself in Vermeer's *Woman with a Pearl Necklace*. We meandered through the rooms, not looking for anything in particular. And then we stumbled upon Caravaggio's *Amor Victorious*. All of the other paintings were now static in comparison. "This is so damn alive," I said, and Elissa moved closer to me. "I know him," Elissa said, smiling at both me and Eros—timelessly impish, sexual, nude, mocking. At his feet, discarded, a violin, a lute, pen and paper, a square and compasses. He was mocking our material folly, mocking even art and music. *They have nothing on love,* Eros and Caravaggio were telling us.

Suddenly ravenous, we drove to nearby Kreuzberg, looking for a Turkish kebab stand, for a chicken pita and "roof rippers," what we called their version of the Greek spanakopita. On Oranienstrasse we had our choice, and picked one by a small park.

"*Crybaby,*" Elissa said.

"Am not."

"Yes you are, but look," she said, pointing down a side street toward a little movie theater, its marquee displaying John Waters's new film, *Crybaby.*

"Of course," I said, laughing. We finished our perfect street food and followed the sign: 1950s-Baltimore fantasia with a rebel Johnny Depp, and all those crazy cameos—Iggy Pop, Patty Hearst, Traci Lords, Mink Stole. We filled up on expensive popcorn, but I didn't care—I hadn't seen Elissa laugh so deeply since we'd left New York. Stepping outside, my head was filled with images of Baltimore row houses, the native "Balmer" drawl echoing in my ears. Where the hell was I? How could I be in the here and now when my entire past was here as well? I thought of a character in another movie, *The Adventures of Buckaroo Banzai,* quoting Confucius, saying, "No matter where you go, there you are."

In a daze, I drove us back into the East, the setting sun dissolving in the rearview mirror. Back home, I threw on my running shoes, then ran to the Wall, scampered up and over newly toppled slabs that were like giant dominoes. The last of the sun illuminated the tips of standing barriers and reflected back off the guard tower windows. The Eastern side was still mostly graffiti-free, and there were stretches of the partition where everything looked as it had for nearly thirty years. My injured knee ached, so I slowed, then stopped in a desolate section of No-Man's-Land. A year before I would have been shot for being there. Now I was going for a run, as if this were Baltimore or Aspen or New York. No: *Be present,* I demanded. But even in No-Man's-Land, I couldn't escape myself.

33

"I wanted to be a secret agent and an astronaut, preferably at the same time."

—David Byrne

Soundtrack: Talking Heads, "Heaven," 1979

"PRETTY PERFECT," my father said, raising his cranberry juice toward Red Mountain, where the Aspens were sparkling in the direct, low sun.

"I'm going to miss it," I said, and my father nodded. He was on break between rehearsals for the festival's last few performances. Like the week before, and the week before that, I let the silence hang. I desperately wanted to talk to my father about sex, about him being gay, but was terrified. I thought that if he wanted to talk to me about it, he would have. Or maybe he thought that I obviously knew. I wondered if there was some kind of protocol for gay or bisexual fathers. Like, *Hey, son, how do you feel about me dating other men?*

In the days after Mark told me that my father was gay, I kept waiting for the world to change. But it didn't, maybe because the concepts of "sex" and "father" didn't have anything to do with each other, either straight or gay. The closest these came to touching was two years before when we were still living together and he was dating his old college friend Joyce, the last woman he would see before finally admitting to himself that he was gay.

We would drive the four hours to Saratoga Springs, where we spent the weekend with Joyce and her daughter, passing as if we were a normal, happy nuclear family, which was pleasant for a couple of days, pretending to have an older sister who indulged me with boring board games, going to the farmers' market, seeing an outdoor concert by Sonny and Cher (and Chastity, whom I had a crush on). But even with him spending the night in Joyce's bedroom, the idea of Dad having sex was abstract—companionship, yes, but my imagination went no further.

After Mark brought into the open what I already subconsciously knew, I kept thinking nothing should be the same. I wondered if I was in shock or denial, but in the weeks after, I stuck to my routine, which was that nothing around Aspen was routine and that everything was possible. I biked around town and out to Woody Creek, climbed the Ute Trail overlooking town, and scrambled up the Hunter Creek Trail and bushwhacked back through the aspen groves on the side of Red Mountain. With Mark and Tommy, fellow faculty brats, I snuck into the Continental Inn and would jump into the pool from the second-story balconies, practicing for when we went to the Grottos, six miles above town, where we plunged into icy water from jagged cliffs and where kids were always breaking legs or arms or necks.

When I wanted to be alone I walked up toward Independence Pass and fished in the Roaring Fork. I sat in the bright sun breathing in a mixture of strong smells—the fishy rot of my salmon-egg bait, the sweet scent of coconut suntan lotion, and the cool, clean smell of the spraying river. The boulder had a fissure running through it, about a half-inch wide, and a family of black snakes would poke their heads out to watch me and steal stray salmon eggs. I could pass hours there, and was content to catch one or two trout, or even zero trout. These moments of just being, where I had no thoughts, where I simply existed, were bliss. But they would be interrupted by worries. Why wasn't I passionate about anything? How could I not have known my father was gay? Was I gay?

Late afternoons I cleaned up and went to the music tent for the afternoon concert. Or maybe my father would go over alone and I'd start manning the balcony for the start of the Sunset Society. Watching the sun go down before others arrived, I'd say aloud what I had felt but had never been able to put words to: "My father is gay." I'd say it again, waiting for it to change me; maybe there would be some kind of molecular shift brought on by repetition.

Still, no matter how I added up the facts, the logical equation came out wrong. If A equaled B, and B equaled C, therefore A equaled C. But A didn't equal C. I had been around gay people my entire life and had no problems with homosexuality, either in general or specifically with my father, so why was I freaked out? Maybe it was Peter himself. But I liked Peter. *Although,* I thought, *he could be my dad's son. My brother.* I felt I'd been replaced and sent into exile. But I couldn't be mad at my father. He was all that was good and perfect and magical. My father had made paradise for me. I loved my father. I would die if he went away.

And what if I was gay? I didn't think so, but I was going to drive myself crazy unless I seriously studied my own reactions to attractive men. For the entire summer I had been drooling over every girl in town—but what about the guys? So I looked, I mean really looked, at my friend Bill. He was three years older than me, from Oklahoma. Slender, red-haired, with freckles, he had come out that summer, and I guess I could see why gay guys were attracted to him, but I didn't get any tingling or weird feelings around him like I did around pretty girls. I figured maybe he wasn't my type, so I went to an opera rehearsal and checked out Dan, the choreographer, who was more classically good-looking, as in San Francisco queer–looking—petite, short-cropped hair, always dressed in tight, fashionable black clothes. Again, no disorienting sensations like when I was around attractive girls.

I tried to think if there were any famous musicians, athletes, or actors that made me feel off balance. There was one instance I could think of, and that was at a cast party early in the summer, when someone put on David Bowie's concert film *Ziggy Stardust and the Spiders from Mars* and my mouth went dry and my head felt like it wasn't attached to my body. But most everyone in the room, straight or gay, was in some state of swoon. I figured that Bowie was a category beyond heterosexual or homosexual—just sexual.

"I wish we could be here when the leaves turn," my father said.

I knew he had to leave for a dress rehearsal soon, and that this might be our last alone time on the porch for the summer. Here's what I wanted to ask: *Why do I have to go back to Baltimore? Are you replacing me with Peter?* This is what I said: "Why would you live anywhere else than Aspen?"

My father smiled and looked up and down the valley. "It *is* beautiful," he said, "but you'd run out of people to talk to. When the festival ends, Aspen will be a ski town again. Without culture, this place would get pretty dull pretty fast."

"No way," I protested. To me Aspen felt like its own oasis, like a temporary Berlin, but devoid of danger, or history. It was a beautiful, gay-friendly, safe island in the mountains where culture was dropped in for months at a time. Wouldn't it retain some of this when the circus pulled up stakes? I wanted to ask him. Instead I waved as he got up to leave.

34

"I don't believe in fate or destiny. I believe in various degrees of hatred, paranoia, and abandonment. However much of that gets heaped upon you doesn't matter—it's only a matter of how much you can take and what it does to you."

—Henry Rollins

Soundtrack: Black Flag, "Rise Above," 1981

AS THE MOUNTAINS SLID into the haze behind us, the road ahead rippled, the temperature and humidity rising with each eastward mile, creeping up almost imperceptibly as the elevation gradually fell. But I felt every mile of the slow slide into the eastern funk. Another trip, another silent handoff from one parent to the other. As we drove into Goodland, Kansas, I wondered how many times I'd been handed off. Every beginning and end of summer. Every holiday.

With each mile east the world outside of our bathysphere grew hotter and more humid, and also uglier, as we traveled from the simple beauty of the sunbaked Kansas wheat fields to the chemical-clouded skies over Joliet. The threshed Midwest fields blurred by, then the strip-mined Pennsylvania hills, and, at last, the reward for two thousand miles of driving: the filth-covered streets of Baltimore, with boarded-up row houses and listless, half-naked citizens sprawled on stoops, the air so still and hot and damp you could swear that the mosquitoes were stuck in midair.

It was as if I were watching a movie and the frames start jumping and all of a sudden there I was, numb and alone in my room on the third floor of 2819 St. Paul Street. But at least there I had sanctuary. I had the third floor to myself, and my mother rarely ventured upstairs. The month before, while I was finding out that my father was gay, my mother had called to tell me that my cat Linus had developed a bladder problem and had to go live on a farm where it was okay if he peed all the time. I believed her.

Outside of my room, the house had to remain immaculate. No mess, no noise. My mother banned shoes indoors, for both the noise and the dirt. My room was directly over my mother's bedroom, and even without my shoes, I worried that I would be heard, so I never lifted my socks off the floor, silently sliding my feet on the old floorboards. I aimed to be so quiet, it was as if I weren't even there.

We had left David's small house in rough, blue-collar Hampden for a bigger row house near Johns Hopkins. Ten blocks north were the mansions of Roland Park; ten blocks south, east, or west you stepped into the crack- and poverty-blighted world that would be so well depicted in *The Wire.* Borders were porous, and the poor public-school kids made easy sport of dorky private-school kids like me. Waiting for the Baltimore city bus on rainy or icy days was terrifying. Clear days I rode my bike four uphill miles to the city limits and the suburban Boys' Latin campus. The 7:52 A.M. city bus stopped at Calvert and Twenty-ninth Streets, around the corner from our row house on St. Paul. The probability of getting mugged increased exponentially with each minute that the bus was late. Black kids on their way to their metal-detector high school thought it was hilarious to shake down the white kid in his stupid wide tie. "Let me hold your watch," one said the first time. I stared at the kid like he was speaking a foreign language, and then a slash appeared on my forearm and my watch was ripped from my wrist. I never saw what produced the long, thin cut.

Once safely on the bus, I was usually the only white person on board. The other passengers headed out of downtown were mostly older black women who had gotten on before me, around North Avenue, and were going to clean my classmates' big suburban houses, as well as a few black grade-school kids using city passes to get to the last public school before you hit the strip of private high schools—Roland Park Country School, Friends, Gilman, Bryn Mawr, and Boys' Latin.

As the bus made its way up Roland Avenue, the houses grew larger and larger. The black kids got out at their school, then the black maids got off at the next few stops, and I was the lone remaining passenger at the end of the line, which still left me with a three-quarters-of-a-mile hike to Boys' Latin. One morning early in my freshman year, I was thinking glass-half-full thoughts like *At least it isn't raining too hard* as I trudged through the muggy air, my fellow students whooshing by in BMWs, Mercedes, and Jeeps. I kept an eye out for a shiny green dune buggy driven by a kid named Dennis. At the beginning of the week the shaggy blond senior had taken pity on me, pulling over and yelling out, "Hey, Germie, need a lift?" That was the best my classmates could do—"Germie," because I had lived in Germany.

No Dennis on that rainy day, but a gold BMW wagon changed lanes and slowed down. I hoped it wasn't some Boys' Latin joker about to toss a beer bottle at me. Not this time. It was another senior, a longhair named Luke. Rolling down his window, he said, "Hop in, Shorty."

I jumped in the backseat next to Jake, a junior. *Jesus Christ, be cool*, I thought as another junior in the front, Steven, took a long drag on a short, fat joint. The whole car was filled with skunky-smelling blue smoke.

"Give Shorty a toke," Luke said with a laugh.

Steven smiled and handed me the joint. "Go ahead," Jake said with what I thought was way too much glee.

"Um, okay," I said, trying to look pro as I tentatively pinched the joint between my thumb and middle finger. I sucked on the thin end and hot, acrid smoke raked across my throat and poured into my lungs. I felt like I was sucking down lava. I gagged, but held it, my eyes watering uncontrollably. *Don't cough, don't cough. You're cool. Don't cough.* My lungs were on fire and I started coughing and hacking and I couldn't stop, my three companions howling with laughter. As a thirteen-year-old freshman, I was strictly JV. Yet, what an honor to be in the cool kids' car, even if I was like a stray dog into whose face they were blowing pot smoke.

My anxiety about showing up for school stoned was mild. You could show up dead and still pass. I got straight A's with the barest of efforts. The educational philosophy of Boys' Latin was along nineteenth-century British lines: rote memorization, no questioning, no interpreting, minus any rigor. On the first day of ninth grade, I was given a swift reminder of the rules by Mr. Shriver, a small-eared, narrow-eyed soccer coach who also taught chemistry. He had gone off on a tangent about the chemical properties of a lead musket shot during the Civil War, and I made what I thought was a clever aside about war profiteering. He strode over, kicked my foot off the seat in front of me, and said, "Damn smart aleck."

A good number of my classmates had ended up at BL after being booted from more prestigious schools, mostly for drug use.

Boys' Latin was 99 percent white, 98 percent WASP. The one Italian-American kid stood out and was heckled on the sports fields by opposing schools' fans (most of the schools in the area were also all WASP) with taunts of "WOP, WOP, WOP." If he hadn't been the most athletically gifted kid in school, he would have been taunted at Boys' Latin as well. There were two black kids, both on athletic scholarships, and they were left alone. They posed no threat to the country club, since it was assumed that after graduation they would never be seen again.

The one Indian-American kid wasn't hassled because he was the main drug dealer. Whatever Satish brought into school was quickly snapped up. Five hundred hits of speed: gone by noon. Five pounds of sticky bud: gone by first period. Fifty hits of PCP: well, that was a harder sell after the first Friday of school, when Sammy, a popular stoner, took two hits and wound up on top of his Nova, frothing and ranting incoherently.

Why my mother sent me to a fuckup school, I'll never understand. I had always been a straight-A student and had never had anything resembling a discipline issue. Maybe she thought it was the least preppy of the prep schools. But there were alternatives—like Friends, the coed, liberal Quaker school down the road from Boys' Latin, where I took a typing class, with girls no less, and was surprised to find that the boys and girls could talk casually to each other, without the insanity that gripped single-sex-school students when thrust into the hormonal maelstrom of interschool mixers.

At first I wanted to embrace the school's fuckup image, imagining myself as a Sweathog in a more upscale version of *Welcome Back, Kotter*, or, on more sinister-feeling days, as Malcolm McDowell in *If. . . .*, plotting the destruction of his repressive British boarding school, the fantasy morphing into his brilliant *"droog"* badass in *A Clockwork Orange*. Now there was someone who lived balls-first, unlike me, whose balls were pulled up so tight they might as well have been in my stomach.

But Boys' Latin wasn't a holding pen for outlaws and visionaries. Instead it was a repository for lazy, drug-addled preppies with secure futures—they had jobs waiting for them at their father's law firm, car dealership, and construction company. Boys' Latin was a placeholder as they went through the motions of getting a "proper" education. There were no music or art classes; the one nod to the arts was an after-school theater club, which was strictly for losers like me.

Boys' Latin did excel in one other thing besides drugs—sports. You were cool if you played sports and/or were a stoner. All students were required to participate in two after-school sports per year. The popular kids did the football-basketball-lacrosse triple, with lacrosse being exalted as the ultimate sport. The Johns Hopkins college team was perennially fighting for national championships, and the Hopkins head coach's son, only a sophomore at Boys' Latin, was the star of the upper school team. Soccer was slightly lower in esteem, but still cool, and considering I had played in German leagues starting at the age of four, I knew this would be where I could make my mark.

On the first day of upper-school soccer practice, the coach blew the whistle and we were supposed to scrimmage; he simply threw us into a full game. Back in Berlin, even when I was a toddler, my coaches had drilled discipline, finesse, and power. As we took the field, I thought *Whatever* as I took the ball and danced around two defenders, then streaked down the middle. I was faster than most of my classmates, and no one could match my ball control. Another defender tried a slide tackle and got nowhere near me. I dribbled right up to the box, where the last defender, Gunner, a big, beefy freshman, waited, looking as nimble and clever as a pile of horse shit. I knew that I could beat him, but I slid the ball to my left, directly onto the foot of my teammate Billy, who was surprised by the pass, bobbled it, and was creamed by the goalie.

A few minutes later I got the ball again at midfield and flew toward the goal, shimmied by a defender, Billy running to my right, this time paying attention. All of a sudden I was blindsided and sent flying. I landed on the turf hard. *What happened?* Even by German standards, Gunner's tackle had been a goonish move.

I raised my head from the turf and yelled, "What the hell was that?"

"You're just a fag," Gunner yelled back, then booted the ball upfield.

For a second I thought I was on the school's lawn during free period, when most kids played smear-the-queer. I stayed down, waiting for the coach to stop play, but his whistle remained on his chest.

"Coach, he didn't even play the ball," I yelled.

"Grow some balls, Spillman," the coach/chemistry teacher demanded.

As I hobbled around the pitch, I clung to my German soccer-playing skills, but this was a different sport, a different country. Out on the field no one cared that I considered myself a Berliner. The next day I joined the cross-country team. The lowest of the low, the last refuge for the unathletic, the geeks, and all the other losers, where I belonged.

35

"There are two rules I've always tried to live by: Turn left, if you're supposed to turn right; go through any door you're not supposed to enter. It's the only way to fight your way through any door that you're not supposed to enter. It's the only way to fight your way through to any kind of authentic feeling in a world beset by fakery."

—Malcolm McLaren

Soundtrack: Malcolm McLaren, "Madam Butterfly," 1984

"YOU GOING TO STICK IT OUT?" I asked Hank.

"This sucks," Hank said, slamming down his chipped mug. We were in what back in the East Village would have been considered an old-man bar, but here was a leftover proletariat bar with one kind of state-sanctioned weak and very cheap beer. Ringo had encouraged the grizzled owner to now serve coffee as well, which he did, but it was as thin and watery as the beer.

"How much you have left?" I asked, and Hank reflexively touched his right sock, where he kept his passport, an open-ended return plane ticket, and the exact amount of cash needed for the train ticket to Lisbon.

"Twenty-three marks."

I knew it was bad, but not that bad. All over but the crying, I figured, and said, "It'll be good to get back to your friends." Hank shrugged.

Hank exhaled what I guessed was supposed to be a snort, but it was so halfhearted it sounded like a snore. "Right," Hank said. "Friends go in and out of your life like busboys in a restaurant."

I tried to read his blank expression as the words slowly sank in. I had been there for him, so what the hell was he talking about? "Fuck it," I said, not wanting to engage. "Stay, find some work."

"Easy for you to say," Hank said with a cold glare.

"What?" I said, wondering if he wanted to really get into it.

"Besides," Hank said, looking down at the black silt at the bottom of his mug, "there are no jobs to work. The natives have nothing. Ringo and the bar owners are it."

"When the going gets weird . . ."

"Whatever," he said, not in the mood for a pointless pep talk.

"What about all the furniture and junk from the streets? Figure out a way to sell it back in New York?" I asked, thinking that if *my* safety net were gone I'd find something, anything to stay here.

"If we could get it back, we could sell it for a fortune. We'd need capital, my man. And that would make us the man, man."

"What about your East Village–East Berlin art exchange idea?" I asked.

"I don't have the means or interest to be a gallerist," Hank said. "I'd like to help the local artists, make introductions, but I'm not the one to take on organizing exhibitions or sales. . . ."

"Communist Frozen Moments!" I yelled out. The jumpy bartender looked our way, still clearly unhappy that we were there. "If you can capture mundane crap like beer bottles and spaghetti, why not real history?" I asked, semiseriously.

"What, epoxy a tourist's hammer stuck into a piece of the Wall?"

"Someone's going to do it," I said.

"Not me," Hank said, and pushed away from the table. "I'm going to go sketch the Wall some more. I'll use the last few marks for food, then I'm out."

"All right," I said, not knowing what else to say.

"Want to walk over with me?" Hank asked, not making eye contact, a tentative overture, an invitation to try to repair what might be irreparable damage. Since Zambi, nothing had been quite right with us. Before he had overstayed and stepped all over my trust, we had been simpatico. I thought back to New York the year before and on a brutally cold night we had gone to see Sonic Youth at CBGB, the band going full-on for two hours, a collective knowledge that we were all part of something transcendent, artists compressing a time and place and feeling into one perfect performance.

During "Hey Joni," Thurston, Kim, Steve, and Lee went off into an extended, exalted riff, and when it was no longer sustainable Lee Ranaldo looked up from his guitar and spread his arms wide as if to embrace the moment and all of us, or perhaps the gesture meant that he had done everything he could and now had to take his hands off his guitar. In his flannel shirt with the sleeves rolled up, he looked exactly like the iconic photo of Jack Kerouac spreading his arms wide while reading in a Lower East Side loft in February of 1959, almost exactly thirty years before and only a few blocks away. I looked over to Hank, who looked right into me. He was seeing what I was seeing, he too was feeling the continuum.

As Hank slung his messenger bag over his shoulder, I doubted we'd ever have a moment like this again. "I need to find a place," I said, half-hoping that Hank would want to come with. "A music store from when I was a kid," I added.

"Godspeed," Hank said. Outside the bar, I watched him lope toward the Wall, his sketch pad sticking out of his bag. I turned and walked the opposite direction. I had wanted to jog through the neighborhood to cover more ground, but my two Berlin runs had been too much for my knee, which now throbbed with a dull, steady ache. Toward the end of the last run through No-Man's-Land, I had come close to the old feeling of obliteration, the negation of my self. It was something like writing on those rare occasions when the writing was going so well that I disappeared and the page alone existed, a feeling I hadn't experienced since I left New York.

So now instead of a run, I set out on what I thought of as a Situtationist *dérive*, what Guy Debord called "a mode of experimental behavior linked to the conditions of urban society: a technique of rapid passage through varied ambiances." This was the Situationists' way of rebelling against the predictability and dehumanization of urban spaces. They would make it new, and their own, by randomly walking through cities, not following any preplanned routes. East Berlin was ready-made for the *dérive*, its predictable routes disrupted daily as roads, bridges, and walls disappeared and buildings were torn apart or repurposed for impromptu art galleries, music venues, or communal living spaces. No one was waiting for what would officially be done come October 3, still two-and-a-half months away.

But this part of Prenzlauer Berg was still predictable, hardly changed from the mid-nineteenth century, some parts bombed, but rebuilt to be exact replicas of the way they were before the war. I had left Elissa back at our apartment, where she was either sleeping or writing, which had become her two modes of existence as of late. She had disappeared. She was either totally crashed out, or fully, sometimes a little scarily, into her work. I gave her as much space as she needed, but sometimes I worried that she was concentrating too intensely. She would sit for hours at a time, not moving, just writing. I didn't know how, in the midst of all the chaos and excitement, she was able to fix anything to paper.

Or, if I was honest with myself, I didn't know why I wasn't able to. As I scanned the familiar-looking building façades, I told myself that I was in the recon phase, gathering material, and that I would of course hammer this experience into art, and do so any minute now. She hadn't let me read anything she'd written in Berlin. In Zambujeira sometimes, when I was in bed and was working at the kitchen table, out of nowhere she'd read a page or two of what she was working on. Maybe Elissa was writing something so brilliant that she'd sell it and then we could move . . . My thoughts trailed off as I spotted a storefront. I crossed the street. It wasn't the music store, but some kind of industrial laundry facility, one of the giant machines slowly sudsing.

I had to get my head out of the clouds. It was up to me to make Berlin work for us. The international track meet at the Olympic Stadium was coming up soon, and I needed to get my ass in the car and drive over to the West and use a pay phone to call *Sports Illustrated,* get a press pass and contacts for the athlete reps. Around the corner I nearly ran into a woman who was animatedly talking to two men. *"Entschuldigung,"* I said, and then I had to explain myself, how we were trying to live in the East. They wanted to talk some more and one of the men invited me to have lunch with them. I begged off. *"Mein frau,"* I said with a "What can you do" open-palmed gesture.

A few steps past, I wondered which one of them had been a Stasi informant. It had just come out in a West Berlin paper that one in three citizens was paid off at some point to inform on a neighbor. I imagined that when the Stasi files were opened, a whole lot of ugly secrets would spill out. I wondered if those three worried about that, or if they were more concerned about whether they'd be able to live in their neighborhood after reunification. Rehashing the Cold War endgame was probably not a pressing concern when you were being forced out by moneyed hipsters from the West, or worse, by the clean-cut autocrat speculators waiting to swoop in with their piles of cash.

I realized that I'd had nothing to eat since Elissa and I had split a doughy blob of peasant bread with honey that morning, and that I should head back to pick her up and find some dinner. I set off on a different route home, thinking about that trio and the others caught up by the historical transition, like the two guys we had met the night before at the CV, who had worked at a now-shuttered shoe factory for twenty years each, using machines from the 1930s, and who were now deemed unemployable.

And pity those who had misjudged history, like Winfried Freudenberg, a thirty-two-year-old engineer who, the previous March, only five months before the Wall was breached, had flown a homemade methane-filled balloon out of Prenzlauer Berg to the West and freedom, but had plunged to his death in the West Berlin suburb of Zehlendorf, landing in the garden of a big, beautiful house not far from Barry's home. Ralf had crossed paths with Winfried, and others at the CV talked about Sabine, his widow, and how she was trying to make a new life for herself. Their plan of escape had not been a spur-of-the-moment dash. It was a long, thought-out process. Winfried took a job at a natural-gas-processing plant in the neighborhood, and he and his wife spent two months sewing together a balloon made of strips torn from old army tents. In the middle of the night of March 9, as they were filling their balloon, they were spotted. As the police closed in, Winfried and Sabine realized that the partially filled balloon could carry only one of them. Winfried got in. Sabine stayed behind. What was their conversation? Was there a conversation? Were they panicked? Levelheaded? Were there promises? How do you leave the one you love behind? Was he thinking that she'd find a way out later?

Winfried was a scientist. He had calculated the necessary ballast, which was the combined weight of the two of them. Even three-quarters full, the balloon shot up over a mile in the air. He flew past the airport in the West, his intended target. He spent six hours floating. It isn't known how or why he fell. His balloon was found a few blocks from his body. Winfried was the last person killed trying to get over the Wall.

36

"Behind the masks of total choice, different forms of the same alienation confront each other."

—Guy Debord

Soundtrack: The Animals, "We Gotta Get Out of This Place," 1965

MORE THAN TWO MONTHS into the school year, I still couldn't shake the feeling that I was a fraud. Second period—what a joke: a kid born and raised in Germany taking Advanced German at the all-girl Bryn Mawr School. But I was studious. I wanted to know every fact and figure about each and every one of the eighteen girls in their plaid-green school uniforms and those painfully arousing short white socks. Even the teacher, Ms. Semple, was latent with sexuality, confusingly so as she waddled up to the blackboard, heavy with child. At Boys' Latin I could take Latin, French, or Spanish, but we were allowed to take German at Bryn Mawr. I was the lone Boys' Latin student who took advantage of the deal. You'd think my testosterone-drunk classmates would've been dying to join me, but they were too scared. The work was too hard for them, and for all of their bravado, they didn't have the guts to be in a roomful of smart girls.

Bright November sunshine flooded the room, probably the last day before the weather turned, and I knew I was being checked out, yet I could never quite prove it. I could feel eyes on me, but when I looked at any of the girls, they were intently focused on their notebooks or the blackboard. It was a nonstop game, and maybe once or twice a class I'd make eye contact, but even then they acted uninterested, as if I were an empty desk their eyes had randomly passed over.

Three of the girls were hippie-wannabes, a challenge for them with their school uniforms, which rendered everyone a prepster. They had long hair and funky cloth messenger bags with peace signs and patches stuck on them. A sophomore in the corner, a tall girl with long black hair and a Grateful Dead skull patch on her army bag, was always sketching. Whenever I went to the board to parse some German phrase, I tried to see what she was drawing, but she covered it up whenever I came near.

As I barely got back in time for third-period algebra at Boys' Latin, Gunner asked—as usual, for the benefit of the rest of the room—"Get any this morning?" I laughed along with everyone else, and Gunner looked faux surprised. "What? All those girls in heat in one room and you didn't get any? What're you, queer or something?"

I kept laughing. Outside of Gunner and the major jocks, I got along with most everyone. I could fit in anywhere, could slide into any local accent, had picked up enough knowledge to talk lacrosse, beer, bongs, girls. Most of my classmates appreciated my humor, as long as it wasn't directed at them. But even though they tolerated me and thought I was funny, I'd never be part of their country club. I could dress like them, talk like them, date girls from the same all-girl schools where they were going to find their wives who looked like their sisters, and still I was the weirdo clinging to the freakish idea that there was a world beyond Baltimore. They were all going to stay and have comfortable jobs and careers and send their kids to Boys' Latin.

I passed as one of them, but my overriding urge was to be everything they were not—black, queer, intellectually curious, foreign, musical, artistic, creative. I saw myself as a walled, weird city where nonconformity is the norm, where adaptation and creativity matter. Baltimore was a square blip in world history, a place to be from, a place to be mocked in John Waters films. While I watched Mr. Chubb robotically recite formulas, I had no idea that Waters had also gone to Boys' Latin for the end of his high school years. I wouldn't learn this potentially lifesaving fact until many years later.

If I had known that Waters had survived Boys' Latin, I would have felt better about my own chances. I'm certain I wouldn't have questioned myself so much. And maybe if I had grown up in Baltimore, I might have had a very different high school experience. I might have made the best of what was to be found on the fringes, like Waters, who made art out of what respectable Baltimore considered human trash. But I had lived where high culture was integral to the community.

On the bus home, I wondered if I was a narrow-minded snob. What if West Berlin's walled-in cultural foment was a historical blip? Worse still, what if its creative/intellectual life was deviant and wrong, and Boys' Latin and the simple materialism of Baltimore's upper-middle class was on the winning side of history? What would I do—give in, or fight to the death? Would it be possible to reject my father's world of life through art and try to fit into this preppy materialist world? And what happened to your soul when you became something you loathed? I could have assumed my rightful place within White Male Privilege, but I wanted nothing to do with it, and instead identified with everything that was not White or Male or Privileged.

Halfway home, I hopped off the bus in front of the Roland Park Country School, where Celine, my first real girlfriend, was waiting for me. No matter that I had walked her home a dozen times already—I was still stunned to see her there waiting. I had met her at one of the interschool mixers, dragged there by my sophomore friend Jack. He and his freshman brother lived in nearby Hampden and I caught rides with their mother, who worked as a secretary in the lower school so that Jack and his brother could get free tuition.

Jack was one of the few other nonprepsters, his parents proudly working-class. Unlike me, he didn't try to fit in, not giving a damn about the country club kids. He was into the occult, Dungeons & Dragons, science fiction—not a black-cloak kind of loner, but more like he did his own thing and if others wanted to join him, that was okay. He was afraid of nothing, not even girls.

Jack took me to the Roland Park Country School mixer and he danced with a bunch of different girls. Emboldened by his example, I screwed up my courage and asked a shy, light-skinned black girl to dance. Celine's long, straight black hair hung over her face so that it was hard for me to tell if she really had said yes. Too scared to leave each other and risk rejection by the other kids, we danced together the entire night. At the end of the evening, when we were waiting for her mother to pick her up, my entire body screamed, *Kiss her, you fool.* But I was too timid, and the tension petrified both of us.

But everything was different away from the dance. We couldn't kiss when we were supposed to kiss, but did kiss when we weren't supposed to be kissing—getting a slushie at the Wawa market, walking home from school. I worried that I would catch flak from some of my racist classmates, the ones who wore "DISCO SUCKS" buttons and made fun of the black scholarship student's stutter. I kind of wished they would say something, so that I could defend her honor and show my self-proclaimed moral superiority. But I heard nothing. Celine was popular at her school. And if it hadn't been for her light brown skin color, she would have looked like just another nice preppy girl in her blue plaid uniform. But she wasn't like the other girls. She wasn't giggly, didn't try to impress, and wasn't caught up in social games.

As we walked, I took off my dorky tie and slung my beige corduroy blazer over my shoulder. Celine took off her blue sweater and wrapped it around her waist. Semi-shod of our school uniforms, we still looked respectable enough for me to meet her parents, and before we did I stole one last kiss. Past the old water tower on the border of Roland Park, we were now within sight of her row house, set back from the road across a large swath of yard. Celine froze. Hanging out on her porch were several young men in Poly Tech football jackets, her brothers and their friends, I guessed.

"You better stop here," Celine said. She pulled her hand away and took two quick steps to the side.

"Why? I'll walk you up," I said.

"No, it'll be dangerous for you."

"Dangerous?" I laughed. Celine didn't smile back.

"They might get the wrong idea. They might think you're trying to take advantage of me."

"Oh," I said, stunned.

"You better go before they see you with me. You can meet them later, after you meet my parents. Some other time. Just go."

"Okay, I'll see you," I said as Celine sped ahead. I crossed the street, wondering if they had seen me, and if they had, if they would chase me down. Would her brothers really rip me to pieces to protect her? What must it be like to have a sister worth fighting for? Once I was safely out of sight, it hit me how screwed up the situation had been, that a white boy going out with a black girl meant there had to be some kind of exploitation going on.

I stewed about this all the way back to St. Paul Street and our house, which felt cryptlike as usual. My mother and David never had any friends over to visit. NPR was the default radio station, but only for *All Things Considered* while making dinner and on Saturdays for the opera broadcasts from the Met ("Busman's holiday," my mother would joke). But we rarely listened to other recorded music, and the house was noiseless except for when David warmed up for his nightly gig at the symphony, or when my mother sang or had a student over for a lesson.

To be with David, my mother had left behind a tenure-track position in Lynchburg. In Baltimore she picked up teaching work at various colleges, but there was nothing on the level she had given up in Lynchburg. She continued to sing, performing with the Baltimore Symphony and giving recitals at the Baltimore Museum of Art, at the Peabody Conservatory of Music, and at various other places around town. But Baltimore wasn't Berlin or New York.

She met the lack of opportunities with her usual steely practicality. She went back to grad school, this time for a degree in business management. On top of giving private voice lessons, she went into music management with a pianist friend of hers. The two worked with a handful of other musicians and also did volunteer work at nursing homes, where they sang tunes from the turn of the century, like "Meet Me in St. Louis," the old-timers loving every minute of it. This was what she had to do to express herself, but as I was judgmental and didactic, I didn't really get what it had to do with art. She also expressed herself by managing artists and by assembling performances. She was so adept a manager that she was hired to run the Baltimore Children's Museum, a deft career swerve I didn't see coming. Somehow she had reinvented herself and was now one of the city's cultural leaders.

No one was home, which was a relief. I couldn't remember if it was my night to "carry my own weight." On those days, my mother gave me a recipe and then it was my "job" to make the meal. And it wasn't a collaborative effort—it was me, alone in the pristine kitchen, wondering what I was supposed to do. Sometimes I would save my allowance and buy pizza. But even then I had to make sure to be neat and orderly. I was allowed two cookies for dessert; no crumbs. I was expected to clean up after dinner twice a week. I cleaned the dishes by hand, then my mother inspected my work. With the seriousness of an assembly-line foreman, she held the dishes up to the light, one at a time, and looked closely for any specks of soap or food, then stacked the "unclean" dishes back in the sink, although for the life of me I could rarely see where I had failed.

I guessed that she was overcompensating for what she thought was my father's slack parenting—not that she would know, as they didn't talk to each other. Away from the house we got along better. I went with her to shop for fabric, which was kind of interesting, observing the clothes-making process from the huge bolts of cloth to the finished product, but while I was impressed with her ability to sew anything, how exciting was it to pick out beige corduroy and complementary brown leather for elbow patches for what would become a school blazer?

She also took me to classical-music performances and arty movies, once accidentally taking me to the uncensored version of *The Man Who Fell to Earth* with David Bowie, both of us squirming through a scene where a handgun became a sex toy. David, on the other hand, was less concerned with the highbrow, and happily escorted me to an early Woody Allen triple feature.

Even though cross-country season had ended the week before and I had no reason to keep running, I quickly changed into shorts and ran out the back door, then past the bricks and ivy of the stereotypically East Coast college campus of Johns Hopkins to the trail by Roland Creek, a secret green passageway through suburbia where, if I stared off into the middle ground and didn't focus, I could imagine that I was running through the Colorado mountains. I hurled myself up and down the slippery, muddy hills, falling, rolling my ankle, but not stopping, not slowing, pushing myself until my lungs felt like they were going to explode out of my chest. I was muddy, sweaty, angry— everything that I was not at home.

My mother didn't understand why I had suddenly gotten so into running, this messy physicality so far from her own experience. She didn't get why anyone would run, though we were in the middle of a running boom. *The Complete Book of Running* was on top of the best-seller lists, and the area around the college was lousy with joggers. I loathed joggers, half-assed fatsos in velour suits, creeps who were roller-discoing the year before, the kind of self-indulgent trend followers Hunter S. Thompson savagely mocked in *The Curse of Lono*, in which he hurls insults and beer cans at the mid-pack joggers in the Honolulu Marathon. To me, the difference between a jogger and a runner was everything. It was the difference between a poseur and an authentic soul. Discomfort versus pain. Donovan versus Dylan. Endurance versus self-inflicted suffering in order to attain a higher level of consciousness.

Though I was maddened by the whole craze, I had just read and loved Jim Fixx's bestseller. When I banged in through the back door, drenched with sweat, my mother was sitting at the dining room table, reading *The New Yorker* with a cup of tea. She gave me the usual puzzled look. I took off my shoes and ran quietly up the stairs, thinking that Fixx was able to articulate what I was feeling but couldn't put words to. Fixx nailed how you could lose yourself running, when the "runner's high," that rush of endorphins, kicks in after thirty minutes. And he captured the crash that follows that euphoria, the exhaustion and yet at the same time the overwhelming urge to run more, longer, harder. As I scampered back down the stairs with the book in hand, I thought, *This will explain me to her; she'll finally understand.*

"Mom, you've got to read this!" I said, and dropped the bright red book in front of her.

My mother looked at the lean, disembodied legs caught mid-stride on the cover, then up at me, her face souring. It was as if I'd presented her with a plate of worms. Or maybe she was simply confused, as I was. But I was more than confused—I was flustered, my cheeks burning. "Uh, well, it kind of explains why people run and you've, you know, asked me why I like . . ." I couldn't read her puzzled expression. It either was saying, "Go on, help me make sense of this" or she wasn't getting it, wasn't forgiving me for crashing her peaceful *New Yorker* time. I decided on the latter and slid the book off the table and slunk upstairs.

37

"If you're writing anything decent, it's in you, it's your spirit coming out. If it's not an expression of how a person genuinely feels, then it's not a good song done with any conviction."

—Alex Chilton

Soundtrack: Big Star, "September Gurls," 1974

AFTER MY FAILED SEARCH for the music store, my knee was sore but I could bend it without too much pain. On our landing, I thought that I really should write up my East Berlin *dérive*. But who in New York would want this? Why not write it for the new Berlin? Start a magazine here. Of course, this would need capital, something we didn't have.

"How was it?" Elissa asked, not looking up from her yellow notepad.

"Fun. Below the Kollwitzplatz park, there was a pothole so big it took up the entire street, and it was filled with five Wartburgs."

"Hilarious," Elissa said, still focused on her notepad.

"They looked like . . ." I waited, but she said nothing. "How goes it?" I asked. She shrugged. "What're you working on?" Elissa shrugged again.

"Food?"

"Sure, Big Chief Hotwater," Elissa said, finally looking up.

I went down the hall to fill Sparky, our dubious Soviet Mr. Coffee. I had found the contraption on one of our foraging expeditions, and had a hunch that we could pair it with the oblong metal tub I had found a few days before. Sparky was a bulbous glass pot affixed to a primitive machine that looked like a hot plate, and we guessed that it was a Soviet version of a Mr. Coffee, and for the most part, despite odd pings and blinking lights, it worked. For bathing, I heated up pots of our icy tap water that I then poured over myself as I stood in the tub. For this, Hank had given me a name promotion from "Chief" to "Big Chief Hotwater."

After cleaning up, we searched for food, and stumbled upon yet another phoenix-like drinking space, two blocks from the now firmly established wine bar. The funky new bar was a gutted floor-through with exposed bricks, wires, and piping. The tables were made out of industrial-sized saw blades, some four feet across, that were riveted onto the tops of old cable spools. The well-worn steel surfaces had an oily, purplish sheen. Although the curved tips were dull, they were still menacing, and I was careful not to pull my rickety chair too close.

"I miss it," Elissa said as she put down her bitter beer.

"What?" I asked, although I knew what she meant.

"Home. I miss home. Back there. Home."

"Really?"

"I do. I miss bagels and pizza, the Sunday *Times* and movies, I miss Film Forum, and I miss my friends. Remember those?" she said. "Don't you?"

"Sure, sort of," I said. "But friends are fluid, you know? And anyway, they should join us. We've invited them. They could come, you know. Anyone who says they want to be an artist . . ."

"They have jobs," Elissa said, exasperated.

"So did we. But this is the place to be. This whole neighborhood is going to be amazing. This is ground zero in the battle between commodification and artistic utopia. We can be on the winning side of history, or, if we lose, we'll be like the heroes of the Spanish Civil War, having fought the fascists way ahead of those who fought them in World War II. We're part of the international intellectual and artistic army, the true avant-garde. . . ."

Elissa smiled at me, her "This is why I fell in love with you smile," but it was fleeting. "I'm tired," she said.

"Maybe we're drinking too much," I said. It was possible she was. I was fine. Fatter than I'd like to have been, but that wasn't drinking, that was not running. "Maybe it's time to cut back. Not altogether, but, a little."

"No," she said irritably. "It's not that. It's not the drinking. The drinking is fine. I have no problem with how much I'm drinking. Drinking is the thing I do best here. Drinking is just ducky. All I said was, I'm tired. I'm fucking tired and my stomach hurts."

"Like *return of ulcer* hurts?"

"Like *tired* hurts," she snapped. I drained my pint, not realizing how thirsty I was. Slouched in the sheet-metal chair, she looked small, and she looked exhausted.

"Maybe you should take a break from your work," I said. "Take a few days off . . ."

"No way," Elissa said, her eyes angry.

"A day—"

"You don't get it."

"Whoa, sorry," I said, holding up my hands. I did get it. She was tired of being deprived of her bullshit creature comforts—her comfy bed, knowing what she was going to eat for breakfast; she was tired of . . . blah, blah, blah. "How about we go over to the West and get a decent meal."

"And what? Get another cash advance?" Elissa asked, sitting up straight, now fully charged.

I had miscalculated her mood. "We're okay," I said.

"Are we?" Elissa said, smiling brightly, tilting her head—bad signs. Threat display. "Did you call *Sports Illustrated*?"

I hesitated, thought about lying, but she'd know; she always did. "I forgot," I said.

Mistake. I could sense a strike coming. "Like you forgot the name of the first girl you slept with?" Elissa asked.

"Whoa," I said, stung by the perfect low blow, one simple fact encapsulating all of my failings as a human being. "Where'd that come from?" I asked.

Elissa leaned back, and said nothing as she glowered at me, drilling me with her stare as she drained her beer.

"At least I remember the experience," I said.

"You remember the experience but not the person you had it with?" Elissa asked, and waited for me to further incriminate myself. She should have been a lawyer.

"Let me get you another beer," I said, and grabbed her glass before she could assent. At the bar, which was made of cleverly interlocking industrial gears, I got two fresh pints and asked the bartender, a young woman wearing dangling black screws for earrings, who had put this new place together. There were a dozen East Germans ordering drinks, and she held up a finger to indicate that she would get to me when she could, and so I had to weave back through the saw blades to our table, where Elissa still smoldered.

"Give it just a little longer," I pleaded. Elissa sipped her new beer, not saying anything. Her fire was dying down. She looked tired again. "Okay? Just give it a little bit longer," I said. I didn't want to sound like I was pleading, but I was. I needed her to believe. She had to believe; she'd always believed. She knew, much more than I did, what this "it" was—my romantic need to be in the cultural moment and my need to feel like I had my own home, which was also tied to my early history in Berlin. If I could get "it" right, I would return to being a Berliner, which would define me and make me real, not some nebulous amalgam of other people's histories and creations. She sighed. She was now fully cooled, resigning herself.

"It's a party," she said, running her fingers along the edges of our saw-blade table.

I took her hand. "We're going to be great," I said. Relief mixed with nausea. She was relenting, but she didn't believe in me. She didn't think that I was meant to be in Berlin. Or rather, she didn't think that "we" were meant to be in Berlin. But I was certain that everything was still going to work out for both "me" and "we."

38

"I try never to wear my own clothes, I pretend I'm someone else."

—David Byrne

Soundtrack: Velvet Underground, "Rock and Roll," 1970

NONE OF THE BOOKS WERE WORKING. I tried hiding out
in the tree house with *The Prince of Central Park*, where the
teenage-runaway hero lives, but that felt too real, as did Hunter
S. Thompson's *Hell's Angels*, so I switched to sailing across the
Narnian sea, but that was too familiar and childish, so I tried to
float down Ken Kesey's Oregon logging river, but instead of a
gentle current under my back, I felt like I was on a raft rushing
through whitewater toward a waterfall. Warm springtime air
came through my open windows and I could smell the mix of
cherry and magnolia blossoms that were exploding pink and
white all the way up the broad avenue that led to Boys' Latin.
I should've been asleep, but I switched on my Tandy all-in-one
stereo, hoping to find a radio play from the forties or fifties
coming from a station that seemed to materialize after midnight.
I liked the anachronisms—trolleys and milk left on the front
steps—and got into the hokey stories, which were suspenseful,
but not so scary that they weren't easy enough to drift off to.
Sometimes I was awakened by David's turning off the radio,
then pulling the blankets over me.

Now, tuning in, I found one. The story about the blind woman alone in her house and the bank robber at her door. I had heard it a bunch of times. It was good, like the one about the snowstorm-stranded couple with the mysterious noises on top of their car, but I had heard it once too often. I was curious about what was over on the left side of the dial. I'd moved it right a few times to listen to 98 Rock, which played everything my classmates loved—Springsteen, Aerosmith, Led Zeppelin. I'd listen to it quietly, so my mother couldn't hear the lowbrow noise. I rarely moved the dial left, into the classical music and religious-nut zone. My ear against the black fabric covering the speaker, I inched the dial slowly through the static. *Whoa. What's this?* An eerie, simple guitar with a lone male voice, high-pitched and pinched, singing about being tense and nervous and that he can't relax.

I didn't get it. *What* is *this?* The singer was uncomfortable and the delivery awkward, which made me feel awkward and uncomfortable, made me want to turn it off, but I also kind of identified with the singer's awkwardness so I also wanted to keep listening. I pressed my ear to the speaker and listened and listened and listened, the song staying weird and true, the words about someone not fitting in, but the music making me want to dance. I was excited but confused, wanted it to keep going until it made sense, but then the DJ came on. "Hey folks out there in B-more. It's one o'clock and you are listening to the mighty ten watts of WJHU, pumping out furious sounds from the basement of the AMR *numero dos* dorms. That was Talking Heads doing 'Psycho Killer.' K-Rock we are not, my friends! And I'm going to shut up now and play some Clash."

Clash? "I'm so bored with U.S.A.," a pissed-off Brit snarled. My mind exploded and kept exploding—the Sex Pistols, Joy

Division, the Ramones, Blondie, Television, one after the other they poured into my brain, and then the Velvet Underground were singing about all tomorrow's parties and then about how Ginny was saved by rock 'n' roll and it was like they weren't singing about Ginny, the Velvet Underground were singing about me—no, they were talking *to* me, in my own house, and I couldn't believe that there were people out there who knew what I was thinking and feeling and that they knew that I was up in the middle of the night and that I was freaked out and alone and wanted to escape but was worried that everyplace that wasn't a fantasy like Aspen was going to be like wasteland Baltimore, and I didn't think I could ever be like these truth-tellers, so brave and cool and weird.

This music was my Narnian wardrobe, my portal to an alternative universe.

If this music exists I am not alone. There were others like me. Other kids listening. But it also meant that these people making the music—these seers, these freaks, these prophets, these fuckups—they'd survived whatever messed-up childhood they'd had, and had grown up and now were creating art, and they were living the artist's life.

39

"Ah-ha-ha. Ever get the feeling you've been cheated? Good night."

—John Lydon, January 14, 1978, after the Sex Pistols covered the Stooges song "No Fun." This was the concert's encore, and the last performance by the Sex Pistols before the band broke up and Sid Vicious died.

Soundtrack: Public Image Ltd., "Poptones," 1979

WE CHRISTENED THE NEW PLACE The Buzz Saw Bar. Everything in the East was so new, nothing had been named yet. If we named these new places, then we would be part of the history, we could control the narrative. I thought this as Elissa went back to our flat, wanting to work before we headed out to the CV for the rest of the evening. I was taking her dose of reality and got into Dusty and drove over to the West and my favorite phone booth, a few hundred yards across the former border on a quiet side street off of Köpenicker Strasse. In New York it was not quite noon, so I could catch my editor at *Sports Illustrated*, could ask him to get me a press pass for the track meet. Last I had heard, before I left Portugal, was that Arturo Barrios was going to try to break his world record in the 10,000 meters, a record he had set at the previous summer's meet in Berlin. That would be enough of a story, but this would also be the first meet in Berlin where former East Bloc athletes could compete on their own, not beholden to their politically controlled governing bodies.

I gathered up my hoarded coins and started feeding the phone box. I looked at the 212 area code in my notebook but punched 303 instead, dialing my father in Aspen.

"Hey, Dad," I said through the buzzing line.

"Hey, kiddo," my father exclaimed after a lag.

"Guess where I am? Off Köpenicker Strasse. The Wall is right at the end of the street."

"Wow. Still standing right there?"

"Mostly, but there are sections missing where we can drive right through the Wall."

"I can't believe it."

"It's a different kind of wild than when you were here," I said.

"Will you see Peter?" my father asked.

"I don't think we're going to Cologne anytime soon," I said. Even through thousands of miles of crackling wire, I could hear the lingering heartbreak. Peter had taken a job in Cologne, and for two years they had tried to make the relationship work long-distance, but it was too much distance. When they broke up, my father was devastated and vulnerable, and talked more openly with me than he had ever done before, or since. We finally talked about how he had only accepted his sexuality at the age of forty, despite being certain from childhood that he was gay.

Until we talked, I had assumed that after the split from my mother he was fully liberated. It was, after all, the swinging sixties, and he was in the center of a cosmopolitan, international circle that included many openly and flamboyantly queer artists. Yet Berlin hadn't been all that swinging for him. I was stunned to learn that even then he had been deeply fraught about homosexuality.

At the time, he considered himself religious. He had grown up in a liberal church—liberal for central Kentucky, that is—that had preached tolerance and support for civil rights. When he reached Eastman he joined the InterVarsity Christian Fellowship. In Berlin he volunteered as the musical director of an American Presbyterian church. As far back as I could remember I had been unmoved by all religions, had come to view them as enemies of art, and saw little evidence that my father felt differently. So I had thought this was just another gig. But my father wanted to make grace-filled music.

He believed that homosexuality was a mortal sin. He claimed that his gay experiences were brief and mostly unsatisfactory. In high school, a few minutes with a college student in a practice room, and in each of the places where he lived thereafter, single brief encounters: in college, at West Point (where he had gone after Eastman to avoid the draft, landing in the U.S. Army Band, with which he played USO shows alongside patriotic celebrities like Bob Hope), in New York, and in Berlin. And each time he was sure that he was committing a mortal sin. He told me that he had hoped the army would "discipline the faggot out of me."

Until his father died, a few months after my grandfather had told me about his time in India, my father believed that he was going to hell for his desires, not merely his actions. At the funeral he thought back to a college classmate whose own father had died while they were in school. She'd told him that when she saw her father in the coffin she knew that it wasn't actually her father, that he was somewhere else now. But when my father looked at his dead father, he thought, *There is my father. He is nowhere else. He's there, right there.* That's when the certainty of heaven and hell evaporated. As my father put it after he and Peter broke up, "That's when I knew there was nothing over my head. It was no longer a mortal sin." *It* was now okay.

"I never thought . . ." my father said into the static-filled line.

"Hardly anyone did. And we're staying over in the East, in Prenzlauer Berg."

"No kidding. Is it safe?"

"Sure."

"You come across the music shop we used to go to?"

"What street was that on?"

"Bizet, I think. In that area with all of the musician street names—Bizet, Gounod, Chopin . . ."

"Right, right." The line thrummed, and I pictured him looking out over town to Red Mountain, getting ready for a rehearsal. "How's Aspen?" I asked.

"Good—busy," my father said.

"You missing Jan?" I asked, his best friend and the mother of my old friend Mark having died a few months before. I couldn't imagine the Aspen festival, or Eastman, or my father without her. I thought the line had cut out, but it was the silence of surprise.

"Yes," my father finally said. He still hadn't talked to me about her death, about the quack doctors with their crystal therapy until it was too late to check her cancer. "You writing there?" my father asked.

"Trying to," I said, wanting him to ask me more. I fed another handful of pfennigs into the box and waited. I had a strange sense that he had once stood where I was standing, also in his twenties, making a life for himself in the tumult of Cold War–era Berlin. "I saw Barry, who hasn't changed at all," I said.

"Oh, good. I'd like to see him again."

"I didn't know you did seventy or eighty concerts with him."

"We had quite the run. . . ." my father said.

"Would you ever want to . . ."

"Of course—to visit."

"But you'd never live here again?" I asked, and the line hummed while my father thought.

"I already did. That was an important, necessary time for me. When are you going back to New York?"

"I don't know yet."

"Oh, really?" my father said, and I was surprised to hear worry. He of all people would know about working without a net.

"I'm running out of change, Dad."

"Okay, kiddo. You take care of—"

The line went dead. I had, indeed, run out of coins. I really needed to call my editor. I knew I could go to a nearby Laundromat to get more change to make the call, but I stayed in the booth. My limbs felt like they were full of lead. I thought about what my father had said, about how Berlin had been an "important, necessary" time for him. Was this an "important, necessary" time for me? Staring out of the phone booth, down the alley to the graffiti-covered Wall, I told myself, *Yes, of course it is. Just keep affirming it and it will be true.*

40

"Nevertheless the passions, whether violent or not, should never be so expressed as to reach the point of causing disgust; and music, even in situations of the greatest horror, should never be painful to the ear but should flatter and charm it, and thereby always remain music."
—Wolfgang Amadeus Mozart

Soundtrack: Lou Reed, *Metal Machine Music*, 1975

ON A LUGUBRIOUSLY HOT JUNE DAY I went for my usual after-school run, the magnolias wilting, my new constant soundtrack of punk bass and drums pounded out by my Asics Tigers. In the 1920s, the so-called Lost Generation embraced hot jazz, breaking from the confines of leftover Victorian stodginess. In the 1930s, Cole Porter's suave, fatalistic songs were the sound of the new sophisticated and transient cosmopolitans. In the 1940s and early 1950s, bebop was the driving sound of the Beats and the New York School painters. Late 1950s—rock 'n' roll, leather and swagger. Mid-1960s, the British invasion, then 1968, the May Day student revolution in Paris, with a Hendrix soundtrack. 1979, as a rebellious fourteen- and then fifteen-year-old, I was perfectly placed to get swept up in punk, then new wave.

The Clash, Joy Division, Buzzcocks, Gang of Four, Ramones, and then Minor Threat, Fugazi, Bad Brains, Black Flag, and X—their music went straight into my veins. Most of my classmates were still listening to Led Zeppelin, Aerosmith, Journey, Foreigner, Bob Seger. Punk gave me some crude tools to bash at my classmates' shallow party music, and it also articulated what my utterly inarticulate rage-filled teenage brain could not articulate about the world I was trapped in, which punk helped me to define as homophobic, consumeristic, racist, and conformist.

I listened to the Johns Hopkins college radio station whenever I was in my room, then bought whatever new punk music they had played. Ken Kesey now seemed like an impractical utopian and a dreamer, and I wanted nothing more than to be Hunter S. Thompson. But I looked around and saw nowhere to engage. And even the thought of engagement made me queasy. Confrontation would mean coming out of my defensive armor.

George Orwell, in his essay "Why I Write," says:

"I had the lonely child's habit of making up stories and conversations with imaginary persons, and I think from the very start my literary ambitions were mixed up with the feeling of being isolated and undervalued. I knew that I had a facility with words and a power of facing unpleasant facts, and I felt that this created a sort of private world in which I could get my own back for my failure in everyday life."

That's me, I said as I read this, except that I didn't have the "power of facing unpleasant facts." I ran from anything unpleasant. I faced unpleasantness not with my self, but through the words and songs of others. My rebellion was internal.

As I ran hard across Roland Avenue, I felt taunted by Baltimore and Boys' Latin. The school's motto, *Esse Quam Videri*, means "To Be, Rather Than to Seem." But I was not being, I was seeming. I pumped my arms harder, leaned forward, willed my-self faster along Roland Creek Trail, where I knew every notch of every lichen-covered hawthorn. I danced across the jagged rock path through the creek, then rushed along next to the ribbon of water, sweat soaking my black Joy Division T-shirt, jumped up to smack the metal "NO PARKING" sign at four-point-five miles—*ping*—and then raced back around, retracing my steps faster and faster downhill home.

Home. How did I get there so fast? I tried to catch gulps of air, slow everything, make sure I hadn't tracked any mud into the house, heaven forbid, and get to my room and shower as quickly and quietly as possible.

"Whoa, hey, Mom, didn't see you. Or hear you," I said, surprised to see her by the kitchen table, a handful of unsorted mail in her hands.

"Did your coach give you any breathing lessons?" my mother asked, her voice tinged with incredulity.

"Breathing lessons?" I managed.

"The way you're choking down air, you aren't getting much into your lungs."

"Just . . . ran . . . hard."

"Still. Try this," she said. My mother put her right hand on her diaphragm and pushed in. "When you breathe in, breathe from your diaphragm. Fill the bottom of your lungs first, then when you breathe out, push in with your diaphragm."

"Really?"

"I can't believe you don't do this. Singers are taught this early on. Without breath, you can't sing. Try it."

I pushed out my diaphragm, air rushed into my lungs, and I exhaled it all loudly.

"No, no. Slowly," my mother patiently corrected me. "You'll get a lot more in if you slowly pull the air in."

I tried again. I pushed my diaphragm out gradually, and she was right—I was getting a ton more air into my lungs.

"Good," my mom said, smiling. "Now exhale slowly, pull your diaphragm in. That's it," she said, pleased that I had caught on so quickly. "A good way to practice is to lie down on your back and focus on your diaphragm."

"Wow, Mom," I said. "Thanks. Thanks a lot." I felt like I should say something more. Where did this kindness come from? She'd never been to any of my races, had never shown interest in my running, so this gift was from left field and I didn't know what to do with it. My mother kept smiling as she sorted the mail. What else was I supposed to say? I edged toward the stairs, but lingered for a second, looking at my mother, thinking that she didn't look that tough, that in fact she was really small, thin-boned, like she was made out of matchsticks and could snap apart right in front of me. I wanted to say something, anything. She had given me an opening, but I couldn't form any words. Instead, I took a few more deep breaths, using the technique she had showed me. My mom nodded her approval, and I slid quietly back to my room.

A few weeks later, on my last run before my escape into summer, my legs burned as I sprinted up the steepest part of Bellona Avenue. My fourth half-mile-hill repeat, I was trying to get ready for the Fourth of July road race in Aspen. This time up the hill I wanted to run right out of Baltimore, wanted to run right through the apex of the hill and up into the heat and clouds and hyperspace, where I'd blow through three years and leave high school and Baltimore in the rearview. I crested the hill, earthbound, but with the sudden realization that I *could* go into hyperspace. I *could* compress three years into two. If I took extra classes, I could graduate a year early, knocking twelve months off my Boys' Latin sentence. I wouldn't turn sixteen until halfway through my senior year, but so what? I would be a free sixteen-year-old.

"Do you think you can handle the extra courses?" my mother asked after I spit out my plan, sweat dripping onto the kitchen floor.

"Of course," I said, my hand on my abdomen, trying to use her technique, though I was gasping. "The classes are easy."

My mother frowned like she wasn't so sure of my plan. She was driven as a child, so I was betting she was thinking that I was like her—eager to get to college as soon as I could. She watched my hand moving out with my diaphragm as air rushed into my lungs, then in as I exhaled, and again three more times, slower with each breath, and finally said, "I know that you can do anything you set your mind to. As long as you can maintain your grades, you can try it for the year and see how it goes." My mother looked concerned, but proud of my determination to take on such a challenge.

"I know I can do it," I said with the certainty of someone who has just paid his life savings to be smuggled out of some poor, violent country, not caring where he will land or what awaits him there. All I knew was that I was going to get out. I now had a two-year life plan. Past that, I didn't care if I went to college or wound up on the street. Whatever happened, it would be away from Baltimore.

41

"I cannot conceive of music that expresses absolutely nothing."

— Béla Bartók

Soundtrack: Béla Bartók, Piano Concerto no. 3, 1945

AFTER THREE WEEKS with no laundry, our clothes were moldering. The Easterners didn't have Laundromats; they washed their clothes in sinks, but we only had icy-cold tap water. Unfortunately, the Soviet Mr. Coffee didn't heat enough water to truly wash clothes. We tried a few small batches and laid them on the granite windowsills to dry, but in the damp, cool Berlin air, the clothes simply festered.

So we piled our clothes in Dusty and went in search of a Laundromat. While it would have been easy to find one in the West, I wanted to make a last-ditch effort to do laundry in the East, to support our East Berlin brethren, who were starved for cash. I also wanted to avoid going back into West Berlin. It wasn't the same place I had grown up in. Where were the artists? Where were the black-turtlenecked artsy-fartsies who attended my father's concerts at the modern museum? West Berlin had turned into one big shopping mall populated by smug cretins who looked down on us. Maybe they thought we were from the East. In one of the West Berlin newspapers I saw a cartoon with the title "My First Banana" underneath a drawing of an Eastern factory worker trying to peel a cucumber. The second time we crossed over, the same cartoonist's daily offering was titled "Channel Surfing," showing the same Easterner pointing a television remote at a washing machine.

This was my chance to walk the walk, to effect real change in the lives of our new brethren. A few days before, while searching for the music shop, I had seen what looked like an industrial laundry facility, with huge machines that I assumed were used for cleaning uniforms and hospital laundry. Since the prewar factories were closing down, they might let us clean our clothes there. If I could find it again. So up and down Bizet, Gounod, and Chopin went Elissa, Hank, and I, with me also keeping an eye out for the sheet-music store. Each long block of five-story apartments with arched entryways leading to cobbled interior courtyards looked familiar, yet unspecifically familiar.

"Really close," I said, even though we had been down the same block three times. Hank and Elissa carped, both of them saying they were hungry. "And it's Saturday," Hank reminded me. Shops would close at noon, not to open again until Monday morning. So if we were going to buy any basic food, it was now or wait thirty-six hours. Somehow Hank had made his twenty-three marks last five days. He wasn't drinking, unless someone bought him a beer. Potatoes and bread—how long could you live on that diet?

Then I spotted it, on the ground floor next to a small grocery—the unmarked industrial laundry. Through the window was a row of eight enormous washing machines, steel behemoths each six or seven feet in diameter, with only one in use, a white whorl of what might have been nurses' uniforms.

Behind a dull white Formica counter, a middle-aged man with a thick mustache stared at us, baffled, as we entered.

"Guten Morgen, mein Herr," I said, as formally as I could. Squat and muscular, the man tugged at his blue worker's cap and took a step back. He squinted at us, as if trying to decide if we were real. We must have looked like American boho scum in our black jeans and T-shirts, so he was clearly confused by my clean Berlin accent.

"Morgen," our worker friend said, then asked what we were looking for, if we were lost.

"We have a problem and proposition," I said, half-expecting the man to flee before I could make my pitch. We'd encountered a few Easterners like him, hunkered down in their small shops like Japanese soldiers holed up in caves in the South Pacific, refusing to believe that the war was over.

"We are Americans, working and living in the East, and our apartment has no water so we cannot wash our clothes. There are no places that we have found in the East to wash our laundry." I said this in one breath, and so far so good—he was still listening. "We are hoping to pay you to use your machines. . . ." The man soured, and looked like I'd asked him if we could defecate in his machines. I quickly added, "Or pay you to wash our clothes."

"But we do big jobs, hundreds of uniforms," the man protested, not harshly, more like an invitation to keep talking, to help him make sense of the world.

"Yes, I see, but we have all of our laundry and we would pay you for this service, this convenience," I told him. He narrowed his eyes at the word "convenience," an alien concept before last October.

"Wait there," the man said, then headed into the interior of the building.

"But . . ." I protested.

"It is okay," he said in thick English. "I get my supervisor."

He disappeared, and I could hear him talking to another man, debating; then there was a pause, a long silence, and more discussion.

A tall man in a newer blue uniform led the other man back. "*Guten Morgen*, I am Herr Mueller, the manager here. What can we do for you?"

Hank was rocking on his heels, and I could feel his impatience. Elissa's smile was frozen in place, her jaws tightening. I calmly repeated our proposition. Herr Mueller listened, snuck a distrustful peek at Hank and Elissa, then looked to me, unsure of what he should do.

"Let me see the items in question," Herr Mueller said.

"Pardon?"

"We need to examine the clothes in question in order to determine if we can undertake this job," Herr Mueller stated.

"Get the clothes," I said to Hank, who sped out to Dusty and pulled our East German army duffel bag from the minuscule trunk.

"I see," Herr Mueller said when Hank handed him the duffel. Herr Mueller gingerly carried the bag with both arms like he was carrying a sleeping child, placed the bag on the counter, and slowly undid the rope fastening.

"*Bitte,*" he said to his colleague. The underling nodded, then carefully excavated a stiff white running sock, caked with dirt and sweat. The underling held it up for Herr Mueller and Herr Mueller nodded. The underling put it down on the other end of the counter, then returned to the duffel bag. He pulled out a purple T-shirt, smelling like caged sweat suddenly unleashed.

"*Ja,*" Herr Mueller said, after his colleague had held it up and rotated it. He placed it on top of the stiff sock.

"My God," Hank said.

"Good, I am very happy that this is going to work," I told Herr Mueller and his underling. "The rest of the clothes are much the same."

"Yes, I am sure," Herr Mueller said, then turned back to the bag. "But we have never done this kind of public work before. We must see every item to be certain."

There went stiff sock number two, now some more soiled, stiff socks, followed by underwear (much to Elissa's embarrassment), jeans, more T-shirts, sweatshirts, GDR army fatigues, East German flea-market pajama tops made out of an impossibly stretchy synthetic fabric and in inadvertently hip patterns like fuchsia and cotton-candy-pink diamonds on a background of black-and-white spirals—one by one, they were dragged from the bag, each examined, approved, then placed on the pile.

"*Ja*, all is clear," Herr Mueller said.

"Whew," Hank sighed, and Elissa's smile reanimated.

"Wonderful," I said. I wanted to hug them. I was doing it—engaging. And more than that—changing and cocreating a new world. "Now," I added, "all we need to understand is how much time you will need to do the job and how much to pay you."

The two men looked at each, the senior one concerned, the underling perplexed. "Excuse us," Herr Mueller said, and guided his colleague into the back room. They were deep in debate, but I couldn't make out anything. I stared straight ahead. If I made eye contact with Hank or Elissa they were going to erupt with laughter. To them this was a lark, but to me . . . it was everything. It was why we were here in the East. I focused on the calendar next to the door. It had a picture of a boy in a hospital bed, his left leg in a full cast, a paternal doctor standing over him with a grave-looking nurse in the background. The words underneath: "Recovery, yes. Germs, no—GDR hospitals are the cleanest in the world."

One of the few stories my mother had told me of her time in Germany was about when she and my father lived in Stuttgart, when she was nine months pregnant with me. They lived in a typical German three-story city dwelling meant to house two generations on the first two floors and boarders on the top floor. My parents were the boarders. One frigid December day, the woman of the house, who lived on the first floor, came knocking.

"You have terribly embarrassed the house," she said, trembling.

"How?" my mother asked, mortified.

"You have not been washing the windows."

My mother looked around at her squeaky-clean windows. "The windows?" she asked.

"Yes. Inside and out. It must be done every other day."

"But the windows are not dirty. And I'm very pregnant."

"So was I. I missed no days. With none of my four children. It is what we do."

"It isn't what *we* do," my mother said.

She would not have suffered these East German functionaries lightly. But I could. I wished she were there to see me succeed.

"Yes," Herr Mueller said as he reentered. He was serious but smiling. Junior beamed behind him. "Yes, we are confident that we can do this task," Herr Mueller said as if he were unveiling the UN Charter. "It will be accomplished in eight days."

"What the—" Hank sputtered, but I cut him off with a look.

"Excuse me," I said. "You don't seem to understand that we have no other clothes."

Herr Mueller's smile deflated like a leaky balloon. "Yes, but we cannot . . ."

"There's got to be a way," I said, quickly adding, "if you are going to survive. There is a clothes-cleaning service in the West called 'fluff and fold.' You bring your clothes in and the people there wash your clothes in half a day. Or, you can use their machines and have everything done in an hour."

"Impossible," Junior declared.

"This must be for the very rich, yes?" Herr Mueller said.

"No, not at all. It is for anyone who can't afford to have washing machines *in* their homes. Most middle-class Westerners have washing machines *in* their homes," I said. I was trying not to sound angry. How the hell could I make them understand the danger they were in, the abyss they were about to fall into? *C'mon, folks, I'm on your side.* I wanted them to live in utopia with us, and if they didn't adapt, they were going to get squeezed out. "I want to help you here," I said. "You will soon be surrounded by people with washing machines and with Laundromats and competition. Do you understand?"

The two men looked at me blankly, as if I were speaking Latin.

"Is there no way you can do this today?" I asked, trying to bring everyone back to the immediate problem of the pile of stinking clothes between us. This was all that stood between them and a happy, prosperous post-reunification future. *Seize the day,* I willed them.

"We . . . we examined our schedule and workloads and we cannot understand how the project can be completed in less than eight days," Herr Mueller said. There was doubt in his voice, a tiny little crack.

42

"I've been studying a map of the world, noting places that give a name to one's yearning, a dream to share with another traveler when everything falls back into place."
—Tove Jansson

Soundtrack: Ludwig van Beethoven, Grosse Fuge in B-flat Major for String Quartet, 1826

THE WHITE LINES ROLLED AHEAD as my father drove, me matching words to the lines, ticking off everything that had been happening to me at school, with running, with my two-year escape plan. My father nodded and listened, nodded and listened.

"Stuckey's on the left, home of pecan brittle," I said.

"Six hundred and twelve miles to Meramec Caverns."

Inside our orange space capsule, we were now into our driving rhythm, taking breaks for gas and food, but otherwise keeping the car moving west. At diners, over burgers and fries, we played Boggle and other word games. I was always happy to squeak out a rare victory against my father, who could do *The New York Times* crossword puzzle in five or ten minutes, in pen.

When he'd picked me up in Baltimore, I wanted our journey to last forever, but also, for the first time, I had the simultaneous wish for the two thousand miles to Aspen to disappear and for the Pacer to be there now now now, my body a battering ram that could be used to bash into a different dimension. If

I could hurl myself hard enough against the mundane I might break through to something transcendent. Within minutes of unloading the car, I raced up the steep, rocky Ute Trail, then bushwhacked still higher, through the tree line and onto the exposed glacier field. The next day I ran off of a different trail, found my way home, then, scratched up and sore, leapt off the third-floor balcony at the Continental Inn, narrowly missing the concrete lip of the pool.

It wasn't enough. It never was. So I jumped off railroad trestles into rushing rapids in the Colorado River. I went on long solo hikes where I followed animal paths and hoped and prayed that I would get lost. I pedaled my bike up to Maroon Bells and Independence Pass, ten-, twenty-mile climbs, then bombed downhill, hitting fifty miles per hour, passing cars inching their way along the narrow, twisty mountain roads.

The Saturday before the Fourth of July weekend, as I was racing down-valley toward the Woody Creek cutoff, an eighteen-wheeler rumbled and whooshed past, inches away, the wake shaking my whole bike, sending me sliding through a gravel embankment and into the thick trunk of a cottonwood tree, my front wheel folding over like an omelet. Bloodied and dazed, I hauled my bike up the embankment, then dragged the wreckage across the road and knocked on a farmhouse's weathered blue door. A quiet older townie took pity on me, threw the mangled bike in the bed of his battered blue pickup, and drove me into town. When I entered our ski condo, Sharon, a leggy brunette soprano from Lubbock, Texas, who was waiting for my father to show up for a rehearsal, dropped her score and rushed over to me.

"Sit down. Where's your alcohol and tweezers?"

"I'm okay."

"Shut up. Where's your alcohol and tweezers?"

"My dad's bathroom," I said, trying to look stoic, but feeling exhilarated.

"Sit," Sharon ordered, and was back quickly with the alcohol, cotton balls, and a pair of tweezers. She swabbed out my scraped knee and elbow as I tried to be manly. Then she went at me with the tweezers, slowly pulling black and gray pebbles from my left palm. This twenty-one-, twenty-two-year-old woman was leaning over my arm and painstakingly digging under my skin for each little rock. Her hair smelled like almonds, and I tried hard not to bite the four long, stray strawberry curls near my mouth.

"All done," Sharon said.

"You sure there aren't more?"

I wanted her to keep digging into my palm, to make me feel something, anything. But at the same time I wanted to be so on the physical edge of danger, risk, and exhaustion that nothing else could exist, not even myself. Sometimes I succeeded, and there would be brief moments of obliteration and the bliss of no thought.

A little after dawn on the Fourth of July, I gulped down a banana and dashed down the street for the annual Independence Day road race. The five-mile loop started and finished in the center of Aspen, in Wagner Park, a two-block-long rectangle of green that skirted the town's pedestrian mall. The course went right under our balcony, and my father was up there, waving with one hand, his other clutching a coffee mug. My white-and-blue Tigers skimmed the cool black tar as the course veered left at the edge of town, following the Roaring Fork downstream for two miles, my feet rushing faster and faster, the three leaders dangling thirty feet in front of me, the image of my improbable victory clear. I had visions of being the next Frank Shorter, the American who won the 1972 Olympic marathon in Munich, the city where he was born, his father having been an army doctor. I dreamt of East and West Berlin hosting the Olympics when I was thirty-two or thirty-six, and, of course, I would win just like Shorter.

When the course turned back toward town, up the brutally steep Cemetery Hill, I was ready. I had found a hill in Baltimore that mirrored the one in Aspen, and I had been doing repeats in the heat and humidity. I tapped the Clash, synced my steps to the beat of fighting the law and winning. I was a punk, I was a gangster, and I was going to reel these dudes in. But as the road tilted up, the song skipped the groove, and I felt sweat burning in the scabby scrapes along the outside of my right knee, the three leaders steadily pulling away as reality came back into painful focus—*I'm a fourteen-year-old kid, not Frank Shorter, not a British punk, and definitely no gangster.* No matter how much I willed myself to suffer, I couldn't keep up. As a handful of other runners passed me, my legs and lungs screamed at me for my fast, foolish start,. My quads were on fire and at the top of the hill I wanted to drop right in the middle of the road. My whole body was burning—and then it wasn't. I was floating, in more pain than I had ever been, but also beyond the pain, my legs pumping as fast as they could. The last two miles: thoughtless.

I crossed the line, stumbled off the road, and sprawled onto the green grass. Gary, the winner, all legs and a yellow Coors singlet, pulled me to my feet. "Good job, kid," he said. "Top ten's not bad in this field, and you were right there until the hill."

"Yeah, that killed me," I gasped.

"Keep it up and you'll get it," the real runner said, then tossed me a light-yellow can. "Refuel, kid."

I pulled back the tab and took a deep, long drink, then tossed the can and looked around for my father. The liquid yo-yoed in my esophagus. I put my hand over my closed mouth, willing the beer to stay inside me.

"You okay?" my father asked, appearing out of nowhere.

"Okay. I'm okay," I managed to say. "Dehydrated."

"Here," my father said, handing me a synthetically red Gatorade and my Specials "Rock Steady" T-shirt. "Proud of you."

"Died on the hill," I said.

"Drink," my father said, then went off to his full day of rehearsals. Art and opera trumped Independence Day.

I changed out of my sweat-soaked singlet, then sat down in the grass, and would have stayed there for the rest of the day if my friends Ted and Bill hadn't found me after an hour. The town was beginning to swarm, and they dragged me to a nearby bench on the pedestrian mall to watch for newly arriving cute boys while I watched for cute girls. I sometimes wished that I were gay, would have loved nothing more than to be embraced by queer culture, but I felt decidedly, overwhelmingly hetero. Maybe I was overcompensating, but my raging hormones were pointing me in only one direction. Where did they all come from? The whole valley was suddenly filled with beautiful girls. I wanted every one of them. I took it as a personal insult when any girl went out with another guy. Most of the girls in the festival were slightly too old for me. Or, I should say, I was too young for them. But there were also townies and locals and tourists, many of them my age or a year or two older.

"Nice," Ted whispered as two buff townies walked past. Ted was recently out but was still shy and hid behind Bill, a flaming and self-confident Juilliard sophomore.

"Really like your peaches," Bill sang, loudly.

"Want to shake your tree," I finished the phrase, not as loud, somewhat directing my words at a girl my age, I thought, though it was hard to tell how old she was with her whiteface makeup.

"Enjoying the show?" Bill asked.

"Mmmm . . . mimey," I said.

Ted looked around, confused, and then finally noticed the Christian mimes twenty feet in front us.

"What *are* they doing?" Ted asked.

"Looks like the Resurrection," Bill ventured. "Oh, I just love it when they rise up from the dead."

We watched a pimply Christ being raised by other earnest teens, silently, with large gestures. They then bowed to a handful of unenthusiastic claps and the three of us cringed as the Christian teens fanned out, armed with pamphlets.

"Oh, please, Mary Magdalane, walk my way," I said.

"No, no, we want Christ," Bill said, and sure enough, the pimply Christ was handing out propaganda at a nearby bench, looking nervous as he glanced our way.

"It's okay," Bill said, almost loud enough for the frightened mime to hear, "you can come over, though I doubt you suck non-Christian dick."

The three of us burst into hysterics as the poor mime reversed course and began handing out pamphlets far, far away from us, the unsavable. How I would have loved to drop my Boys' Latin classmates here, to show them my world, though I'd still need Ted and Bill, braver souls than myself, to shield me.

The day kept happily unspooling, hours disappearing with friends and beer and Frisbees, and I wanted the day to be endless but it was now sunset, our balcony crammed with friends, new and old, a violinist named Kimi next to me, her small hand clamped into mine, my father and Peter working the blender nonstop. Over Red Mountain a towering cumulus cloud was aflame. Red, pink, and purple streaks bled out north and south, dissipating down-valley and up toward the Continental Divide and Independence Pass.

Somehow it was time to don sweaters to ward off the suddenly icy air, the stars sharp and pressing down like stalactites, time to make our way to Wagner Park with drinks and blankets, the grass covered like a crazy quilt, strangers stitched up next to strangers. We wedged ourselves in and the fireworks shot off Ajax Mountain and over the town. The dry, high-altitude air nearly nonexistent, I felt as if I could reach out and grab the red and blue bursts above me.

I was happy. And I let myself be happy.

Midnight come and gone, our ever-expanding band of revelers traipsed from party to party, and right at the peak of communal happiness, I stole away, back to my balcony. Below, cowboys and stoned violinists staggered along Durant Street. Overhead whizzed rogue Roman candles. My eyes ached. All I wanted was sleep. But, then, that would mean that this perfect day would be over.

43

"Music is your own experience, your own thoughts, your wisdom. If you don't live it, it won't come out of your horn. They teach you there's a boundary line to music. But, man, there's no boundary line to art."

—Charlie Parker

Soundtrack: Charlie Parker Quintet, "Dexterity," 1947

FROM THE INDUSTRIAL LAUNDRY FACILITY in the East to the Western side of the Wall was, at most, a fifteen-minute drive if I drove straight shot down the wide-open Prenzlauer Allee. But I didn't want to rush from the 1950s to the 1990s. I took the backstreets instead, zigzagging toward the Wall. I wanted to get lost. Which, sadly, was virtually impossible for me: My internal gyroscope from years of running into the wilderness was unshakable. If I got lost, I wouldn't have had to admit defeat. Once we crossed over into the West I'd have to accept my failure, that I couldn't convince the East German laundry guys to save themselves. If I couldn't do a simple thing like that, what could I accomplish in the East?

"I'm sorry," Elissa said from the backseat.

"Me too," I said, and caught her eye in the rearview mirror. She felt bad for me, but I could tell by her newfound energy that she was looking forward to a break from the East, was anticipating clean clothes and maybe even a real meal. I wanted these things for her, but was also annoyed that she needed them. I wanted to stay pure, like some stubborn Luddite. I was determined to be a full citizen of the new East Berlin, no matter how hard that would be.

"Where are we?" she asked, leaning forward to get a better view.

"The Wall's around the corner."

"No way."

"Way."

And sure enough, there was the grainy gray barrier. While I knew exactly where we were along the Wall, a couple of four-foot slabs were newly missing. I could now drive right through the partition and wouldn't have to cut back along No-Man's-Land like I had planned. I guided Dusty through the narrow hole, and we found ourselves in a Deutsche Bank parking lot filled with hulking BMWs, Mercedes, and VWs, the vanguard of the old Wehrmacht. It felt like the blotchy black-and-white documentary we'd been in had lurched into a lurid Technicolor spectacle.

Even the people were shinier, brighter, but not pleasantly so—they were too loud, too colorful, like Plasticine figures.

My internal map told me that we were not far from Kreuzberg, the old hipster neighborhood, where I was sure we'd find a Laundromat. I kept expecting to be enveloped by memories, by remembered smells—the Turkish street vendors with their lamb spits; the doughy, salty pretzels, the damp, earthy air—yet it all felt hazy and distant. Each time we crossed into West Berlin, I wanted to be reembraced. I wanted to feel like a transplanted tree returning to its native soil. Instead I felt like a dandelion fluffball skittering across concrete. And if I was, indeed, a windblown seed, I would've much rather put down roots in East Berlin's crazy swirling dust storm.

Faced with our real clothes crisis, I shook off the poetic non-sense and found a Laundromat on the edge of Kreuzberg, close to Schöneberg, where Marlene Dietrich was born and raised. The Laundromat was down the street from a decent kebab stand, where I grudgingly enjoyed a gyro that I couldn't have had back in our neighborhood, the Turks yet to cross over into the East, afraid of the racist skinheads.

"Hey, check out the record store," Elissa said, pointing to the flyer-covered window across the street.

"Let's go," Hank said, already crossing over.

"I'll watch the clothes," I volunteered.

"Oh c'mon, lighten up, Francis," Elissa said. "They'll be all right for a little while."

"It's okay," I said, not feeling okay, and doubly not okay, as I knew that I was sulking.

Fifteen minutes later, Hank and Elissa returned, Elissa beaming.

"What?" I grumpily asked.

"Brits in there," Elissa said. "Sweet, sweet native English." Despite my best effort to suppress it, I laughed. "*And,*" Elissa added, "they're going to the track meet. Which is *tonight.*"

"What?"

"The one you said you were going to cover," Elissa said. "Remember?" she asked, her eyes narrowing, readying for another strike.

"I can't believe I spaced it out," I said. Elissa's eyes widened as she realized that I meant it. Her anger turned to confusion. "I really did want to write about it," I said.

"I believe you," Elissa said. "And it's not too late."

"Okay, let's just go then. I'll figure something out when we get there," I said.

"Right," Elissa said, halfway hopeful.

Since it was only two o'clock, we had time to kill before the meet, and Hank suggested that we hike over to the nearby Reichstag. "First time since the war that people are allowed to look inside," he said, reminding me of the confident and resourceful Hank who seemed to have vanished in Portugal.

The Reichstag had been burned in an arson attack in February 1933, a month after Hitler took office, and Hitler blamed the Communists and used the fire as a pretext to suspend all civil liberties and consolidate power. Minimally repaired before the war, in early 1945 it was once again heavily damaged, this time by U.S. and British bombers. After the war it was partially repaired, but never used. We walked around the hulking shell and found the one open side room, ringed in scaffolds and braces. In front of the scaffolding there was an exhibit of photographs of the dome before and during the war, including one sequence showing the bombing of the building we were standing in. The black-and-white photos showed the bullet-shaped bomb falling from the B-17, closer and closer to the dome in each picture until most of the dome disappears in billowing clouds of expanding smoke.

I looked at the photographic evidence, then up at the scaffolding, trying to imagine the terror. I thought of the Berlin Philharmonic, playing their "last concert" on April 12, 1945, three months after the bombing in the pictures, in the nearby and already heavily damaged Beethoven Hall, under the orders of Albert Speer, who chose the program, including Wagner's *Götterdämmerung*. With the Russians on the edge of the city, Hitler Youth stood at the exits holding baskets filled with cyanide pills. Party officials took the pills, but not the musicians. They would die for their art, but not for the Führer.

A few hours after we left the Reichstag, we bought cheap seats to the track in the massive Olympic Stadium, a quarter occupied on this rainy, windy evening, huge klieg lights illuminating the low clouds so they looked like swirling Creamsicles.

"Speer designed this stadium so that it would crumble into spectacular ruins," I said, grasping at remembered facts.

"Why not Rouen?" Elissa asked, and it took me a minute to figure out that she was talking about the French cathedral we had visited only a month before, but which felt like a lifetime ago.

"They wanted to take it all with them," I said. Forty-five years after the end of the Third Reich, and fifty-four years after Jesse Owens ran there, the stadium was still fully intact and functioning, once again host to an international track and field meet. "Speer planned all the Nazi monuments with ruins in mind, hoping for the enduring grandeur of the Roman Colosseum."

"Creepy krauts," Elissa said. She was energized by the clean clothes, real food, and our first decent cup of coffee in a long time, and was visibly more relaxed among the Westerners; no threat of riot police or skinheads here.

In the two front rows an oompah band in lederhosen had been placed solely for me, I knew, because they played "New York, New York," and then "Brazil." How did they know *Brazil* was one of my favorite movies?

Down on the track, Arturo Barrios, the Mexican world-record holder in the 10,000 meters, was trying to set a new mark. He'd have a tough time out there tonight, with the rain and puddles. *Why hadn't I got it together to interview him?* I thought, wondering why I was self-sabotaging. I needed Arturo in order to stay in Berlin. *Am I running to or from my true self?* My legs twitched in time with his fluid strides as he ran behind the pace-setting rabbits, two world-class runners paid to set a record pace for as long as they could before Arturo took over. Man, was he smooth—no wasted movements, his entire being focused on forward momentum. Four years before, I had been running ninety miles a week, with my eyes on the New York Marathon. I became stronger the longer the distance, increased suffering equaling increased mastery, and knew I could have been a competitive marathoner.

Barrios gamely splashed ahead once the last of the rabbits fell off after the fourth mile, gutting out the last two-plus miles solo. Everyone in the stadium stood, clapped in rhythm to his strides. We all kept cheering after he crossed the finish line in 27 minutes, 18 seconds, only 10 seconds off his world record, set on the same track the summer before, but under ideal conditions. Everyone in the stadium cheered the noble effort, his determination against the elements. What was my excuse? What was I chasing?

If I wanted to stay in Berlin, I needed a plan. I needed to get serious about my work—I needed to start reporting stories, and interviewing people like Barrios. I knew it, Elissa knew it, and I told her I would. I lied. Or, to myself, I said, *I would prefer not to.* I wasn't sure how we were going to stay, but it wasn't going to be by the old ways. There had to be some other path. I hadn't found it yet, but when it appeared, I knew I would be ready to run.

44

"Put down the pen someone else gave you. No one ever drafted a life worth living on borrowed ink."

—Jack Kerouac

Soundtrack: The Knickerbockers, "Lies," 1965

ON A MILD LATE-NOVEMBER NIGHT I was all dressed up—black jeans, black-and-white Converse high-tops, a white button-down shirt, a skinny black tie, and a black dress jacket with a Selecter pin stuck in the thin lapel—on the cusp of a life-changing decision. So often our crossroads moments aren't clear to us until long afterward, but this was a moment where the paths—and the consequences of my potential choices—were clear. Robert Frost in "The Road Not Taken" or Robert Johnson meeting the devil in Clarksdale, Mississippi, at the corner of Routes 61 and 49—they would know what to do. Me, I felt like an idiot standing on my stoop, paralyzed, unable to decide which direction to turn.

In truth, I had three places to go, or more accurately, three distinct Friday night choices: 1. See a safe hippie band with my intimidatingly sexy new girlfriend; 2. See a real punk band for the first time; 3. Get safely smashed at a school party.

Three months into the school year, three weeks before my fifteenth birthday, and officially a junior on my two-year life plan (Boys' Latin giving me permission to skip my sophomore year),

I was still trying to find my balance. I was a skinny fourteen-year-old cross-country runner and all the other juniors were seventeen-year-old football and lacrosse players who shaved and looked at me like an unwelcome little brother. Sex was their main subject of discourse and I didn't have much to say. Sure, I knew the lines, the exaggerations, the double entendres, but not what went with the words. It was like knowing how to play a basic twelve-bar blues—C to F to C to G to F to C—but without having lived through any experience worthy of a blues song.

One of the childish things I had to jettison was the *by* at the end of my name. I was now Rob, not Robby. When I came back from the summer my friends Danny and Joey were now Dan and Joe and looked five years older and tougher. They had discovered punk and hardcore, and declared all other alternative music "hippie shit."

I wasn't so sure. I spent all of my allowance on music—Patti Smith, Talking Heads, David Bowie, Adam and the Ants, early Who, and especially ska: Madness, the English Beat, The Selecter, and The Specials. I hung around Edith Massey's thrift store in Fell's Point, where Divine and other John Waters "stars" congregated. I stayed on the periphery, but did find my new wardrobe there, including the mod jacket and tie, and my prized find—a British belt buckle.

My fellow juniors, much older and hardened than me, crashed cars, were arrested for DWI, got into fistfights in bars, screwed around, and sweated out pregnancy tests. Yet they still clung to the same bands they had been listening to in middle school—Aerosmith, Styx, REO Speedwagon, Boston. I hated their casual, lazy fandom. To me, my newfound music defined me, was life and death. The music was as holy as the battered Kerouac, Kesey, and Thompson paperbacks I read and reread.

They made life worth living. How could one listen to music casually? Music was what helped them down a Natty Boh beer. My classmates were amateurs at life. Of course, this was a ridiculous stance for an almost-fifteen-year-old. What teenager *isn't* an amateur? And I was certainly no pro. I had delusions that I was looking for transcendence and epiphanies and a life through art while they were amateurs in the true sense of the word, following enthusiasms simply for their pleasure.

I was unable to see that I was frustrated by a system that created and coddled these semidecent humans-in-formation and so I hated them. I hated them because I had no tools to change them. I hated them because I wasn't one of them, hated them for having functional families. Rather than hating myself, I hated them, deeply. Yet I didn't let it show. I went to their parties, drank their beer. Sometimes, when watching them smugly singing along to "Dazed and Confused," I wondered what it would be like to not care. To not have to worry if you have a place in the world. I envied that they were going to blissfully go through life listening to their stupid party music with the privilege of tossing beer cans from their BMWs. My rage and envy turned them all into the worst of their species. They didn't have to use turn signals, so therefore my twisted logic dictated that they were date-rapists and fag-bashers, and they would go on to fill toxic waste dumps as corporate creeps, would keep the Cold War running, would become the guardians of institutional racism and sexism and would be the biggest boosters of the Ronald Reagans of the world.

Through punk and reading and running I was channeling my disillusion inward. But wasn't there something creative I could do with it? My heroes had figured out how to turn their rage outward, to share their misery, or even better, turn their misery into art. Where was my tribe, people like the ones I read about in *On the Road* who "burn like roman candles"?

A few weeks into the semester, in Advanced German II, I intentionally dropped a pen and pounced out of my chair before the Deadhead girl in the corner could conceal her drawing. I saw enough—Abby was sketching me. I looked at her hard, seeing her for the first time even though we had been in the same classroom for over a year now. She was two or three years older than me, but carried herself like a confident twenty-year-old. She smiled at me, not a girlish smile, but a "So what" smile, a "What are you going to do about it, boy?" smile.

After class, in the minute I had to linger before having to rush back to Boys' Latin, I waited for her.

"Nice drawing," I said.

"Thanks," she said with a hint of a blush, then brushed back her long, wavy black hair. Over the next two months I competed for her attention with her pothead crew. Abby was a stoner, but still pulled straight A's. I hadn't smoked pot with her because I was doing well in cross-country, but now that it was almost December and the season was over, I thought that I might. And this possibility would be a near-certainty that night if I chose to meet her as planned, in half an hour. When we kissed, Abby always tasted like resin, burnt and bitter. I felt like she was going to catch on to my inexperience at any second, but the week before she had taken me to her secret place, the Bread and Roses Coffee House near Greenpoint, a long, low barroom where a band called the Charm City Reactors was playing. ("Charm City" was one of the many slogans Baltimore had tried to adopt in the seventies. A few years before, two separate studies had shown that Baltimore had the country's highest urban teen pregnancy rate and the highest urban teen illiteracy rate.

The city tried the slogan "The City That Reads" to combat this, painting it on city bus shelters. Industrious kids amended it with the letter "B" before "Reads," so that the slogan read "The City That Breads." *Sic transit gloria mundi.*)

The Charm City Reactors were a bunch of longhairs, three guys in their twenties with wispy beards and a sixteen-year-old female lead with long, straight black hair and a purple-flowered peasant dress. Most of the girls in the club wore ankle-length flowing flower-patterned skirts and swirled to the music, and the air was thick with the sweet smell of patchouli and sandalwood, the occasional earthy stench of pot base-noting the essential oils. That night the Reactors played the Animals song "We Gotta Get Out of This Place." Singing along, I thought, *I could do this. I could live here.* We were all dancing together and uptight Boys' Latin was as far away as Aspen. I was wearing a white T-shirt with a thrift store black suit jacket, a few black-and-white pins stuck in the lapels, and even though everyone else was in hippie garb—tie-dyes and flowers, Birkenstocks and Mexican ponchos—I felt welcome, part of the club.

The following Monday I told Dan and Joe about the cool band I had seen on Friday night. "We were at the Marble Bar seeing DOA," Dan said with a sneer.

"I've never been," I said. I had been intimidated about seeing punk bands in the basement of the Congress, a notorious old transient hotel in a sketchy part of downtown.

"Nothing like Bread and Roses," Joe said. "Any of those hippie losers step in, they'd get slammed into paste."

"What's so bad about them?" I asked. "They aren't bugging anybody."

"That's just it, man," Dan said. "They're part of the fucking problem."

"This Friday, the Circle Jerks are playing at the Marble Bar," Joe said.

He didn't need to say that I'd be a loser if I didn't go.

Okay, then—that was path number two. Marble Bar, Circle Jerks, paste.

Path number one was still clearly Abby. A reggae band was going to be playing Bread and Roses that same night. "Sally's scoring hash oil, and her parents are going out of town. We can party at her place before, okay?" This is what Abby said, and what I heard was *I'm going to take you to Sally's and get you really stoned and jump your bones.*

Path number three was pretty lame in comparison, but a lot safer than the other two. My cross-country teammate Russ was having a party, his parents also out of town for the weekend; I guess it was Parent Abdication Night. The last time Russ had had a party, his huge Roland Park house was crammed with kids, the bathtubs filled with ice and expensive beer. How could his parents not have heard about the noise and mayhem from the neighbors?

But even when Russ's parents were around, they were clueless about their son. Once, after practice, when I was over for dinner, as we were sitting down to the table, Russ leaned over to me and whispered, "I just dropped a tab of Windowpane." His mother talked to his father about the day at the firm while Russ stared at his peas. Russ was mesmerized by his peas. I nudged him and he smiled at me, took a bite of his pork chop, then froze, his fork hovering over the peas. He remained like this for a minute, and I kept waiting for his parents to notice. Suddenly Russ mashed down his fork and pummeled the peas, then ran away from the table. "I'm sorry, Mr. and Mrs. Jensen, I think Russ's not feeling well," I offered to the mildly surprised parents. "If I could be excused, I'll go check on him."

Three would be the path of least resistance.

But when the going gets weird, the weird turn pro. I stepped off the stoop and followed my feet. Twenty minutes later, before I lost my nerve, I strode across the transient hotel's lobby, past the overstuffed chairs and sofas with sleeping winos, the once-opulent grand hotel bar where Edgar Allan Poe was said to have gotten sauced. I descended a flight of stairs, pushed through thick folds of black curtain which reminded me of the front curtains of the many stages I had been on, and *bang*, I was slammed with a wall of pure noise. Up on the Marble Bar's small stage the four scrawny Circle Jerks were launching into their first song, and the entire bar was in a black broil—bodies bouncing off of every surface, the white marble columns, and the white, eighty-foot-long eponymous marble bar. Arms pinwheeling, leather-clad punks hurtled themselves at each other in front of the low stage. Kids were being shot out of the mass, ricocheting back into the mosh pit.

Chaotic lunacy. I couldn't believe I was in it, and all of a sudden Dan was inches in front of me, smiling. Blood crept from his right nostril, yet he was smiling a contented, beatific smile. I wanted to contemplate this incongruous image of blood and happiness, but Dan grabbed my lapels and threw me toward the pit. *Blam*. Ouch, damn it—my back. I was going down. No, hang on. *Smack*, my ribs, but at least I wasn't on the ground. I spun around and sidestepped the kid with a foot-high green Mohawk. Pissed off now, I grabbed a handful of leather and shoved, surprised by how far I threw the kid, and for a split second I worried that it was too hard, but I was smashed into and had to push some part of someone else's body off me and damn, got hit in the back again. Tried to jump to the music, which was too fucking fast. I couldn't understand a word. Into the chorus, they were repeating it. Listen: "Live fast, die young, live fast, die young."

One more time . . . and is the song over? Yes—and they're ripping right into the next one. I pushed, I bounced, I lowered my shoulder. I got Dan! And he was smiling. Now here he came back at me. Good one. Don't get blindsided. *Never* close your eyes. Another song. And another, and another. Slam-dancing was like running—self-inflicted pain. But different. I was also inflicting pain on others, and they were all enjoying it. It was licensed aggression, but with no premeditation, no thought. It was violent Zen. Nothing else existed. I ran into whoever was near me, I ran into the walls, I jumped up and I jumped sideways into anyone near me. I was a charged particle attracting and repelling all other particles.

The band stopped. The four sweat-soaked Circle Jerks dropped their instruments and left the stage. I was drenched, adrenaline rushing through me. Dan reappeared.

"Yes," I said.

"Yes," Dan said, and led me outside into the cool air.

I kept walking, toward home, alone. Soreness crept into my arms, legs, back, ribs, head, my ears still ringing. I felt as if I was vibrating. I had seen the Way and the Light. All I wanted was the Truth. At Bread and Roses I had been offered a watered-down religion, a thin Presbyterian broth of "Love Thy Brother" platitudes. At the Marble Bar, the Word was handed down to me, a stout Catholic meal of individual and collective rage.

45

"She has feelings; what she calls her feelings are only her ideas of what feelings should be: She is full of ideas about feeling."
—Peter Handke

Soundtrack: Birthday Party, "Nick the Stripper," 1981

"HOW LONG CAN WE LAST?" Elissa asked.

It was a drizzly Monday afternoon and, with the exception of a droopy guy in a damp turtleneck reading a paperback in the corner, we were alone in the CV.

"Tell me the truth." Elissa shut her eyes and pretended to brace herself. "How bad is it?"

"It's fine. We can make the money stretch," I said. We'd done it before. In Boulder we lived on eggs, onions, and potatoes, and apples stolen from a neighbor's tree.

She opened one eye. "How much do we have left in overdraft?"

"A few hundred."

"A few hundred?" She blinked. "Are you fucking kidding me? That's not possible. A few hundred?"

"I can get work, you know, as a stringer. . . ."

"Really? Like with the track meet?"

"I can still write that piece."

She rolled her eyes. "Like you're going to get your driver's license renewed? No, excuse me, *were* going to get your license renewed."

Elissa had intended this as a stinging jab, but I was proud of my suspended license, revoked because the uptight asshole Baltimore cops hated my art car and gave me tickets just for driving it on their streets and so I refused to pay their stupid tickets.

"And how long is *this,* how long do you think *all this* this is going to last?" Elissa asked, waving at the fake-wood-paneled walls of the CV and beyond it Prenzlauer Berg.

"What do you mean?"

"I mean what's going to happen when West Berlin takes over? What's going to happen to our place?"

"Squatters' rights."

"You're sure?"

I wasn't. "But can't you just see how amazing this place will continue to be, and we'll be the pioneers, we'll—"

"Do you really believe that?" Elissa asked, her look slightly shifted from hostility to curiosity.

"I am sure of it," I said, and Elissa nodded, took a sip of her beer to gather herself for the next assault.

"Aren't you afraid," Elissa said, "that it's going to be like home—just like the East Village? Look, the theater people are already fleeing to Odessa to wait tables at the Russia mafia resorts. Artists are like the tree frogs of society—when they start disappearing you know that gentrification has entered its final stage."

I reached for my beer, and Elissa said, "Don't you dare smirk at me."

I hadn't seen her this animated in weeks. She hadn't engaged at all the previous night when we were here. When a big group of us were talking about agitprop theater, she had put her head on the table.

"You really don't think," Elissa continued, "come October 3, the West isn't going to swallow the East? And the East is not going to fight, but welcome it. You've seen those Mercedes trucks driving around with guys tossing cartons of 'West Brand' cigarettes to the Easterners. They're excited about bananas. They're throwing out Bauhaus furniture."

"You don't have any faith, do you? In any of this," I said, wondering when she had given up hope in this place, hope in me. "So what if you're right, that the worst case scenario happens? If it does, we should be here to fight."

Over her shoulder I could see people trickling into the CV, including several people I'd been talking to last night, musicians and this girl who'd told me about a new dance space. They nodded at me, but they could tell that we were deep into it, sadly.

"What are you talking about? This isn't our fight, Rob. This isn't *our* home."

"It could be," I protested, wanting to be anywhere but here now. It was like being trapped in quicksand—the more we talked, the faster we sank.

"Seriously?" Elissa said.

"Think of the Spanish Civil War."

"Wouldn't it be pretty to think so," Elissa said. "Please. Spare me the Hemingway histrionics."

"We should be writing about this," I said, stung. "You can't argue with that. It's what artists do—report, reflect, give voice to the voiceless."

"Of course. It's material. And if you got your shit together you could write something about it, but guess what?" Her eyes flashed. The question hung in the air between us. She shrugged and looked at me like I'd been lying to her. "I don't think your heart is really into this reporting business, is it?"

"It is," I said, hearing the lie out loud for the first time. "Well . . . I do think it's important for this"—I waved my hand to indicate the CV, which was filling with people—"for all of this to be documented. To bear witness."

"I came here to write fiction, not be a foreign fucking correspondent. And what do you mean, 'bear witness'?"

Hank was late. I could've really used him now. And Elissa had liked his idea that the CV could put in a gallery and local artists could sell their work and we'd help hook them up with New York galleries. Hank could take care of the wiring and carpentry while—

"We have lives," Elissa continued, "friends, things we *really* want to write about. This is a great and wonderful diversion, but we have to think realistically about what's going to go down next month. Honestly. What we're going to do with no money, no citizenship, no—"

"Why do you always have to look at the downside?"

"Somebody has to."

"Why?"

"Wouldn't it have been nice if Colonel Kurtz had someone pointing out the dangers of going upriver?"

"Right," I said. "I'm just paddling us upriver into—"

I felt a hand on my shoulder. Günther, one of Ringo's fetchers, was wondering if I had seen his boss. We spoke in German and Elissa rubbed her temples. I felt like going with Günther to search for Ringo. Instead, I turned back to Elissa. "Do go on," I said in my Grey Poupon voice.

"All I'm saying is you're not opening your eyes to the reality of the situation."

"And that's a bad thing?" I said, joking but not joking.

"Oh, Rob," Elissa said with an exasperated smile. If this had been a chess match, I'd have declared a stalemate, more out of fatigue than an actual deadlock. For one of us to win, the other would have to give up.

"We should go," I said. "We don't want to be late."

"We're already late," Elissa said. She was right. Of course she was right. We silently nursed our beers, the mutual dissatisfaction lingering until Hank finally showed up. It was a relief to get up and walk the half-dozen blocks to Ralf's small, clean apartment, where he made us dinner, something resembling Hamburger Helper washed down with jelly jars of a lighter-fluid-like German cognac which made Ralf all the more serious, and Hank uncharacteristically mute. It's possible he was too busy enjoying his first real meal in days.

"No, you do not understand," Ralf said as he topped off our drinks, the four of us wedged around his tiny, black-painted kitchen table. "We want the socialist experiment to continue."

"L'Oréal puts lipstick on rabbits," Elissa said, "and shoots hair spray in their poor little pink eyes."

Ralf looked confused.

"All in the name of vanity," Elissa continued. "Disgusting."

"Animal testing," I said. "She's tired of this conversation. Go on. Ignore her."

"We in the New Forum advocated for the removal of the corrupt government, but not socialism," Ralf said.

"So you wanted the Wall to stay?" I asked.

"Not then, of course, no, but now, yes."

"Really?" Hank asked.

"Your unchecked capitalism will crush socialism."

"Wait," I said. "You don't think the elections—"

"No. I'm most worried about the people in the streets, the workers. What happens when you bring in your twenty-four-hour 'convenient stores'?"

"What's so bad about convenience?" Elissa asked.

"Exploitation of workers."

"But most of the 'convenient stores,'" Elissa said, making air quotes, "are family-run businesses owned by immigrants—imagine generations of a family working together in harmony."

"Elissa, even if it is someone's son working from midnight until eight in the morning, the son is still being exploited."

Elissa shook her head.

Hours later, after Ralf had once again done his best to explain the importance of accurately measuring the number of neutrinos emanating from the center of stars—"the very foundational knowledge of the universe depends on this"—the conversation drifted to the East Village, the music and art scene, and our own troubles with gentrification.

"Didn't you say that artists are being driven from New York?" Ralf asked me.

"Yes, somewhat—" I began, but Hank jumped in.

"We're like rats there," Hank said, slightly slurry. "We move away from the poison of gentrification and find the blighted spaces where only we will live. Now it's Brooklyn."

"What happens when there are no more blighted places?"

"In New York? That'll never happen," I said, for the first time feeling nostalgic for the city. I had to admit that I missed the energy, the tenacity.

"I have only been to West Berlin, and once to Rome for a conference where I had a Stasi escort. I would very much like to see New York," Ralf said.

"Then you must come stay at our home," Elissa said. "We'd be happy to show you our city. Wouldn't we, Robby?"

46

"I know something about dread myself, and appreciate the elaborate systems with which some people manage to fill the void, appreciate all the opiates of the people, whether they are as accessible as alcohol and heroin and promiscuity or as hard to come by as faith in God or History."

—Joan Didion

Soundtrack: Bad Brains, "I Against I," 1986

A FEW WEEKS AFTER seeing the Circle Jerks, I was at a party of stoners, Abby in another part of the big house, off with some other guy, my Marble Bar evening not forgiven. Someone handed me a white marble pipe and I was surprised by how hot is was and by my taking another hit, since I was already stoned and didn't even like pot that much. I hated the clawing in my lungs and the floaty, stupid feeling afterward. I preferred the angry numbness of alcohol. Yet I liked the stoners, the Deadhead types, better than the prepsters, and wanted them to like me as well. I had just turned fifteen and punk was an answer. But it was only one answer. Peace, love, and understanding was another. So was art, but at the moment my creative thoughts were being asphyxiated by the pot, and, in a stoned revelation, that Baltimore was asphyxiating my creativity. Before any more deep thoughts could develop, the sofa swallowed me. It was so soft I felt like I was inside of it. It was an aquarium and everyone else was outside of the glass.

How in the world was I ever going to get off the sofa, or home? I was a mere mile and a half from my house, a distance I could have easily run in nine minutes. If I'd had legs. And all these fucking fish couldn't give me a ride. How could fish drive?

"Don't ever get in a car if the driver has been drinking or smoking pot." I could hear my mother. "I'll come get you, anywhere, anytime." Oh, Jesus, not that. I was going to have to call her. She knew that I went to parties where there were drugs and alcohol, but she never asked if I drank or smoked pot. I wonder if she was afraid of the answer.

"Mom, my ride has been drinking and I don't feel safe." My voice was echoing in the black rotary phone.

The silence was sickening. I could hear the synapses firing in my mother's brain. "I'll be right there," my mother, far down the tunnel, said. "Don't go anywhere."

I held on to the phone, thinking, *She knows, she has to know.*

"Hey, Bass, I mean Cass, can I have some of your gum?"

I was a cottonmouth bass chewing a stick of cinnamon gum. *Not good enough.*

"Charlie, you carrying your Binaca Blast?" *Of course The Tuna is carrying his Binaca. Peppermint on top of cinnamon. Mom will never smell the beer and pot.*

Outside of my classmate's sprawling Roland Park house, the air was like glue. *Must move legs. Keep pushing. Shit, there's Mom's Camry. How long has she been out here?* The car door was so heavy, but I made it inside.

"You okay?" my mom asked, but didn't look at me. She jerked the wheel and sped away from the party.

"Fine—tired," I said, and slumped against the window.

She knows. She has to know. Say something, Mom. Anything. C'mon, Mom, say something.

I thought this all the way home.

47

"Anger is the blanket that comes around me, and that blunts and blurs my sense of proportion."
                                                    —Pete Townshend

Soundtrack: The Who, "Substitute," 1966

TOWARD THE END of what should have been my sophomore year but was now my junior year, Jack and I went to our classmate Bob's house for a party. We usually avoided the Boys' Latin parties, even though I could play the chameleon and blend in. Yet I never felt comfortable or welcome. Russ and Bob were the exceptions. I had liked Bob ever since an eighth-grade English class, when we'd had an assignment to use twenty vocabulary words in sentences and my classmates went through the motions, doing the least amount of work possible. One even wrote, "My teacher gave us the assignment to use EXPENDABLE, CONTEMPTABLE, EXERABLE, [etc.] in sentences and I did it in one." Ballsy, with bonus anti-points for misspelling most of the words. I wove all of the words into a story about a lost unicorn, and after the teacher called on me to read it out aloud in class, Bob turned to me and said, "That was really funny." I hemmed, I hawed. I didn't know what to do with a compliment even when it bit me in the ass. "Yeah, it was silly," I said.

"No, Robby, that was funny," Bob insisted.

Now, two years later, Jack and I were on the second-floor landing of Bob's rehabbed Federal Hill row house, literally looking down at the beer-swilling future frat-boys. Bob walked upstairs, and he had the same look as in English class—serious, unsmiling, scary calm.

"What's up, Bob?" I asked when we were face-to-face.

"You guys think you're above everybody else," Bob said.

"We are," I said, and waved my beer at our classmates below.

"You act like you're superior or something just because you're different," Bob said, and I realized he wasn't joking.

"No, man, I don't . . . I mean . . . the jocks."

"Not just the jocks," Bob said. "You're above everyone, you know?"

"I don't—"

"No," Bob insisted without raising his voice. "And you're not. You're just not."

"Okay," I said, and Bob pushed past us and into the heart of the party.

Jack shrugged and headed downstairs toward the keg, and I tried to follow, but I was stuck. I couldn't move my legs, as if I had been pithed. Bob was right: I was comfortable up on my perch, looking down, far down, on the scum below me. And those who were scum were a "they." Not a Bob or Russ. It was easy to throw up a blanket condemnation—*Boys' Latin is filled with rich cretins who are homophobic and racist and classist and I hate every one of them.* It felt good to say.

But what about Bob? What about Stan Gann, the smart Jewish kid who transferred to the Park School? What about Juan Bendia, the shy, kind South American kid? What about Fred Chalfant, the nerdy cool kid who played ridiculous board games with me and Jack? Dan and Joe, my punk friends? What about the teachers who tried to reach out to me? Mr. Duff, the Latin teacher who, on the weekends, took me along to Habitat For Humanity projects where I set myself apart with my enthusiastic work with the sledgehammer. Or Mr. Becker, the history teacher who gave me extra credit for reading historical novels, letting me plow through the entire Horatio Hornblower series of seafaring sagas, all eleven, from cabin boy to admiral. Or Mr. Silver, my English teacher, who pushed a paperback of *The Shorter Novels of Herman Melville* on me. I was surprised to find myself getting teary when he handed me that book. *Bartleby, the Scrivener,* with the title character's refrain of "I would prefer not to," blew my mind. To opt out, to not go with the flow, to the point of passive suicide—the idea was an incredible revelation, and to receive such gifts, such life-changing kindnesses . . . how do you write that off?

And if I hated Boys' Latin so much, why didn't I leave? Why didn't I transfer to Friends or Park?

And what of my mother and father? So often I put them in neat categories: Father—good, giving, endlessly loving; Mother—abandoning, cold, and distant. Clean divisions. Neat compartments. But what if the truth was messier? What if my father had abdicated? What if my mother was the one who had tried to create a stable home for me and I was making her job as a parent a grueling slog? Then I would have to ask myself what my role in my misery was. Remaining silent is a form of communication. Passivity is a choice.

Bob's rebuke had unlocked a door. All I had to do now was walk through and away from passivity. On the other side was engagement. I could see this new life on the other side, one that was complicated and messy, one that risked sentiment.

This possible new life could be so much richer than the closed, judgmental one I was hunkered down in. *Move*, I told myself. But I was a coward. I followed Jack downstairs, my legs not quite right, and made my way to the keg and poured myself two beers.

48

"Don't be a writer; be writing."

—William Faulkner

Soundtrack: Bronski Beat, "Smalltown Boy," 1984

ELISSA AND I HAD HEARD that there were Sunday-night dances at the former neighborhood socialist youth headquarters. We were expecting a dismal gray box, not a modest nineteenth-century church that would have been right at home in Dubuque. The church's large oak doors were ajar, cold white light spilling out onto the steps. Inside three- or four-dozen East Germans in their late teens and early twenties were dancing where the pews should've been, their outlines still ghosted on the hardwood floor. Folding chairs were propped beneath six panels of stained glass on either side of the church. Sections of the stained glass were missing, replaced by clear glass, so that each of the twelve apostles was crippled in one way or another—Paul missing his left arm, Peter his upper-right leg, Matthew most of his head except for his right ear and some long locks of black hair.

The altar was intact. On top of it records were spinning on a turntable connected to a boxy gray amp and receiver held together with electrical tape. Speaker cables snaked along the wall and into the balcony, where tinny speakers did their best to crank out Bronski Beat's "Smalltown Boy." Along the face of the balcony were six identical posters of Lenin, a classic white bust on a red background, but each poster was altered with black marker, someone having added granny glasses and a T-shirt that read "I♥NY."

I stared at the Lenin-to-Lennon posters for a few seconds, the Bronski Beat song ending, and as New Order's "Temptation" switched on, Elissa pulled me to the dance floor, the young Easterners giving us room and shy smiles as we joined them. At the altar, the female DJ replaced the record in its pink-and-black slipcover and glared at us. I smiled and she continued to glower. Everywhere we went at least one resistant local refused to engage the interlopers. Yet here, like mostly elsewhere else, the majority of people were trying to be cool, dancing while stealing glances at us. Elissa ignored the glare and pulled me close.

49

"Audiences like their blues singers to be miserable."
                                                —Janis Joplin

Soundtrack: Janis Joplin, "Kozmic Blues," 1969

"EMBANKMENT." An awkward, bulky word. Rachel couldn't turn the car in time and then we were sailing through the air. A good twenty feet above concrete, my one thought was *I might die.*

But then everything slowed, the Mustang stuck midair, like a fly in amber. *How did I get up here?* I wondered.

It was two weeks before my sixteenth birthday, and my father had given me one and only one piece of advice about girls: "Watch out for redheads." When he had told me this, I thought, *You've got to be joking,* but let it go at that, thinking that maybe because he was gay he didn't feel qualified to hand out any further, or real, advice. Or maybe he thought I was doing all right on my own. That summer, age fifteen, about to be a senior in high school, with a fake ID so that I could get into bars, I found that girls in the festival now thought I wasn't too young. Sixteen-, seventeen-, and eighteen-year-old girls tuned in to the fact that I was the son of one of the most popular teachers at the festival. And none of them cared about attachments. They were driven musicians, the summer festival a rung up the ladder to the best music schools; I was a fun, temporary distraction.

Which suited me fine. I guess my father thought I didn't
need any practical advice, though I would have liked a little
more to go on than "Watch out for redheads." But now, hovering
twenty feet over hard pavement, about to be killed by a redhead,
I realized that his one incontrovertible piece of advice was more
useful than a platter of pablum.

Rachel was a wild Bryn Mawr junior I had been dating for
a couple of weeks. She had been given the mint-condition black
1964 Mustang Convertible, an infinitely bitching ride, for her
Sweet Sixteen by her yacht-building giant of a self-made gazil-
lionaire father. On that particular grim, slate-gray December day
we drove downtown, to a bar near the strip clubs where Rachel
knew we could get served. We were, indeed, served—a lot.

Toward closing time she said, "Let's go fool around," and
we stumbled to her car. She cranked up Zeppelin's "When the
Levee Breaks," peeled out, then swung the Mustang left around
the corner, quite smoothly, but also heading the wrong way on a
one-way street. She clipped the front left headlight of a behemoth
white Cadillac waiting at the light, bouncing her Mustang hard
to the right. Dazed from hitting the dashboard, I turned around
and saw the middle-aged, beer-gutted Cadillac driver jump out
of his car, yelling at Rachel, who stormed out of her seat, ready
to shriek back, then registered that she had turned the wrong
way. "Shit, let me get my wallet," she told the Cadillac's driver.
She reached through my window and across me for her purse,
rummaged around, then yelled out, "Shit, shit, shit!" as she ran
to her side of the car, then jumped into the driver's seat, started
the engine, and floored the gas. "I don't have my real license!"

"This isn't a good idea," I said as cars swerved out of our
way. I turned around and saw the Cadillac driver get in his car,
do a U-turn, and take off after us.

"Shit, shit, shit," Rachel said again. She peeled around a corner, floored it for two blocks, and slid through the on-ramp to the Jones Falls Expressway, the main artery out of the city. I looked back and the Cadillac was right behind us.

"This isn't a good idea," I repeated, clutching the dashboard as the speedometer climbed past 70 to 80 to 90 and up to 100.

Rachel repeated her mantra—"Shit, shit, shit"—each time checking the rearview, and seeing that she wasn't shaking the Cadillac on the wide-open, empty highway, Rachel yanked the wheel to catch the Twenty-eighth Street exit, and barely missed a concrete divider. The rear tires skidded and she locked the brakes and we screeched around the sweeping turn. I was sure we were going to roll. Everything slowed. I wasn't scared; I was curious about what rolling in a car would feel like, to have no control, spinning as if on a roulette wheel—black, red, black, red, death, life, death, life. But, instead of rolling, the Mustang's squealing wheels held the concrete through the turn and the road straightened out. Rachel exhaled and punched the accelerator. I was thrown back and felt relieved, yet disappointed. A fleeting thought as we both noticed, and both too late, that the ramp curved again after the brief straightaway. The Mustang rocketed through the apex of the turn and we went soaring off, twenty feet above the ground.

So there I was, up in the air, weightless. Removed from the earth. I didn't want to descend. *Nirvana. How can I stay here forever? Don't look down. Don't look down. Don't look at the pavement.* But the pavement did, sadly, rush toward me. A few feet past a black Dodge Dart we smacked down hard and each of the Mustang's tires blew, *bang bang bang bang,* almost simultaneously. I bounced all over the plush interior as the Mustang careened forward, the metal tire rims grinding against tarmac. Silence for a split second. We were stopped. And alive. Then a roar of sounds which funneled into one sound—the hissing engine, steam pouring from the edges of the black hood.

Rachel looked over at me. *God, she's beautiful*, I thought, her long, curvy red bangs clinging to her sweaty forehead. I wanted to lick the sweat from her forehead. *"Marry me and be my wife,"* I sang in my head. I couldn't speak, and we both looked back, half-expecting to see the Cadillac right behind us, but the driver had stopped at the edge of the embankment. There was no way down on foot. He was out of his car, screaming. I thought that if it had been Hunter Thompson in that Cadillac like the one he drove at the beginning of *Fear and Loathing in Las Vegas*, he would have made the leap and then taken a golf club to our heads.

But we were alone in the middle of a mostly empty parking lot next to a nondescript gray office building. *How did we miss that Dodge Dart?* I wondered as Rachel downshifted into first and limped the Mustang on its rims through the lot and into an alley two blocks away.

"My father is going to kill me," Rachel said, still gripping the leather steering wheel with both hands.

I nodded, wondering how I was alive, much less uninjured. *Do it again, Rachel. Do it again.*

"And he'll dismember you if you're around when he gets here," Rachel added.

"Right," I managed. "You going to be okay?" I asked as I unfolded myself out of the Mustang.

"My father is going to kill me," Rachel said, staring straight through the cracked windshield.

At that moment, there were two things I knew for sure: I would never have another date with Rachel. And this was as great as any sex could ever possibly be.

I walked away from the crash unscathed, feeling like I could sprint all the way home, but after a few blocks my head began to pound, a persistent ache that throbbed with each footfall. With each slow step, spikes shot through every muscle in my arms, legs, and back. The world looked smeary for several minutes and then my vision coalesced in time for me to realize that it was late Saturday night, and I was a scrawny white kid wobbling across the borders of four gang territories, at North Avenue and Charles Street, featured in that month's *Spin* magazine as the "most dangerous intersection in America."

As I walked under a burnt-out street lamp, an improbable image came to me. I'd always thought I had no memories of my parents being in the same room at the same time, yet the image that came to me was from when I was five years old, waking up in a West Berlin hospital, in a criblike bed, and looking through the slats at my parents, who were behind a glass partition worriedly looking down on me. I'd been with my father at the ancient, ornate home of a famous voice teacher named Mauz. Blind, with bright white hair, Mauz was revered, treated as if she could connect her students with all that was musically profound and beautiful.

While my father was playing piano for her, I was quietly playing tag with one of her students, and I ran silently but full tilt toward a gate that blocked the second-floor landing. I leapt onto the railing along the side of the gate, slipped, and plummeted onto the stairs below. Berlin blurred by, a black world lit by the ambulance's red strobe light. I passed out, then woke in a crib in the middle of a sea of cribs, in what looked like a picture of some third-world orphanage. My head was throbbing and I was confused—not by the wide-open children's ward, but by the presence of both of my parents. They had separated just six months before, yet I had already wiped clean any memories of them together, had already forgotten what it was like to live in a "normal" family.

50

"It is better to make a piece of music than to perform one, better to perform one than to listen to one, better to listen to one than misuse it as a means of distraction, entertainment, or acquisition of 'culture.'"

—John Cage

Soundtrack: John Cage, *4'33"*, 1952

A YEAR AFTER my Berlin concussion, my father took off my training wheels and gave me a gentle push and all of a sudden I was doing it, really riding a bicycle, fast, flying across the pavement, the Turkish kids from the neighboring *Gastarbeiter* complex taking a break from their soccer game to watch me pedal madly past their dusty pitch. "Turn, Robby, turn," I heard my father yell behind me, but I was too scared. I kept the handlebars locked in place and pedaled and pedaled, right into an open garage and toward the back wall. Before impact, I had a moment of clarity—the garage's cement wall was the exact same shade of gray as the Eastern side of the Berlin Wall, which was only a mile away from the apartment where my father and I lived. "Stop, Robby, stop," I heard my father yelling, but I couldn't stop. "Turn! Stop!" my father called out, and then I was sprawled across the garage floor. I jumped up, dazed and shaken. And proud. I could do it: I could ride a bike, even if it was straight into a wall.

51

"If You Want To Rebel Against Society, Don't Dull The Blade."

—Ian MacKaye

Soundtrack: Minor Threat, *Minor Threat*, 1981

THE FLASH OF SILVER was going to hit us. I had to turn the wheel. Too late.

My head cut through the windshield as easily as if I were diving through cool, clear water. I flew free from the car. Airborne, I noticed blue, clear sky, and that I was flying toward a beautiful, flowering willow.

I shouldn't have been in college. I was seventeen and a half at the end of my first year. I wasn't yet sixteen when I'd applied to colleges. I was so focused on my Baltimore exit strategy that I hadn't thought about what I would do once out. College? I guessed that was what I was supposed to do. Everyone did it, right? Or at least all of my classmates did. Both of my parents had been of limited help in counseling me about college, about where I could go or even how to apply. Their choices had been Eastman School of Music, Eastman School of Music, or Eastman School of Music. For me, there was no such clear-cut choice, nor any clarity about why I was even going. My mother's contribution to the cause was to take me to a college fair, where hundreds of schools had booths with pamphlets about how wonderful their campuses were. "They all look good," I told my mother as I gathered up dozens of pamphlets.

UCLA and USC were perfect in that they were palm-tree-decorated havens 3,000 miles away from Baltimore. The University of Puget Sound, on the very edge of Washington State, and the country, was slightly more perfect in that it was 3,200 miles away. Puget Sound looked like a decent liberal arts college, but this was of secondary importance.

"You'll only be sixteen," my mother said when I told her my first choice.

"I'll turn seventeen in December," I protested.

"You need to be a little closer to home," my mother insisted.

Instead of Puget Sound, I applied to another nice little liberal college—Drew University, in central New Jersey. At Boys' Latin, my senior adviser was the same English teacher who had given me the Melville novellas. "Drew?" he asked. "That's a perfectly good school, but why aren't you looking at Yale and Princeton? You'd do well at Princeton. Or Brown."

"Me?" I said with a laugh. "No way could I get in there."

"Why not?" he asked. "You're what—third in your class and have skipped a grade, managed the after-school theater club, run cross-country, started the Ultimate Frisbee team . . . why not?"

Because I am nothing. My classes at Boys' Latin had been jokes. The Yales and Princetons only took the squeaky-clean rich kids who had gone to schools like Gilman and St. Paul's. Art schools only took kids who had taken some art classes. And even if I did manage to get into a Yale or Brown, how could we afford it? By "we" I meant my father. He paid for all of my school bills, but wasn't exactly great at saving money. Before Christmas during my last year of high school, my father asked me what my favorite city was. What the hell does a fifteen-year-old know? I said London, which was my father's favorite city. So we spent Christmas in London, going to the theater every day—seeing Diana Rigg briefly naked in Tom Stoppard's *Night and Day*, *Macbeth* with no intermissions at the Royal Shakespeare Company, the original Broadway cast of *A Chorus Line*.

London at the time was cheap, hit hard by recession and spillover from "The Troubles" which kept tourists away. An IRA bomb had injured a handful of people in Hammersmith in early December and afterwards airlines chopped their Christmas airfares. Cheap as it was, I was still worried. On the flight over I said, "This is a really cool way to spend my sixteenth birthday. Are you sure you can swing this?"

My dad looked out the window and said, "Don't sweat it, kiddo."

Even though I knew my mother had some money, I assumed that she wouldn't pay for a nonpractical, liberal-arts education. I didn't even ask her, afraid of the probable negative answer. I got into Drew, but my father said that he couldn't afford it and that I would have to go to the University of Rochester; it was affiliated with the Eastman School of Music, so I could go for next to nothing. Student loans? I didn't even know they existed. No one told me, and I didn't ask.

At Rochester, students had to declare an intended major upon entering. You weren't locked down, but even a provisional decision was ridiculous. Astronaut studies? D.C. hardcore music? Drinking? Bomb throwing? Over the summer I had read an interview with the German filmmaker Rainer Werner Fassbinder where he said, "I don't throw bombs, I make movies." I was angry enough to want to throw bombs, but I was a coward, not to mention a pacifist. I had never been in a fight.

But Fassbinder's quote was a clue; maybe there was a way to harness my undifferentiated rage into art. I knew there was a way past self-defeat, a way around the self that was afraid to be seen or heard. Hunter Thompson had started his writing career as an editor on the air-force newspaper. What would he do at the perfectly square University of Rochester, a campus known for its engineering and premed programs?

So I entered the U of R unsure but determined to make something out of the experience, though I felt like I needed to take care of core curriculum before I even thought about looking for anything creative. I started by declaring economics as my major. It sounded better than premed or engineering. My mother had advised me that I could study whatever I wanted, as long as I got a "useful" degree and had a "set of job skills" to support myself. What the hell does this mean to a scattered sixteen-year-old?

I was too young for the cross-country team, which was a serious Division III team, and which might have preserved my liver and brain cells. The drinking age in New York was still eighteen, and a college ID was usually good enough at any bar. And alcohol flowed in the dorms. Since I wasn't running competitively, I "trained" haphazardly. And acted upon impulses like *Why not try acid?*

The Grateful Dead tour acid called "Space Invaders" lived up to its name. I dropped with my geeky friend Albert, a fellow freshman who likewise had never taken it before. While we were in the Commons game room watching kids playing Centipede, mesmerized by the flowing green orbs, Albert vanished. But this was fine, because I ran into another friend, a jazz pianist who took me into the concert hall and sat me down in the middle of the orchestra section. There was a piano onstage. I wish I could tell you what he played, but the notes weren't notes, but rather a kind of chocolaty ooze, and his head was on fire, huge flames shooting up into the rafters. *I want to have flames shooting out of my head and make someone as happy as he is making me.*

I slipped outside, and I knew it was very cold by the sound of the snow crunching underfoot. The Science Building melted into an ice field. I brushed my teeth for an hour. I was so blissfully gone that I knew I had a clear choice: permanently stay in this state of grace and become an acidhead, or never dare come back.

My increasingly binary outlook to all aspects of life allowed for no middle ground.

Monday morning I was counting ceiling tiles in the lecture room of the narcoleptic calculus teacher's class. Then listening as the Indian macroeconomics teaching assistant's thick accent and uninterested monotone combined into the incomprehensible. *What am I doing here?*

I teamed up with Albert and a few other engineering geeks who had mapped the steam tunnels running under the campus and out to the university hospital on the other side of Mount Hope Cemetery. Their master map was intricate and mesmerizing. It was art. Subversive art. A Situationist-style intervention. This I could do. At ten below zero, we would sneak into the tunnels and explore the subterranean universe, popping into buildings and surprising bundled-up students as we emerged in our sweat-soaked shorts and T-shirts.

When I received my first-semester grades, I called my parents with the dismal news. I was surprised when my mother said, "I know it is hard at your age. But you can rise to the challenge, like you did at Boys' Latin." I felt sick that she was rooting for me and couldn't figure out how to tell her that her cheering was futile, as I was in the wrong game.

My father, on the other hand, wanted to talk in person, so he came out to campus on a brutally cold day. As soon as he walked into the all-glass Student Union, I felt the sickening churn of disappointment.

"So what happened?" my father asked, calmly, concerned, which made me feel even more wretched about myself.

"I guess I'm just having trouble making the transition," I said, not having the guts to tell him that I was in the wrong place, that I was wasting away while trying to pass deadening subjects like calculus and economics. "I'll do better next semester."

"I know you can do it," my father said.

Second semester, I took an English class—The Postwar American Novel. A book a week, and so many great books by such strong men—for they were all men, the course taught by a rumpled professor much like the Donald Sutherland character in *Animal House*, a ruined writer, who throughout each class tapped a sad, unlit cigarette on the face of his gold wristwatch. *The Deer Park, Portnoy's Complaint, Ragtime, Catch-22, Gravity's Rainbow*, one after the other. How I ate them up, even though the meals were too rich for my limited palate.

My enthusiasm was far greater than my intellect, but what I did understand, more than anything, was that these writers had sensibilities that were in tune with my own. This feeling was a much stronger and more complicated reaction than when I had first heard Talking Heads alone in my room late at night. These writers saw the American Dream as a mirage in a spiritual desert littered with empty entertainments, material and marital acquisitions, a vast nothingness burying the poor, old, uneducated, blacks, Indians, and anyone else who didn't buy into the dream or who were ignored by its salesmen.

These writers were working Thompson's territory, but in fictional form, and I liked it. I loved it. I wanted to be one of them. I wanted to create, as Robert Frost put it, "a momentary stay against confusion." But to me the gulf between me and these writers was infinite. They weren't humans, but strange gods who had delivered fire to us mortals.

The Postwar American Novel class was the one class I passed that semester.

In other words, I flunked out. And after flunking out, I didn't think that I would ever be a writer. I assumed that the literary world was like the classical music world where most successful musicians went to highly competitive music schools and had mentors. My assumption was that successful writers went to elite schools like Harvard where they worked on the *Crimson* and then got internships in New York City publishing houses where their Ivy brethren looked out for them and gave them a leg up toward literary success. What was I? A literal failure.

Late May, I left town in my father's orange Pacer. My friend Albert was in the passenger seat. My plan was that, after a few days in Baltimore, I would drive to Aspen, where I would search for a summer job before any of the other seasonal slackers blew into town. I didn't know what the hell I would do after the summer. Maybe community college, maybe stay in Aspen and work the ski season. Maybe join a cult.

Twenty miles south of Rochester, on Route 15, I had The Who cranked up. "People try to put us down," I sang out, mashing the gas pedal with my bare foot. Out of the corner of my eye I saw a silver Chevette streaking toward us nearly head-on. I tried to swerve, but had only enough time to turn the wheel an inch to the left. In the split second before the Chevette smashed into the Pacer, I wondered what the impact would feel like. I knew it was going to be harder than anything I had ever felt before. I wondered if it would be the last thing I ever felt.

I wasn't wearing my seat belt. My skull splashed through the windshield, which disintegrated as I soared over the hood and sailed away from the car.

Past the willow tree, I landed on someone's front yard and went into a forward roll. Sitting in the cool grass, I scanned my arms and legs, then felt my face and the top of my head where it had hit the windshield. Not a scratch. I looked up to see a beautiful, flowering willow tree, its long limbs reaching down to almost brush my lips. I turned around to see flames shooting out from the hoods of both cars.

I sprinted to the passenger side of the Pacer, where Albert was holding his head, dazed, blood streaming between his fingers from a gash on his forehead. I dragged him away from the car to the grass, then ran to the Chevette, where the driver, a slight Asian woman, was bloody and unconscious. I unbuckled her seat belt and carried her to where Albert was, his head still in his hands, then came back for her husband, who was moaning and covered in blood. I unbuckled him and he stood up, but collapsed, one or both of his legs broken. I carried him away from the burning cars, then laid him down next to his wife. A truck driver appeared with an extinguisher and put out the fires.

In the ambulance, my heart rate was 60 beats per minute—close to my out-of-shape resting pulse. The EMT said it looked like some safety glass was embedded in my right ear and a cut at the top of the same ear would require a handful of stitches. I had a slight headache. I had failed to die. Again.

52

"History is the present. That's why every generation writes it anew. But what most people think of as history is its end product, myth."

—E. L. Doctorow

Soundtrack: Buzzcocks, "Hollow Inside," 1979

FIVE DAYS AFTER my second near-fatal crash, I was behind the wheel of another car, thanks to New York's "no fault" insurance; fines were pending for the other driver, who had, according to witnesses, blown through a "YIELD" sign. (I would find pieces of the Pacer's smashed safety glass in my clothes for months afterward, and one tiny pebble of safety glass stayed embedded in my right earlobe for years.) With the insurance settlement, my father bought a used silver Chevette. Sore and achy, I drove the rattling little joke of a car out to Aspen to find summer work while my father finished up at Eastman. May in Aspen was a grim time, cold and rainy, the depths of off-season. I couldn't stay in my father's music-festival apartment until he arrived a month later, so I rented a cheap room in a ski lodge down the street. As the storekeepers returned to their boarded-up businesses, I would ask for work.

When I wasn't on the job hunt, I holed up and read. That class had unlocked a torrent of clichés—these books were "only the tip of the iceberg"; they had "opened up the floodgates"; and

now I was ready to dive down into "the heart of the matter." I
lost myself in a novel or two novels a day, suffering the torment of
Ken Kesey's Nurse Ratchet, hitchhiking across the West with Tom
Robbins's Bonanza Jellybean, being terrified by Stephen King's
spooky off-season Colorado lodge, doubly so since I was reading
about it while living in a spooky off-season Colorado lodge.

I read randomly, hungrily, my father having loaded up the
Chevette with a bag of paperbacks, including biographies and
histories of great artistic epochs. As I read these, I wondered why
I had been cursed to be born at the wrong time and place. Every
other era and place seemed so much more alive—New York in
the fifties, when the Beat giants stomped the earth alongside the
drunken New York School painters, with a soundtrack of Bird
and Miles and Monk; or Berlin in the twenties, with their deca-
dent drag balls, vicious theater, and brutal visual art. I tried to
psychically bore into these books to find the answers to my life.
Nothing was more important. Well, maybe girls, and maybe running. But there were few girls around in May, so I read and I ran.

I applied for what I thought would be a shitty job—working
at a self-serve gas station—but it turned out to be a godsend. I sat
in a lawn chair with bills—singles, fives, tens, twenties—wrapped
around the fingers of my left hand, a paperback in my right. I
was basically paid to read all day. Traffic was light. There were the
rich tourists in rental cars, but the locals gassed up down-valley,
where it was much cheaper. Some of the rich locals did stop in,
like Jack Nicholson, who rode a beat-up Harley and paid for his
buck or two of gas with an Amex. We had a routine: I always
asked him for his autograph on the credit card bill and he would
give me a sneer and say "Wiseass" before signing.

Seventeen, a college washout, and working in a gas station.
And ridiculously entertained. The previous summer I had finally

had sex. I wish that it were a good story, but it was drunken, rushed, awkward, in the apartment of a music-festival singer while her roommate was on a beer run. It was so clumsy that we avoided each other afterward. I forgot her name and I hoped that she forgot mine. I thought other girls would be able to tell that I was still mostly clueless, but apparently that first sex attracted other possible mates. Suddenly sex wasn't hard to find, and I quickly became better at it. In one month I went from being a sixteen-year-old virgin to hooking up with college-age girls. My father had only one, unwritten rule—don't date his students. I mostly respected this.

Once the season officially started up and I was able to move into my father's music-festival condo on Durant, summer settled into a halcyon state of running, reading, drinking, and sex. *I could live like this forever*, I thought one late July morning as I went to open the gas station, which was only a block and a half from our condo. There was hardly a soul out at quarter to seven—a few dog walkers, a lone jogger. No cars, which boded well for my reading day. I unlocked the office, pulled out my green-and-red lawn chair, and breathed in my hangover-curing straight black coffee, still too hot to sip in my Yellowstone travel mug. My father had seen me reading "The Snows of Kilimanjaro" and *A Moveable Feast*, so he recommended the biography *Misia*, about the Parisian arts patron Misia Sert, who was integral to almost every artistic moment of the early nineteenth century, a book I inhaled.

When I told my father how much I liked one of his favorite books, he responded by pressing another of his desert-island books, historian Roger Shattuck's *The Banquet Years*, on me. I blazed through Hemingway's Paris, went to Gertrude Stein's salon, marveled at the bizarre, wonderful genius of the pianist and composer Satie, imagined sipping absinthe and coffee at the cafés,

and wondered where this artistic life could now be found and if
a flunk-out like me could ever be in this new Paris or New York.

A morning rush of a dozen cars interrupted my reading,
capped off by a bleached trophy mistress. "C'mon, c'mon, I don't
have all day," she said, her long red nails clicking against the side
of her beige Mercedes. I didn't reply verbally, instead pointed to
the large "SELF-SERVE ONLY" sign hanging over the pump
island. The kept woman humphed, then managed to work the
nozzle and walk the ten feet in her silver stilettos to pay me the
$10. I let her slide on the four cents she was over, even though
it would come out of my pocket.

Then the miraculous happened—my customers all but vanished for two straight hours and I was left alone with Satie: elfin
poet-pianist-prankster, Montmartre cabaret player and friend of
Ravel and Debussy, then collaborator with Cocteau on the ballet
Parade, with choreography by Massine and sets by Picasso, performed by Diaghilev's Ballets Russes. Later Satie would befriend
Man Ray, Tristan Tzara, Duchamp, Picabia, Derain, Breton. He
was wherever groundbreaking art was happening. And funny.
His "incidental music," performed during the intermissions of
plays, confused everyone—it was too alluring to be background
music, but Satie urged everyone to get up, to mill around, to
talk while he played the piano.

One of Shattuck's lines burned itself into me. Summarizing
the avant-garde in Paris between 1885 and 1914, Shattuck wrote
that "the fluid state known as bohemia, a cultural underground
smacking of failure and fraud, crystallized for a few decades into
a self-conscious avant-garde that carried the arts into a period of
astonishingly varied renewal and accomplishment." Sitting in
the Aspen gas station's lot while reading about Satie, I wanted
nothing more than to be in prewar Paris.

What was I coming of age into? Baltimore. Aspen. The United States of late disco, punk, malaise—nothing but "failure and fraud." But there had to be something else, didn't there?

My shift over, I packed up my books and sped home, changed into my running shorts and shoes, and dashed into the mountains. I ran to the other side of the valley, to the trail-head of Hunter Creek, which snaked up into the valley between Red and Saddle Mountains. The trail was steep and rocky, with a quarter-mile stretch covered with Volkswagen-sized boulders which I pinballed, ricocheting past hikers who were carefully inching their way up the trail.

After, to cool down, I snuck into the Continental Inn's pool, where my friend Andrea was hanging out in the Jacuzzi. She was light-skinned, with freckles splayed across her nose. Black Irish, literally. Andrea was a phenom, a freshman singer at Eastman, the youngest student of legendary teacher Jan DeGaetani, who also happened to be my father's best friend. Andrea could talk her way into any party in town, and excitedly told me about two parties in the hills that were on the agenda, and the trio of rich townie girls who would be going with us to ensure that we got in. Andrea swept you up in her wake, leaving you little choice but to either get out of the way or follow.

"Sounds good," I said, "but let's ramp it up."

"Ohhhh . . ." Andrea sang out a low note of curiosity.

"Let's add to the mix," I said. "I've got some crazies, some wild cards."

"But what if they don't—"

"Let's call it a little critical-mass experiment," I said. "The elements might blow up, but they might combine into something much more potent and volatile."

"You're wicked," Andrea said.

"We're going to have the greatest time ever or we'll all hate each other and it'll be a spectacular mess."

That evening, Andrea joined me, my father, and Peter for Sunset Society, which I still loved, but found a little quaint and subdued. I couldn't wait to get to Andre's, the unabashed disco around the corner from the gas station where we were going to meet the rest of that evening's elements. On the way we stopped to pick up Katrina, a twenty-six-year-old New York singer who thought I was "amusing."

Andrea and I had fake IDs, procured from a local teenager who had converted a walk-in closet into a photo studio, with a Colorado driver's license blown up and mounted on the wall—when you sat in the chair in front of the picture, your head was in the corner box and he would shoot the license, then crop and laminate it.

At Andre's Andrea and Katrina commandeered a booth away from the flashing dance floor, and soon were joined by Andrea's townie friends, whom I recognized but had never met. They were effortlessly put together and politely indifferent to us. Old money. They were quickly followed by my friend Steve, just out of state prison for larceny, and his sister Gwen, who was his de facto parole officer, and Olivia, her purple buzz cut freshly shorn. Andrea gave me a "You asshole" glare during the awkward intros when it looked like this was going to be a disastrous experiment, and I slipped off to the bar for a round of Stolis (Katrina's choice), squeezing between an oily guy in an open-collared black Armani suit and a Chanel-bedecked woman who had gotten her makeup spackling tips from Zsa Zsa Gabor. I did a double take, not because the guy was cutting a couple of lines on the bar with an Amex, shielding them by the brass rail to be somewhat discreet, but because the Chanel-aholic was the same snooty Mercedes driver from the morning, who now didn't recognize me as the gas station attendant.

"Hey sweetie, want a little toot?" the woman asked. I looked to her oily friend and he shrugged and handed me his sawed-off straw.

"Sure, thanks," I said, not really wanting it. The few times I had accepted a line or two, coke had made me mellow, not amped liked it was supposed to. But I'd do a little bump—rich cretins deserved to have their drugs taken.

The evening's mixture was strange and uncomfortable, but also exciting for its unpredictability. I hung back and watched as everyone else tried to make it work. With another round and a few more lines, the group loosened up and we took over the dance floor. Watching militantly queer Olivia dancing with one of the superhetero townie girls and both getting into it, I had an inkling that my creativity might lay in assemblage, in putting together groups of people who wouldn't naturally come together, but which I could blend into easily.

Before I could further examine this theory, Andrea had talked the Armani-Chanel couple into giving us a ride to a party on Red Mountain—Andrea, me, Katrina, and Olivia in Armani's Range Rover, the rest in Chanel's Mercedes.

Pricey cars lined the driveway of a long, sleek house and Rod Stewart asked if we thought he was sexy from the huge open windows. Andrea was sure it was Jack Nicholson's party, and she marched right around to the back patio and the bar by the pool as if she lived there. Andrea talked up everyone and anyone, telling them fabulous tales of her life as a backup singer for the Rolling Stones. She was a believable bullshitter—open-shirted men were drooling over her as she recounted her fictional adventures with Mick and Keith.

In front of the pool house a handful of men and women in catering whites were sweeping up ice and glass, the remnants of the pool house's floor-to-ceiling picture window. Jagged shards poked out of the black-rimmed edges of the window's frame, looking like a giant shark's wide-open mouth set to swallow the party guests.

"What happened?" I asked the bartender.

"Dude, it was crazy. We're running out of ice and all of a sudden Hunter Thompson shows up with the back of his Jeep filled with ice and he drives it right into the fucking house."

Thompson, here? I thought. My hero, this close?

"Where is he?" I asked.

"Dumped the ice and took off."

Damn. Yet what could I have possibly said to him?

In the middle of telling Katrina about Thompson, Andrea deemed the party to be nearing its peak. Since Andrea subscribed to Andy Warhol's party dictum of always leaving before the crescendo, and even though the party was packed with beautiful people, and the booze and drugs were flowing, Andrea marched us right through the throngs and out. "Another party, ta-ta," she announced to one of her admirers, who happily offered us a ride. Her townie friends and my friends decided to stay.

"Mission accomplished," I said to Andrea, who gave me a low five as we got into some guy's Jaguar. I begged off the second party, so he dropped me and Katrina at the Red Onion, where my friend Tom was playing the piano, and where we could cop a free nightcap. Tom was a good Mormon gone bad, a million-watt chick magnet with his Utah pickup truck and his shaggy Western good looks and his Aw-shucks-I'm-just-a-nice-Mormon-kid-who-likes-to-go-camping spiel. Katrina and I walked in first. It was one in the morning, an hour before closing, and as I looked around the crowded room, I counted seven other women I had gone out with or was still seeing. Maybe the evening would blow up after all. I pulled Katrina to me and kissed her. She laughed and petted me like a puppy. In front of all of those other women, I grabbed the back of Katrina's head and kissed her again. I didn't care. I didn't care if they turned their backs on me or slapped me. I didn't care if Katrina dropped me then and there. And I didn't care if I stayed in Aspen past the summer or went back east.

Two steps toward Tom, I felt all the lightness leave my body. Four gay male opera singers were singing along to Tom's soppy version of Marlene Dietrich's "Falling in Love Again." I let go of Katrina and steadied myself on a bar stool. I was overwhelmed by the feeling that my father was about to die. Dan, the longtime choreographer for the opera program, had died over the winter, from what people in his hometown of San Francisco were calling "the gay flu." Gay men everywhere were becoming sick. Very sick. Deathly sick. My father had performed in San Francisco several times over the last few years. Had he slept with anyone from there?

"You okay?" Katrina asked.

"I need . . ." I tried to think of what it was I needed—to run, for her to get me a really strong drink, for us to have sex right then and there?

Whatever she gave me, I would still have to leave Aspen at summer's end. I could keep my gas station job, but I wouldn't earn enough for an apartment anywhere nearby and I didn't have a car. I couldn't go back to Rochester. And do what—work in the run-down city where I had flunked out of college? My father was living with Peter in a tiny one-bedroom downtown, so I couldn't live with him. The few friends I had made in my year at the university were still at school, and how depressing would that be, to be the failed townie hanging with your old college buddies?

Without money, I could see no other option than retreating to Baltimore, a city I had, only a year before, vowed never to set foot in again. Moving back into my mother's house would further the humiliation. A felon who had been released for good behavior, I had blown my one chance in the real world and was now being reunited with my old prison cell.

53

"Every act of rebellion expresses a nostalgia for innocence and an appeal to the essence of being."

—Albert Camus

Soundtrack: Ida Cox and Lovie Austin, "Graveyard Dream Blues," 1923

"EVEN FOR ME, I find bargains there," Ringo had said about the impromptu Saturday flea market he gave us directions to. Flea markets and junk shops and yard sales were a constant for Elissa and me. It didn't matter if we went home with nothing; it was enough to spend the day handling history, spinning stories, and then finally deciding whether or not the chunky Bakelite bracelet, the stiffly posed family daguerreotype, the wide-collared photo-print polyester shirt, and the space-age bachelor party records should become part of our history, our home.

I trailed right behind Elissa as we entered the small, crowded park, caught up to her as she ogled a large amber wedding necklace, the baubles the size of golf balls with hundreds of facets and gradated in color from brownish black to lemony amber. It was laid out on a blanket surrounded by silverware and china, and behind the blanket stood an old Polish couple. The man was impassive, but the woman smiled at us; both of them were haggard, overdressed for the warm morning. They were probably wearing what they owned. I looked around, and there were dozens of couples and families—Polish, Romanian, and Czech refugees—spreading out their worldly possessions for their slightly better-off former East German comrades, exchanging their history for a little bit of Western currency.

"I don't feel so hot," Elissa said.

"This is a bummer," I said.

"All these people," Elissa said. "There are just too many people here."

"Should we go?"

"Imagine how horrible it will be for them in winter. In the snow. And with more of them coming every day."

I knew she was right, but didn't want her to be.

"Why don't you buy the necklace?" I asked.

She shook her head and smiled at the woman, who was looking at us hopefully.

"It would feel like stealing."

Instead, she pantomimed to the couple how pretty she thought their wedding jewelry was.

I wondered what we would have to spread out in front of us fifty years from now, if we had to evacuate our home and dump our possessions. What would we have of value? And where would that abandoned home be?

54

"I became insane, with long intervals of horrible sanity."
—Edgar Allan Poe

Soundtrack: New Order, "Blue Monday," 1983

I ENROLLED IN NIGHT CLASSES at Towson State University, a huge state school— embarrassingly, only two miles from Boys' Latin. If I got A's, I would raise my GPA enough to transfer to the regular school and then could run on the cross-country and track teams. During the day I worked at the Kelmscott Bookshop, which was in an old row house on Twenty-fifth Street, every square inch covered in used books. For five years the owners, two ex–Johns Hopkins literature professors, had been driving their battered van around to estate sales, buying thousands of books at a time. A few of the volumes were valuable, and some were books that people would want to read, but many were odd and unlikely to sell. These freak books the Johansons dumped into a large back room they called "Purgatorio" and designated as a place to be dealt with "later." That "later" would not happen until they hired someone. That "someone" was me.

There were so many books crammed into Purgatorio that the door opened only an inch. My first task was to brave Limbo and shelve anything that could be salvaged. The books at the top of the heap weren't in too bad a condition. The deeper down I plunged, the moldier the books were, and a foul animal smell became more pronounced as I worked my way to the back left corner, the most ancient part of the dumping ground. After a month of digging I found the source of the smell—three dead, shriveled rats. They must have burrowed into the corner and become trapped in an avalanche of books.

The Johansons were still very much absentminded professors, easily distracted by the merchandise they were supposed to be moving.

"What price should I mark this first American edition of *Magic Mountain*?" I would ask.

"Of course, being from Germany, you've read it?" Mr. Johanson would reply.

"No, not yet."

"Really? No?" And off he would go about the sanatorium, the flaws and merits of Helen Lowe-Porter's translation, and Thomas Mann minutiae. ("Rob, did you know that during the war, Mann lived in Los Angeles, where he hung out with Charles Chaplin, Arnold Shoenberg, and Albert Einstein? What I wouldn't give to have listened in on those conversations.") And then the dusty 1927 Knopf first edition would be in my hands, not to be returned until I had finished it. The proverbial "kid in a candy shop" was me. Whatever I touched, I would ask about, and one or both of my bosses would launch into a mini-seminar which I would greedily inhale.

In a sealed cardboard box I found a stack of *Paris Review Writers at Work* anthologies. Over the next week, during breaks and at home, I read about how Faulkner wrote *As I Lay Dying* in six weeks during a break from manual labor, and how he thought that he and his contemporaries "failed to match our dream of perfection. So I rate us on the basis of our splendid failure to do the impossible." I read about how Hemingway counted each day's words to mark his labor, how Dos Passos considered World War I his university. As I worked my through each interview, I fantasized about being these writers, or dreamed of at least being in their orbit, but not for a second did I think I was in any way related to them. Not for an instant did I think I could ever be where they had been, breathe the same way they did.

This pantheon of writers was even farther away than Berlin, which at least existed on a mortal plain. While I hauled around boxes of dusty books, I clung to being a citizen of dazzling Berlin, because if I wasn't, it meant I would be claimed by dead-end Baltimore. If I was a Berliner, my life would have hope, glamour, history; if a Baltimorean, none of the above.

Night school, in comparison to my bookstore education, was superfluous. I learned far more at Kelmscott than in college. No literature class could match the pointed, guided tour through letters that the Johansons were giving me. But the night classes allowed me to transfer into the day school, and even though there were no subjects I particularly wanted to study, I felt that I needed a degree—for what, I didn't know.

I was, however, now eligible for the cross-country and track teams. My new teammates were the opposite of my former Boys' Latin classmates—rugged and down to earth, many of them the first in their blue-collar families to go to college, which none treated lightly. They were from factory towns and farms, and from nondescript Baltimore neighborhoods like Hampden and Dundalk. One was from a trailer park in Western Maryland. The toughest guy, Jack Peach, worked summers in a meat locker, lugging around cow carcasses in a thirty-degree icebox, and then he would run ten miles in the ninety-five-degree wet blanket that was Baltimore summer. A few were born-again, and they tried to school me in evolution and morals.

I learned as much from all of them as I did from the Johansons at the Kelmscott, not about theoretical concerns, but about the real world of the lower and middle classes, a reality I had not been exposed to at Boys' Latin or Aspen or in the rarefied world of classical music. My teammates' uncomplicated dreams—of stability through marriage and finding decent jobs with benefits—were otherworldly to me, as unlikely for me as living in a Parisian garret writing novels.

My collegiate focus quickly turned toward the track and cross-country teams, where it stayed for the next four years. For 1,622 days, I ran every day. And on many of those 1,622 days, I ran twice a day. I averaged thirteen miles a day, ninety miles a week, week after week, month after month, year after year. Though I ate pasta constantly, my weight never deviated from the 138-to-140-pound range, my body fat dangerously low.

With my teammates I ran every day in whatever weather, then drank cheap National Bohemian beer afterward, in the van on the way back from meets in dour mid-Atlantic backwaters like Lehigh, Pennsylvania, and Seaford, Delaware, home to numerous chicken-processing plants, which smelled like the Kelmscott's back room before I cleaned it out. Besides the times when I was reading, these were my happiest moments, these moments of belonging.

My new life slowly wrapped itself around me. I told myself that I was catching my breath and trying to come up with what to do next and where to do it, but in reality I was falling into a yearly cycle of summers in Aspen and school years in Baltimore, where I would go through the motions of being a college student. When I'd been admitted to Towson, the regular day college, I signed up for as many liberal arts classes as I could—sociology, psychology, women's studies, and literature courses. When I got a 4.0 on my first transcript, I proudly showed it to my mother. "Must have been easy classes," she said.

I had no reply. As I pushed myself through a workout of mile repeats on the track, the repetitions increasingly painful as my body became starved of oxygen and glycogen, I replayed "Must have been easy," thinking that my mother had felt betrayed by my failure, by her faith in my abilities having been misplaced. Somewhere in her tone was *I know that you can do anything you set your mind to,* but never again would I discuss school with her.

My real education continued at the Kelmscott, where I fully invested myself in Castorp's journey up the Swiss mountain and Gustav's unrequited yearning in Venice. Classes only existed so I could run competitively. Running wasn't a routine; it was discipline. When I pushed myself to the maximum, it was blessed erasure. My nonrunning friends wondered how I could get it up to run every day. "Running isn't hard," I would say. "It's the stopping that's hard."

Drinking also didn't feel like a routine, even though I did it with a passion almost equal to the one I brought to running. Hard-alcohol hangover runs were brutal, so I tried to stick to beer, but would sometimes take whatever was being poured at a party, invariably swearing off the harder stuff for a while after an evening like the Windex incident—blue Curacao, vodka, and pineapple juice turning my vomit blue. Even though there were always women, they were also not routine. I wanted them all and I wanted them all to love me, or at least sleep with me. Every time I saw a woman I desired with another man, it felt like a rejection. Yet at the same time I was always surprised when any woman wanted me and was also mystified as to why I was rarely without a girlfriend.

My mutability made it easy for me to meet all sorts of Baltimore's substratum—drunks, heroin addicts, anarchists, punks, closeted gays, open queens, girls who thought they were witches, boys who called themselves poets and were beaten up by football players, kids who hung out at Edith Massey's thrift store in Fell's Point and wanted to be Divine, or any of the kids who hung around wherever John Waters was hanging out. It helped that I had one of the few cars among these losers, even if it was a piece-of-crap hand-me-down 1976 Corolla from my mother.

The car wasn't necessary when we went to see punk shows at the Marble Bar, but there were a lot better bands playing down in Washington, where the D.C. hardcore scene was emerging around Ian MacKaye, first with his band Minor Threat, then with Fugazi. We'd pile in my car and drive down to sketchy F Street and the newly opened 9:30 Club, one of us calling out "Fucked up" even though we all knew that the name "Fugazi" came from Vietnam soldier slang for "fucked up" when the action got intense; but this knowledge was a badge of belonging, a barrier between the initiated and the poor squares who didn't know any better. We'd drive down to see any of the bands on MacKaye's Dischord Record label and other local bands like The Slickee Boys and Bad Brains, and a few months after the bar's opening, national punk bands like Hüsker Dü, X, and the Butthole Surfers.

When there were no bands playing, I turned to assemblage. With the success of my small-scale Aspen experiments of radical intent, I fashioned ambitious, advanced critical mass experiments with my ever-expanding assemblage of oddballs. I would gather as many freak friends as I could, add drugs and alcohol, then go out on the town to see how the mixture would withstand the elements. We would gain momentum at the

Club Charles, a glorified downtown dive bar across the street from the one art movie theater in town; then, emboldened, we'd venture to the land of the squares, maybe even out to the suburban Towson bars where the ultrapreppies gathered under crossed lacrosse sticks mounted on peach-colored walls. Who would be the first to be called a creep or fag by some uptight Baltimoron, perhaps even by one of my old Boys' Latin classmates? My money was usually on my high school friend Jack, who had stayed in town to attend Johns Hopkins and was now flying the "fuck you" flag of disdain for anything square. If it wasn't Jack, it was always one of us who was pushed, or hit, or spit on, and then bouncers materialized and started pummeling the combatants.

Casually dressed in black jeans and a T-shirt, looking neither preppy nor punk, I was safely tucked within the group, vicariously enjoying it, never instigating or throwing punches. My friends acted out all of my most extreme impulses. And then, on the sidewalk, bloodied and exhilarated, they'd hug me as if I had been right in the middle of the action, mixing it up just like they had.

My friends were my collective alter ego. And one of them, Sean, could have been my doppelgänger or evil twin. Sean and I were born on the exact same day, same year, the fourth darkest day of the year, mid-December. But while I was being a good boy, sliding through life unobserved, Sean dropped out of high school and was busted for heroin possession. Despite being a junkie dropout, Sean was surprisingly well-read, and I undercharged him when he came into the Kelmscott looking for Russian classics. After his bust, Sean was put on probation and a methadone program, which he found intolerable, so he supplemented his methadone with speed and/or cocaine.

A few days into the modified program, Sean and I crashed a Johns Hopkins frat party. We were without our usual posse, and Sean was unusually tweaked out, sweating profusely as he talked about Marx to the guys around the keg. He could usually pull off a good Marxist rant, but his brain was racing ahead of his tongue and he sounded like Lucky in *Waiting for Godot*, a mostly senseless frothing rant punctuated with moments of profound clarity. Mid-sentence, Sean froze, his brain seizing, and he bolted from the downstairs parlor toward the bathroom at the top of the stairs. I ran after him and was right behind him as we entered the bathroom. I could hear brothers sprinting up the stairs, yelling. Sean slammed the door behind us with both hands with so much force that half the ceiling fell down, a huge plaster chunk splitting on top of Sean's head, opening a jagged gash across his plaster-coated forehead. When the frat boys started pounding on the door, Sean turned and *dove* through the open window.

I was all for throwing myself into the void, but I wanted a decent chance of survival. I dashed to the window, expecting to see a horrible splat of Sean on pavement, but there was grass below, two stories down, and somehow Sean had landed safely and was now running across the lawn toward the woods. No way was I making that leap, so I opened the door and faced a dozen angry brothers, half-hoping that they would beat me up. I was laughing as I said, "That crazy fuck jumped out the window." They asked me if I knew who he was, and I said, "No clue, but I think he's a chemistry major."

A part of me wanted to be like Sean, to live out loud, to be seen. But the anonymity of the chameleon life fit much more comfortably. I could pass almost anywhere—except when I was behind the wheel of my car. My friends, under the influence of many legal and illegal substances, had declared the Corolla's maroon color "profoundly dull, a crime against humanity." They'd endeavored to bring justice with twenty-seven cans of spray paint, covering it with unrecognizable shapes and blotches, our handprints . . . whatever felt right at the moment. For two years I parked the psychedelic mess many blocks away from my mother's house, successfully concealing it from her until college graduation. I was able to hide it from her, but not from the police, who stopped me on any pretext and then searched the car for drugs. I racked up so many tickets, my license was suspended.

Four years of passing as a college student yielded a whippet-like body and a psychology degree, which might've been enough to land a fry cook job. Along the way I had taken enough straight science classes, including a half dozen premed, to get into graduate schools for sports psychology; these included the University of Arizona, which I signed up for. Maybe I'd be a coach, or an academic researcher, or maybe by going to the desert I'd figure out why I was in a spiritual desert.

My plan was to fill my car with books from the Kelmscott and then, after yet another blissful summer in Aspen, drive to Tucson, where the wide-open, dry landscape was an ideal place to run. I assumed there would be plenty of women to choose from, and as long as I could keep reading and keep running, that would approximate a life.

To celebrate my last Baltimore night, I planned to get good and drunk with my friend Jack. In a warm drizzle, I drove to a Fell's Point dive bar full of dockworkers knocking back beer and shots in their well-worn coveralls.

"You ever leaving this place?" I asked Jack.

"Don't have a reason to," Jack said, and we clinked whiskey shots. I envied his combination of wildness and stability. He'd

always lived in Hampden, had persevered at Boys' Latin, had
thrived as a double English and chemistry major at Hopkins,
and now had gotten a scholarship to stay for graduate school
in their prestigious science-writing program. He was working
Orioles home games selling popcorn, taking home trash bags
full of leftover popcorn to subsist on.

"Take care of Sean," I said.

"I'll try," Jack said. "But you know him. . . ."

"Think of me when you guys are getting thrown out of Poor
Richard's," I said, weirdly future nostalgic for a place I loathed.

By closing we had succeeded in our mission. Jack was a
degree less good, so I gave him my keys, which was like putting
a bullet in one of a revolver's six empty cylinders and spinning
the chamber. As he peeled out of the gravel parking lot, I recal-
culated the odds from 16-percent to 100-percent certain that
we were going to crash. It was only a matter of how hard and
where. I hoped it would be a memorable crash, or at least one
that would make me feel deeply again, even for a split second.

Jack accelerated along the old, cobbled street, the tires rising
off the stones, one at a time, up and down, bouncing, the car
sagging and then bobbing as we dipped and rose. We were flying
forward, skipping like a flat rock on a rippled lake. But then the
car skidded slightly to the left, then a little to the right, then
violently to the left, the tail whipping around, spinning the car
across the cobbles toward the side of a brick building. I would
like to say that I was scared, but I wasn't. I knew the drill. Almost
exactly four years after the near head-on outside of Rochester,
I welcomed this onrushing crash like an old, reckless friend
who at least makes you feel alive even as he is putting you back
in mortal danger. With each high-speed revolution I thought,

Jack's side, my side, Jack's side, my side. If the car spun into the wall on Jack's side, he would die. If the car spun into the wall on my side, I would die. Russian roulette, car-crash style. Now the odds were fifty-fifty that the last day of college would also be the last day of my life.

As the wall kept flashing closer and closer, I had to laugh that I'd succeeded in hiding my car till my very last night in Baltimore, and now I was going to total it.

Steel crunching into brick. A joyous sound. The satisfying sound of reality.

Jack's side.

I rolled away from the car and looked back. Where the hell was he? The whole driver's side of the car was caved in and the steering wheel was jammed a foot to the right. I got up and walked around to the other side, where Jack was standing in the gap between the building and the car. Apparently we had bounced off the wall. Jack was staring at the crushed car, dumbfounded.

"Jack?"

"Yeah?" he said, still staring.

"How the hell did you get out?"

"Don't know," Jack said, then turned to me.

"You okay?" I asked.

"My head hurts."

"Me too," I said, and grabbed Jack's arm to move us away from the crumpled car, which was hissing like a pissed-off snake. We brushed away safety glass, then flexed our arms, disbelieving that we weren't broken and bloodied.

We silently agreed to move farther away from the car. Jack didn't talk. I didn't talk. We walked five blocks, stopped, but neither of us had anything to say so we kept walking, silent as we navigated the five miles back to our neighborhood. A block from my house I said, "We'll report it stolen." Jack nodded. We nodded goodbye, then I was in bed. I thought that I should try to stay awake in case I had a concussion. But my eyelids were like slabs of concrete.

55

"History has remembered the kings and warriors, because they destroyed; art has remembered the people, because they created."

—William Morris

Soundtrack: Thelonious Monk, "Who Knows," 1947

"THERE IS THE SOUP KITCHEN," Ralf said.

"Soup kitchen?" I said. Near midnight at the CV, I was turning into a pumpkin. Or crashing, my blood sugar flatlining. I hadn't eaten since a little bit of bread for breakfast.

"Yes," Ralf said, "it is now a bar, of course, but it has some food. It is, how you say, harder than this place."

"You mean *rougher*?"

"Yes, yes, that's it. Under the GDR the soup kitchen was hidden, so it is not easy to find, and it still attracts a rougher type."

"Charming, I'm sure," Elissa said, and Hank shrugged. He was hardly eating, was thin even for him, but he was still getting up every morning at dawn to sketch at the Wall. We followed Ralf across the park opposite the wine bar, then two more blocks past older mismatched buildings that were all slightly off-kilter, as if they'd been drawn by a child. Halfway down the block we turned into a lightless alley, a narrow corridor of strewn paving stones with a five-foot-wide brackish river coursing down the right side, leaving a foot-wide walkway. A plank stretched over the river and into a bright doorway. As we approached, two men danced across the plank, and one with a huge black beard, on seeing us, slipped and plopped feet-first into the foot-deep muck. The man grabbed Ralf's hand and let himself be tugged onto dry land.

"*Danke.*"

"*Bitte,*" Ralf said.

We all skipped up the plank and were met by a thick cloud of smoke, blue and bitter, from Russian and Cuban and East German cigarettes. Long black picnic tables were scattered around the large square room, and along the back wall was an eight-inch-tall slot where, I guessed, the soup was once sloshed.

A single word was hand-drawn on a paper plate and taped over the slot: "PIZZA."

"Pizza," Ralf affirmed, pointing to the sign.

"Hallelujah, Jesus," Elissa said. "See, I knew this place would be charming."

"Amen," I seconded. Pizza would cure Elissa's homesickness, I thought, and for some reason I was hearing this thought as the Wicked Witch of the West saying, "Poppies will put them to sleep."

"Find a seat and I will bring the pizza," Ralf said.

"I'll get the beers," Hank said. I slid him a few extra marks without Elissa's noticing. I knew I shouldn't feel sorry for him, but he was suffering in order to render this world through his art.

Hank cut through the crowd of smaller Germans while Elissa and I found space in the middle of a table near the back, next to a couple of guys playing chess. Despite the chess set, the crowd was, as Ralf had promised, rougher than at the CV, with a lot more facial hair, and a few facial piercings, along with the musky smell of too many manly men in one room. The four or five women were equally tough-looking. If the CV was like a groovy bohemian bar, the soup kitchen was more like a biker bar. But no one took much notice of us.

Ralf cut right through the room, thick with bodies, back to our picnic table, where he proudly presented the pizza. It was about six inches in diameter. The white dough was crossed by two half-inch stripes of plastic-looking white cheese. In the quadrants were, counterclockwise, one dollop of tomato puree, a small pile of corn, what appeared to be two withered mushrooms, and lastly, one canned, color-leached peach.

"Pizza?" Elissa said. I could feel her homesickness returning full force. How many late nights had we had a soul-saving slice from Ray's on the corner of St. Mark's Place and Second Avenue? This was the food of our courtship, the fuel to get us through four bands at CBGB's, the sponge to sop up the mess at the end of another sloppy night at Joe's, Downtown Beirut, the Village Idiot.

"Yes, pizza," Ralf stated, confused by Elissa's doubt in the face of the irrefutable evidence. She took a hopeful bite of the tomato quarter, and her look of abject disappointment should have been enough for me to spirit her back to the East Village. I bit off the tip of the mushroom slice, the surprising taste of hot plastic and grassy mud like getting hit in the mouth with a dirty, errant Frisbee.

"It's an experience," I said.

"Fuck experience," Elissa said. "I want some real pizza."

"That's your problem," I said. "This *is* real."

"Reality?" Elissa said. "Seriously? Coming from you?"

Hank methodically, stoically ate the corn slice, and when Ralf declined the peach slice, Hank ate it as well, while I grimaced my way through my relentlessly plastic-tasting slice.

"You need to eat," I said to Elissa.

"I need a lot of things," Elissa said, not touching the necessary nourishment in front of her.

But before I could say anything, she turned to the young man next to her and pointed to his eyebrow piercing, a silver hoop through scabbed skin. "Does it hurt?" she asked, and the burly kid blushed at her attention and said, *"Nein, und das?"* and pointed to her nose ring.

"Not really. But this . . ." Elissa pointed to the top of her ear, and the raw place where a piercing, despite being nearly a year old, had yet to heal.

Maybe she doesn't need food. Maybe she can just exist on stories, I thought, amazed, once again, by the openness of Prenzlauer Berg.

Elissa seemed fine, so I turned to Ralf. "I'm wondering if . . . well . . ." I fumbled for the right words to ask how this collective exuberance and possibility were going to survive the Western *Anschluss* known as reunification.

"Yes?" Ralf said, but I suddenly felt uncomfortable. The man across the table, a large, bearded man sitting next to Ralf, moved his knight, then stared hard at me, contemplating me as if I were some kind of exotic animal seen in the flesh for the first time. Maybe I had misjudged how much joy we were bringing to the people.

"American?" he asked, pronouncing it with incredulity, as if he were asking if I was an echidna.

"Ja," I answered.

The man's eyes opened wide, and I braced myself for a punch. Instead of punching me, the man leapt onto the picnic table, his scuffed black boots scattering beer bottles. He took off his floppy black hat, clutched it to his breast, then shouted down to me: "Oh, lovely American! How you grace us with your presence. Oh, my poetry is not worthy of you, but I must give you a poem nonetheless." The man paused and swept his hat to take in the entire room.

I glanced to Hank, whose smile belied that his right hand was hovering over the knife in his sock. I would have been terrified except that when I looked to Ralf, he appeared unconcerned, just annoyed; and only half the room was paying attention, the scene apparently familiar; and Elissa was still talking to the scabby punk. I didn't want her to miss this experience, whatever it was, but when I returned my gaze to the poet, he screwed up his face in mock seriousness, then stuck out his tongue with an accompanying loud raspberry, spraying the chessboard below with spittle.

The poet continued to glare at me, his eyes sparkling, challenging, but with a hint of friendliness, as if his raspberry was a dismissal of where I was coming from but also a welcome into his world, on his terms.

"Thank you so much," I said. The man nodded as if I had passed his test, bowed to the smattering of applause and jeers from the rest of the bar, then stepped back down, his opponent never having lifted his gaze from the chessboard.

"Please, Hermann is not so bad," Ralf said, pained on my behalf.

"Don't sweat it," I said, meaning it.

"But, I want to . . . how do you . . . ." Ralf's English was failing him.

"It's okay. *Auf Deutsch,* I'll translate," I said.

Ralf rattled off a quick explanation and I turned to translate for Hank, Elissa's back squarely to us as she leaned in to hear the scabby kid's broken English. "Ralf wants us to know that

Hermann," I said, "is not an *Arschloch*—an asshole. He is a real poet. Hermann believes that the Americans are going to pave over East Berlin and build another Disneyland, where he and all the other poets will have to work in mouse costumes."

"I feel like a prisoner in Disneyland!" Hermann shouted to the chessboard.

Ralf whipped around on Hermann and started hurling compound-noun constructions at him.

"What? What!" Hank asked.

"He's telling Hermann, I think, to at least insult us in his own words, not Peter Handke's. And now Herman called Ralf an *Altkämpfer*."

"A what?" Hank asked.

"A name for Hitler's cronies who were at the Beer Hall Putsch in the twenties, the drunks who tried to take over the country by seizing a tavern. They thought the masses would flock to them."

Ralf and Hermann went back and forth, Ralf, angrier than I'd ever seen him before, finally yelling, "Handke's not even German! He's Austrian, you pompous twit!"

56

"Art is the lie that enables us to realize the truth."
— Pablo Picasso

Soundtrack: Meat Puppets, "Lake of Fire," 1984

"WAKE UP, ROB."

"Mom?"

"Get up, your car's been found."

"Mom?" I tried again, my alarm clock blinking red, 8 A.M.

"Your car," my mother repeated. She was looking at me like I was a hideous insect. I was still in my black jeans and Joy Division T-shirt, my black Converse high-tops unlaced but still on. I reeked of whiskey and beer.

"Really?" I said, trying to muster some surprise out of my gonging head.

"Did you lend your car to one of your friends?"

"What? No. I was with Jack," I said, and got to my feet. "Where is it?" I asked.

"The police found it crashed in Fell's Point," she said.

"Crap," I said. My mother searched my face for clues, and I ducked down to tie my laces.

"We need to go to the police pound," my mother said, and I followed her downstairs and out to her Camry.

Blocks blurred by, my vision not quite right. Jail? Or worse, my mom finding out the truth about me. The police lot, chockablock

with banged-up cars. I couldn't think, couldn't find words to say
to the bored cop with the clipboard who signed us in. What the
hell was I going to say to my mother? I couldn't look at her. Then,
suddenly, we were standing in front of my brutalized vehicle.

"Wow," my mother said, taking in the paint job.

"Yeah, wow," I said, trying to match her shocked tone.

While the cop circled the car, making marks on his clipboard, my mother whispered, "When did you do that?" *She
knows. She fucking knows. Everything. All the drinking and drugs
and women. She knows what a fuckup I am. She knows.*

I turned to her and said, "I didn't do that." I lied like I
meant it, because I was a damn good actor. "Whoever stole it
must have vandalized it."

My mother opened her mouth, hesitated. She knew the
truth. She thought she knew me, but she wasn't sure. At that
moment, did she want to know the real me? The cop looked
inside the car, made a few more notations.

My mother closed her mouth.

The cop walked back to us and said, "This is yours, right?"

"Oh, my poor car," I said with what I hoped was the right
amount of pathos.

"No signs of forced entry or hot-wiring."

"Really?" I said. I hadn't thought about that, but then
again . . . "If it wasn't hot-wired, then how'd they take it?"

"Good question," the cop said, and for the first time looked
up from his clipboard at me, perhaps accusingly, perhaps not
accusingly.

"He must've been really hurt in the crash," I followed.
"Look how far the steering wheel moved."

"Surprised there wasn't any blood," the cop said, genuinely
curious.

There was an inch gap on the trunk's lip, right where I had put red spray-paint handprints. I pried it open enough to gather the handful of Kelmscott books and my 1976 Putt-Putt Junior Championship Liberty Bell putter. I held my breath as I signed the cop's forms and didn't exhale until I was back in my mother's Camry.

My mother slowly drove us back uptown, not saying a word, her eyes fixed straight ahead. My father was already halfway there from Rochester. In a few hours we would drive to Aspen for the summer. He'd take me out of Baltimore for the last time, and I vowed, not for the first time, that I'd never, ever set foot in Baltimore again.

But I was still present, in my mother's car, heading home along Calvert Street. Past North Avenue, I rolled down the window, willing my guts to hold back the vomit. I looked over at my mother, her jaw set, both hands on the wheel. The finality of my leaving struck me full force. What had I put her through? Not just this morning, but the last ten years, all of the shit. Screw these artificial barriers we'd erected between us. Now was the time to tell her that I was sorry for being a fuckup, for making her worry about me, for not letting her parent me, for not letting her into my life, for being distant, for being like my father, for being a coward. Now was the time to tell her that I loved her. Ten blocks from home, where to begin? Why couldn't I just break the ice? *Please,* I silently begged her, *try one more time. Ask me again about the car. I'll tell you the truth. Ask me how I'm feeling. Ask me anything. I'll tell you everything.*

The lights were green the rest of the way up Calvert, and my mother found a convenient parking spot in front of our house. I went upstairs and finished packing. By three, I was gone.

57

"I think life is far too short to concentrate on your past. I'd rather look into the future."

—Lou Reed

Soundtrack: Lou Reed, "Perfect Day," 1972

ELISSA AND I HAVE BEEN DANCING for hours to the nonstop music, the DJs putting together an enveloping sonic tapestry. I still can't believe that we are at a rave, in Berlin—and not just in Berlin, but under the Wall. All night young East and West Germans have found their way underground and now the abandoned subway station is packed with dancers. I hold on to my wife, both of us disoriented by the relentless strobe lights, her back slick with sweat. The drum-and-bass-heavy music too loud for us to talk, I mouth, *I love you*. Elissa signs the same. This is all that I have ever wanted.

58

"Rock 'n' Roll: The most brutal, ugly, desperate, vicious form of expression it has been my misfortune to hear."
—Frank Sinatra

Soundtrack: The Smiths, "How Soon Is Now?," 1985

"THIS IS HELL, ISN'T IT?" I said to the petite girl in all black with the shock of white hair as we crushed into a crowded stairwell on a cool October afternoon, Penn Station roasting, the Friday postwork crowd cranky and pushy as we plunged down to the Amtrak platform.

"The absolute worst," she said. I followed her onto the train and I casually took the aisle seat opposite her, avoiding eye contact, instead taking out Francis Steegmuller's biography of Jean Cocteau and ostentatiously angling it toward her. I was going to play it cool, let her come to me. I stared at the word "ambulance" for a few seconds and glanced across the aisle and Jesus H. Christ I had to talk to her this very moment or I would spontaneously combust. I started talking. About anything, everything. I told her that I was a writer, that I'd dropped out of grad school, that I'd come to New York with $150 in my pocket, the thrift store Harris Tweed coat on my back and a duffel bag of books, that I was working in an art-postcard factory and showed her my bookmark, a postcard of Allen Ginsberg's 1953 photo of a brooding Jack Kerouac smoking on a Lower East Side fire escape.

She seemed impressed and told me she'd grown up in Delaware, was living on the Upper East Side in an illegal sublet with two other girls and was incredibly hungover at the moment. She stared at me with her big green eyes as I rambled on about *The Banquet Years* and she went on about her recent Gertrude Stein jag, and the easy back-and-forth was exhilarating, but I dialed back my hopes after I told her I was going to visit my old friend Jack in Baltimore and she said she was going to see her "old friend" in D.C., not saying whether the friend was male or female.

She had also recently moved to New York to work in publishing and had landed a job on the floor of Tiffany's, selling obscenely expensive jewelry. She'd chat up the customers and whenever she discovered one with a connection to the publishing business, she said, "I pounced on them," eventually snagging a job as the junior books editor at *Woman's Day* magazine, which meant she fueled her literary aspirations by screening unsolicited odes to Alan Alda and typing and retyping her bosses' letters—"I'm a terrible typist"—and writing stories on the magazine's letterhead.

The train was held up in Philly by signal problems, so we shared a handful of tiny vodkas from the café car. Before I stepped off in Baltimore, I told her my friend Carlos was planning on driving to New York City, I offered her a ride with us, and she accepted. I gave her Jack's number on the back of another postcard, Brassaï's *Lovers in a Café*. The plan fell through, but when she called me at Jack's she and I decided to buy return Amtrak tickets together.

We agreed to meet the next night at Downtown Beirut, the East Village dive bar, for a proper first date. By that night I had convinced myself that she had been a delusion, that she wasn't going to materialize, so to keep me company when she stood me up I brought along my postcard factory friend Jim, who was writing intense, experimental novels.

But Elissa did appear, dashing in an hour late, flushed and disheveled as if she had already been to a fabulous party (she would later tell me that she had accidentally gone next door, to the Village Idiot, a mirror-image dive bar, having planned to meet me a respectable half-hour late, but then had had to slam her highball of Pernod on ice and rush next door). When she saw Jim, she gave me a curt nod, but kissed Jim on the lips, then gave me a look that said, "Don't ever make this mistake again."

After a few drinks I offered to take her to the movies the next night to try once more to have a proper date. "We'll see," Elissa said, but the next afternoon when I called, she agreed. The last date I'd taken to the movies was a ridiculously hot decathlete. We'd seen *Brazil,* which blew my mind, but confused my date. "It's like Monty Python meets *1984,*" I said by way of explanation. "Monty who? And what does the year 1984 have to do with anything?" Her hotness didn't compensate for her cluelessness.

I was already falling for Elissa, so why not see what she made of? I took her to IFC to see Godfrey Reggio's documentary *Koyaanisqatsi,* a beautiful and bleak spectacle of man's disregard for the earth, with a propulsive Philip Glass score. I kept stealing looks at her. I thought at one point she was crying.

"Soul-killing, though in the best way," she said afterward. "But how depressing."

"If you think that's depressing," I said, "you should see Atlantic City."

"I've never been," she said. "Let's go. Let's go now."

Any doubts that I was hopelessly in love vanished.

We borrowed a composer friend's crappy Datsun and drove to Atlantic City, which was indeed as bleak as the movie, the money-laundering palaces dwarfing the surrounding slums.

The next afternoon, a Saturday, when I woke up, I was ecstatic. I couldn't wait to go for a long, hard run. Then I remembered. I bent my achy, puffy left knee. No chance. Three months before I had been running ninety-plus miles a week, harder than ever. At the beginning of the summer, my father thought that it would be our last drive from Baltimore to Aspen, so he planned an epic route across Canada to Vancouver and then down to San Diego and then to the Grand Canyon, with built-in stops for crazy adventure runs. Near the Saskatchewan-Manitoba border we passed a man who was pushing a giant cross on a roller, shortly after we'd witnessed a house burn down in a town of twenty houses, all of the citizens clustered around the fire, helpless. A cop stopped us in the middle of nowhere Saskatchewan simply to see what New Yorkers were doing out there. From Vancouver we drove the length of the West Coast on Route 1, all the way to San Diego. Trying to run a trail into the Oregon Dunes National Recreation Area, I was cut up by overgrown blackberry brambles. On the last day of May I ran thirteen miles into Redwood National Park to a stand of the world's tallest trees, where my father was supposed to meet me. I was spent and dehydrated when I reached the end of the rugged and challenging trail. The parking lot and ranger station were deserted. The road wasn't open until June 1, so my father had to find a ranger to escort him into the park to get me, but not before I thought I would have to run another thirteen miles to get out. We then looped back to Colorado via the Grand Canyon. There I ran from the North Rim to the South Rim, twenty-three miles with an elevation drop and gain of eight thousand feet, in five hours, faster than my father drove around the park. When he finally pulled up to the trailhead, he was relieved to see me, knowing that the extremity of this run far exceeded the others.

As we drove up and over Independence Pass toward Aspen, I wanted it to feel different now that I was a college graduate. But it didn't. I again worked at the gas station, again drank, and again ran, for myself and after women. The only difference was that I seriously trained for the New York Marathon. Now that I didn't have to compete in cross-country races, I could devote myself to what I felt was my natural competitive distance. I wasn't particularly fast—my fastest mile was 4:24—but I could sustain a painful pace, clicking out five-minute miles forever. I was still running ninety miles per week. Six of those days I ran twice a day, and on Sundays I ran thirteen to eighteen miles on challenging trails that invariably rose over the tree line.

On a mid-July Sunday, I ran to the end of the Conundrum Valley, where the Conundrum Hot Springs bubbled in pools ringed by jagged, snowcapped peaks—a hard, grinding eight-and-a-half miles, starting at nine thousand feet elevation and ending at over twelve thousand feet. At the top, I took a break for a quick soak, then bombed back down the valley. A half mile from the end of the trail, I felt a pop on the outside of my left knee. I immediately knew it was bad; how bad, I didn't know. My knee swelled and looked like a lumpy grapefruit. At first, rage. Then a quick slide into depression. I had gone four-and-a-half years without missing a day. Now it hurt to walk. I drank to mask the pain. I tested it every few days in Aspen, and then in Tucson, at grad school. I had always been able to run through any pain, but my iliotibial band was damaged, and most likely permanently.

When I ran, I didn't think. Now all I could do was think. Frustration at not being able to run quickly turned into frustration with my entire life. What the hell was I doing? I looked around and realized that I was on a giant state-school campus studying the psychology of sports. How had I let my life drift off into the desert?

I knew that I had to run, but run to a place where the artists and writers were. New York. Immediately. I knew that I could assemble artists and outsiders, and had inchoate ideas about making this a central part of my life. I fantasized about starting a magazine, something unclassifiable that captured the energy and unpredictability of my critical-mass experiments. I didn't have a clue how to do this. All I knew was that it wasn't going to happen in the desert.

A month into grad school, I called my parents to tell them that I was quitting and moving to New York. My father said that he always wondered when I would wind up there. My mother said that she was worried about the sudden decision, but wired me $500 so that I could buy a one-way ticket out.

I jumped on a red-eye with $150 in my pocket, resolved to finally find my tribe and chase creativity and engagement. I slept on my pianist friend Tom's Upper West Side couch for the first few nights in New York, while looking for my own place. I picked up the *Village Voice* and went straight for the cheapest apartment listing, which was for a $270 three-bedroom share on Staten Island (yes, my share was $90).

Using my threadbare Harris Tweed coat for a blanket, I slept on the floor of my eight-by-ten-foot room on the second floor of a falling-down Victorian in one of the few rough neighborhoods of Staten Island, a tiny dark blight in a sea of suburbia. I looked in the want ads for publishing jobs, but there were none, so I answered a listening for a waiter gig in the bowels of the Time-Life Building.

Reading the *Voice* en route to my first day of work, I saw another listing, this one in a SoHo art-postcard factory, so instead of going to midtown, I took the subway to Prince Street and started at Fotofolio immediately, spending the day sorting postcards for shops and museums, getting filthy and sweaty moving around boxes of iconic images of my heroes—Cocteau, Satie, Wilde, van Gogh. With my first paycheck I bought a futon, which left me with two dollars, enough for the ferry, the subway, and a bagel.

Within a week of working at Fotofolio, my coworker Jim and I had conspired to start a magazine called *Moogomboo,* which would open with a manifesto to rip up East Village streets and plant flowers. We'd publish only revolutionary, genius work, by whomever—prisoners, the insane and homeless, junkies. We were going to get inside the machine and blow it up. It would be Erik Satie crossed with Hunter Thompson, whimsy and beauty meet riotous rage. We wrote up dozens of impractical ideas, and then with hubristic certainty declared that our fantasy circulation numbers to sustain such an unsustainable project were 15,000—10,000 from newsstand sales, 5,000 from subscriptions. Of course, we had no money and no access to money, but I was determined to start this magazine one way or another.

I also planned to be at the center of every sexual scandal in literary New York. But, then, Elissa. It was two weeks after our first date, and we hadn't spent a night apart since. We'd tried, but during a late-night phone call one of us would break down and say, "I'll be there in an hour." Usually it was her coming to me. Because her place was an illegal sublet—she couldn't even get mail there—the doorman looked at me funny. It didn't help that her roommates thought I was scum. On those nights when she came to me I'd meet her at the ferry station with my newly acquired beater bike and double her back in the dark through the slum to my room.

Some nights when we were partying late in the city we'd crash with Jim, who lived in a fifth-floor walkup on St. Mark's Place between Second and Third Avenues, a genuine artist on a strip of fakery.

Elissa started keeping a stash of clothes—all of it black—in her filing cabinet at work, along with some expensive silk scarves to fashion an office outfit.

I kept waiting for her to say, *Enough.* But she said, *More.*

She pushed books on me, at first when we were showing off to each other, then with novels and poems that told me she saw me—*The Waves* and *Orlando*, Elizabeth Bishop's poetry, and *The Sun Also Rises*. We went to noir double features at St. Mark's Cinema and Film Forum. Literature and Film and Art—all of it was so urgent, immediate. But she wouldn't have sex with me for a month, and it drove me insane.

Still, this impatience and frustration were nothing compared with my lingering rage—rage at my past, rage at my inability to express myself, rage at all the inequities in the world, rage at being hobbled, rage at my white privilege. Elissa, on the other hand, was filled with a rage to live, to express everything that "good girls" were not supposed to say out loud. Here was the bravest, most intense person I had ever been around. I felt like an utter phony and kept waiting for her to see through me and leave. Instead, she moved in with me.

I resented falling immediately in love with Elissa. I had come to New York with artistic pipe dreams and libertine intentions, but after four months in the city I was living with someone who wouldn't let me get away with my usual gambits of sulking and fleeing. One day she saw me holding a letter from my mother's mother. "It's okay, cry," she said, not waiting to hear what was in the letter. She could just tell.

After I sobbed, I collected myself and showed her the letter, with its shaky poststroke handwriting. The contents weren't emotional or revealing—it was a mundane letter asking if I was having an okay time in school. Elissa patiently unpacked my feelings, eventually getting to the crux. What had crushed me was that my grandmother thought of me in any kind of positive manner, while I had always hated her from afar and borne a grudge against her for her sins against my mother, because if my grandmother hadn't been so steely to her daughter, my mother might have known how to be warmer to me when I was growing up.

When Elissa moved into my tiny room, there was barely enough space for the futon on the floor. After she woke up cranky the first morning with an imprint of *The New York Times* on her ass, I started building a mini-loft, the room's bare-bulb light precariously close to the bed. We spray-painted the walls with angels and slogans, including Hunter Thompson's "When the going gets weird, the weird turn pro." During the day we worked, at night we saw bands or we went home and wrote, candles burning, the Velvet Underground's *White Light/White Heat* blasting, the Pernod straight on ice.

I started writing in earnest, page after page. It was earnest. It was crap. "Don't worry about it," Jim said. "You have to write a million words before you write anything decent." This was like running—common wisdom was that you needed to run hard for ten years before you had the base to *really* run hard.

Elissa, writing, and drinking had replaced running. I channeled my leftover energy into staying up all night walking the city. I went from ninety hard miles a week to zero. My stretched iliotibial band made it painful to walk, much less run. But every few weeks I hobbled around the crack-vial-littered neighborhood park and came back with my knee painfully swollen, Elissa waiting with two cans of Foster's, one to drink, the other to use as an icepack. No matter how much it hurt, I wouldn't stop trying. I kept telling myself it had to heal. It just had to.

When training for races, I could see tangible progress and measurable results, but with my novice writing efforts I could see no progress or results. The learning curve seemed insurmountably steep—much like the learning curve of how to be in a real romantic relationship. Elissa had to tell me to buy a birthday present for her. My family didn't do presents. Elissa was actually excited to go home to Delaware for the holidays. I scoffed when she said I was going, but quickly changed my tune.

How does one behave around a normal, nuclear, happy family? Disconcertingly, after only a few minutes with them in their warm, comfortable house that her father had built right after Elissa was born, I could tell that they were smart and charming and funny and obviously loved each other. They were generous and welcoming to me. It was completely disorienting. I spent the entire first day clinging to their new Siamese kitten, carrying it around as if it were a shield. But Elissa wouldn't let me hide from her family. If I loved her, I would have to love her family. Which was surprisingly easy. I had no baggage with them, and as long as I loved their daughter, they would treat me as family.

For both of my parents, Elissa was like truth serum—they felt compelled to talk to her like they never spoke to me, and I finally was able to fill in some of the gaps from childhood, like how and when my mother found out my father was gay and why she had decided to leave me in Berlin. This knowledge clarified the picture, but didn't mollify my anger. In the picture I was still confused and scared. Why didn't they talk to me like they had talked to Elissa?

At New Year's, we again borrowed my composer friend's Datsun, this time to drive to a party in Baltimore. Halfway there, I said, "I don't really like New Year's parties."

"Well, sure, they're kind of amateur hour."

"Totally," I said.

"Then why are we driving three hours to get to one?"

"Let's drive to San Francisco and back," I said, tossing the idea in the air like a coin, not caring if it landed on heads or tails.

"We have time?" Elissa asked, not missing a beat.

"Six thousand miles," I said thrilled, surprised, and suddenly daunted. "It's five days and ten hours before we have to be back to work. Let's see—that's a hundred and thirty hours. Figuring sixty miles an hour average, that's a hundred hours of driving round-trip, so we'd have thirty hours for sleep and sightseeing."

Elissa smiled. "I'm game if you're game."

After two thousand miles, my friend's crappy little Datsun died in a snowstorm near Glenwood Springs, Colorado, forty miles down-valley from Aspen. A road crew dug the car out and towed us to a garage, which replaced our battery. Having lost a day, we abandoned our goal of making it all the way to San Francisco and instead drove through Aspen, which was buried in ice and snow. I didn't try to find any of my former friends, and instead continued on past Buena Vista, where a vast valley opened up and a hard, cold, winter sunset lit the leafless and snow-covered aspens. Black cows dotted the snow across the valley. The hillside opposite glowed a cool red, like a fading coal. And then it was a thirty-hour blur back to New York in time for a shower before the ferry to work.

That's how we rolled. Hunter Thompson would have been proud.

59

"Write naked. Write from exile. Write in blood."
—Denis Johnson

Soundtrack: Talking Heads, "Take Me to the River," 1978

THE SKY IS A SICKLY PREDAWN GREEN as Elissa and I leave the rave. Even though I haven't felt this physically spent since my last real run, if Elissa gives the nod I'll rally and dance for a dozen more hours. She's jazzed, looks like she could keep dancing, but says, "Let's go home."

I grab her hand and we follow three young Easterners who I'm guessing are heading back toward Prenzlauer Berg. The streets are dark and silent, and we carefully make our way through the strewn paving stones until we reach a nearly impassable intersection. Cobblestones are piled high on one side, and on the other there's a massive hole that's swallowed up a Trabant and a Wartburg. You couldn't drive a tank through this intersection. Yet there is still a working streetlight. The three Germans in front of us stop at the red light and wait. So deeply engrained is their sense of order they can't walk through the red light, even though we're the only people out on the street. We walk past.

"C'mon, you can do it," Elissa says, waving to the Germans. They hesitate, then laugh along and follow.

Fifteen minutes later, the Germans now ahead of us, we're back in our neighborhood. I speed up, but Elissa suddenly stops.

"What?"

"I feel unwell," she says in a funny flat voice, veering toward a park bench, where she flops down.

"We're only a block from home," I say, impatient, then notice that her face is ashen.

"Elissa?" Her eyes are all pupil. "Talk to me. What's going on?"

She opens her mouth, but no sound comes out. She's not drunk—this is something else. Her eyes are unfocused; her breathing is constricted, coming in short, wheezy gasps.

"Let's get you home." I grab her under her arms and she stands stiffly, leaning against me, and lets me guide her toward our building. It takes forever to get her up the stairs, her legs stiff, her steps herky-jerky.

"You okay?" I ask as I tuck her in on the smaller of the two sofas, Hank passed out on the bigger one.

She opens her mouth, but again no sound comes out. Her pupils bounce around the room but don't appear to be focusing on anything. "You're okay," I say as much to reassure myself as her. She raises her right arm slightly, as if she is in school and wants to ask a question. Is she joking? This isn't funny. "Yes?" But she doesn't answer. I take ahold of her hand and she clutches mine fiercely. Slowly I try to lower it, but it won't go, her arm rigid. "It's okay, you're going to be okay, I'm right here," I say over and over, and then she is asleep, her arm still raised.

Through the windows, the sky is lightening. I want to throw up, to punch the walls, to do something, anything. I feel utterly helpless. I could lie down next to her, wrap her in my arms, but I'm too worked up. I pace in front of the three huge windows, first with them on my left, now on my right, now on my left. *What the hell am I going to do? Wake Hank? But what can he do?*

I have to deal with this myself. Get her to a hospital? Did she take something at the rave? The kid with the hoop through his eyebrow that she was talking to. Everyone was hopped up on something. But she would have told me. I walk back to her, gently push her arm down, and it finally yields. *What the hell could cause that? She'll be fine in the morning. This is exhaustion, just exhaustion. When was the last time she ate? Or maybe I should get her to a hospital. What if she's having some kind of bad drug reaction? Shit, shit, shit! This isn't happening. Shit, shit, shit, get on my shoes. Shoes. That's it. Put on my running shoes. Run. Yes, go for a run. Elissa is out cold and a run will clear my head.*

I race up Dunckerstrasse and past the park, the treetops bright with the first light. *This is good. This is right.* My lungs burn but I don't feel my legs. I run past the warehouses and the rave. I wonder if it is still going on. And then I'm right up on the Wall, fully ablaze with the early sun. I run over toppled slabs, golden ramps, into No-Man's-Land. I am a blur of pain but I'm going to outrun it. In no time I'm on the outskirts of the city. I run harder. I could be anywhere—on the mountain trails of Colorado, on the streets of Baltimore; this rush is universal, the feeling of flight and freedom, of getting away from everything and into myself. I'm not living in the future or past. *I'm here, now.*

Miles melt away until I run up on the small village where we had seen the boy chipping at the Wall. The hole has widened in the last two weeks, enough for me to put my leg through and straddle the Wall, then pull the rest of me through. On the Western side, away from the Wall about a hundred yards, is another village, a cluster of modest, well-tended houses, a modest white church spire. There's a smell of baking bread. *I wonder if I can find the bakery? What's going to happen to the two villages once they are reunited?* Looking back to the East, I see the second floor of the boy's house. Growing up, he could peer over to the Western village. Did he have friends on this side?

I try to catch my breath, sweat stinging my eyes. I focus on my racing pulse, try to slow it down, but it is throbbing in my knee. Pain radiates upward. My knee hurts. Really hurts. *What the hell am I doing here? What the hell am I doing running at a moment like this?*

Elissa.

My knee screaming, my heart feeling like it's going to explode out of my chest, I race back to Prenzlauer Berg in minutes, charge up the stairs three at a time. Elissa isn't on the sofa where I left her. I look around frantically, then see her sleeping on the foot-wide ledge of the window. Hank is nowhere to be seen. How did she get from the sofa to the ledge?

I'm afraid of surprising her, afraid of waking her, afraid that she'll fall out of the window. I'm afraid of everything. Carefully I approach her, wrap my arms tight around her, and drag her inside. "It's okay, it's okay, it's going to be okay," I whisper in her ear as I carry her back to the sofa and cover her with blankets.

"So tired," Elissa mumbles.

"It's okay," I say, and stroke her brow. "I'm going to get you to a hospital."

"No hospital," she says, her right arm once again raised.

"Okay, okay, no hospital," I say, and take her hand, her arm lowering more easily this time.

"Rest. I need to rest," she mutters. "Zambi. Take me back. I promise I'll be better."

An hour later Hank walks in, sketch pad in hand, and freezes. I'm sitting next to Elissa, who is asleep on the sofa. I don't have to tell him that something is terribly wrong.

"What do we need to do?" he asks me, looking at Elissa.

"Drive," I say.

"You got it, Chief," Hank says.

Of course he'll come through. Hank at his best—the fixer who mends things to show his love.

We pack our clothes quickly, take some small tokens—graffitied pieces of the Wall we smashed off with a piece of rebar, the front plate of a radio with only East Bloc names, the hood ornament of a Wartburg, Communist pins and patches, a modest string of amber beads that is nothing like the old couple's wedding necklace. The apartment still looks like a home, lived in: the fabulous furniture we have accumulated surrounded by piles of books, framed paintings, and photographs of Lenin, Marx, and the cosmonauts.

As I load up Dusty, I wonder: If I don't take these objects with me, will I still have been here? *Things.* Do any of these *things* matter? Will any of these *things* save Elissa? Will any of these *things* save me?

With the scavenged blankets, we make a nest for Elissa in the backseat. She crawls in, curls up.

Back upstairs for one last check of the apartment, words flood me, but they are not mine. Elizabeth Bishop's poem "One Art," the last two stanzas: disaster and disaster.

When I moved to the States I defined myself as being from Berlin. I was a Berliner removed from Berlin, and I would return home. What the hell was I thinking? Berlin is an idea. It isn't my home. *Elissa* is my home. I'll lose these things, this stuff, this room, this flat, Ralf and the other East German friends, the CV, Prenzlauer, Berlin—it isn't that hard—but I won't lose Elissa.

60

"When one begins to live by habit and by quotation, one
has begun to stop living."

—James Baldwin

Soundtrack: LCD Soundsystem, "Losing My Edge," 2002

HISTORICAL AND ARTISTIC EPOCHS are usually named and
codified after the fact. Yet even Parisian artists at the turn of the
twentieth century knew they were in the middle of a unique
confluence of economic, geopolitical, and artistic forces that
were responsible for a cross-cultural creative explosion. New
York, 1986, was experiencing not an explosion, but an implo-
sion. King Heroin, rising rents, and AIDS were squeezing the
Lower East Side like an anaconda. Tompkins Square Park, a
few years earlier the epicenter of cutting-edge artistic Lower
East Side, was now a homeless camp, covered in lean-tos like
the slums of Rio or Kingston. The art world was gripped in a
reactionary capitalist frenzy, the street energy of Keith Haring
and Jean-Michel Basquiat giving way to Mark Kostabi's assembly
line paintings and Julian Schnabel's bombastic creations. The
New York writing scene was dominated by the drug-fueled "Brat
Pack" led by Bret Easton Ellis and Jay McInerney.

I had moved to New York with visions of going to the Cedar
Tavern to see the modern-day Frank O'Haras and Allen Gins-
bergs stomping around like drunken giants, throwing punches

over the emotional truth of a poem. Instead the visible scene was about limos, drugs, parties, writers fighting over invites to fashion events at Club MK. Sure, there was the lit mag *Between C & D*, which published edgy, grungy fiction and was printed on dot-matrix paper and sold in Ziploc baggies as if it were heroin. The work was annihilating, a negation of everything. Was there nothing to live for?

Or so it appeared to my impatient self, someone who was chasing past versions of bohemia and artistic revolutions. These, of course, are recognized only after the current work has been upturned. At the time I wasn't doing anything to contribute to any kind of new creativity, or engaging in the anti-gentrification battles of our neighborhood, but instead was whining about the lack of a "real scene."

In this toxic sludge, I was at least able to see that one artistic life form was thriving—noisy postpunk bands like Sonic Youth. Throughout the long, grim winter Elissa and I trooped from club to club, CBGB's to the Ritz to the Pyramid, catching Sonic Youth, the Jesus and Mary Chain, Ball, and all the other spine-scraping bands.

Even though I had a job, an apartment, and a live-in girl-friend, I still felt like I was missing the cultural boat, a hard drinker with a bum leg, the same lucky loser who had walked away from three near-fatal car crashes. I wanted out of the black hole. My perception of what New York should be had contrasted so dramatically with what I perceived it to be that I couldn't understand how I had ever wanted to live there. If New York was truly dead, my logic went, why not live and write someplace beautiful like Hunter Thompson did? If there was no collective creative force to tap into, why not tap into natural beauty: unspoiled snowcapped mountains, fields of wildflowers, pine forests big enough to get lost in. It was a simple thought. And with Elissa being my sole tether, it was easy to cut ties and jump into the wilderness. All I had to do was ask her if she wanted to try living in Colorado, and if she said yes, we'd go, jettisoning what little baggage we had.

Elissa had, indeed, been open to adventure. After her stable, rooted upbringing and four years of college, she was ready to risk, to run off with me. Especially if what I promised—time and space to write, and in a beautiful place—was true. When we got there, she was happily surprised that I hadn't lied.

But we were writing in a void. An artistic movement isn't two people creating with no one to share their work with. Thompson frequently left his secluded ranch to engage full force with the world. It took us four months to figure this out. And that we should get married and get the hell back to New York.

In Boulder, we used the last of our money to buy a Siamese kitten (fifty bucks) and a 1965 Volvo 122S (five hundred bucks). We piled what little we had into the bulbous ruster and drove it to New York. The Volvo had been sitting in a hippie's garage for five years with a full tank of gas, so the fuel system was filled with rust and we had to stop every ten or twenty miles to blow chunks of corroded metal out of the clogged fuel filter. If we didn't keep the car topped off, it would stall out, which is what happened at three in the morning crossing the Mississippi. As a policeman pushed us off the bridge with his cruiser, I was sure that I was finally going to get arrested, having gone four years driving without a license. Yet, instead of asking for my ID, he said, "Don't stay on this side of the bridge for too long—we've had some sniper incidents in this part of East St. Louis."

When we returned from Colorado, I wasn't quite ready to kiss the sidewalk, but I was close. I begged New York's forgiveness.

I vowed that I would open my eyes, see it in the here and now versus the sepia postcard images I was projecting onto the back of my brain. It was intoxicating to be around intelligent, creative people, the fall cultural season in full swing with gallery openings and bands playing everywhere.

It wasn't long before I landed my first job in publishing. Even though it was an entry-level job in the Random House publicity department, I felt that I had snuck through the scullery window of the publishing citadel. From in there, anything was possible.

The publicity department was on the Random House editorial floor, which was filled with legendary old-timers. I spent hours in Joe Fox's office playing chess and listening to Fox talk about what it was like being Truman Capote's editor, about the out-of-body experience of reading *In Cold Blood* in manuscript. The first book I had anything to do with was Neil Sheehan's *A Bright Shining Lie*, a passionate rendering of an emblematic Vietnam commander written by the journalist who had secured the Pentagon Papers. The second book was Pete Dexter's gritty novel *Paris Trout*. Both Dexter and Sheehan were kind and generous, and appreciated anything that was done for them. Sheehan had spent seventeen years working on his book; Dexter had lost the first 110 pages to an early computer virus and when he punched the wall in anger he broke his hand, delaying the restart of the novel.

That year Sheehan won the National Book Award for nonfiction and Dexter the National Book Award for fiction. Here were actual role models, normal, hardworking men who had made their own way.

Before we even left Boulder, Elissa had landed a job at *Spy* magazine. As a reporter for the new satirical monthly, she was paid (not much) to make crank phone calls and get shots in the ass from quack doctors. Surrounded by brilliant off-kilter writers and editors, she was very much in her element. There was a pervasive recklessness among the staff, most thinking that no one in straight publishing would hire them after *Spy*, since the magazine had devoted hundreds of column inches to bashing all the powerful people in straight publishing.

After I'd worked on the Sheehan and Dexter books, my boss came to me and said, "Rob, I'd like you to help out on one of the lead titles for next season."

"Great. Which one?"

"*Thin Thighs in Thirty Days*. It's going to be huge, and we're pulling out all the stops to publicize it," my boss said with heartfelt enthusiasm.

Maybe I wasn't cut out for publicity after all.

Rather than pledge my allegiance to *Thin Thighs*, I left Random House and freelanced as a fact-checker for *Spy*, which led to gigs at *Rolling Stone* and *Connoisseur*. I started writing book reviews and author profiles, and the occasional feature for places like *Sports Illustrated* and *Vogue*. Both Elissa and I were now safely inside the publishing-industrial complex. We were surprised by how small this complex was, and how everyone knew each other, and how lateral movement between various magazines and publishing houses was easy and expected.

While I loved being inside the fortress, and was happy to be surrounded by other young, creative people who were trying to figure themselves out, I still felt like I wasn't where I was supposed to be. I still resisted any place that would accept me as one of its own. *This is no Berlin*, I told myself. Of course, this was another projected delusion, yet another way for me not to settle into myself and my life. This unsettling delusion was further stoked by seeing *Wings of Desire* at Film Forum. Angels in Berlin, in black and white, with Nick Cave and the Bad Seeds making a cameo. *This* was a much grittier, more cosmopolitan place. My restless, deluded self was convinced that New York wasn't as real as Berlin.

Yet our tiny East Village walk-up on Eighth Street between B and C had become a shelter for an unruly and ever-expanding circle of hard-drinking artistic friends. We were the one married couple anyone knew, so our place became a default hangout for our single friends, and most weekend mornings there were bodies on our sofa or floor.

Amazingly, we were doing what we had set out to do— move to New York and work in publishing. We were surrounded by actively engaged artists, and we went to shows and galleries. But we were struggling as creative writers. We were both trying to write fiction, and finding it hard to do while also writing journalism. I still believed that it was a problem of place (New York) rather than one of personality (mine). I also couldn't shake the idea that there was something wrong with happiness, or at least contentedness. Artists were never supposed to be content.

61

"To thine own self be true."

—William Shakespeare, *Hamlet*

Soundtrack: My Bloody Valentine, "Soon," 1991

AS HANK AND I PUT THE LAST FEW THINGS in the back of Dusty, Elissa sleeps, showing a sliver of consciousness when I tell her it is time to go.

"Elissa, we're going to get you back to Zambi, okay?"

"Thank you," she says, then falls back asleep.

It is a forty-straight-hour, clearer-than-clear hallucination of narrow roads, oncoming yellow fog lights, bland European pop music leaking from the radio, two dusks, two dawns, and countless espressos back to Zambujeira. We alternate driving, Hank channeling the rally driver he's always wanted to be. When one drives, the other sleeps, though I don't really sleep. Elissa is mute. She's never fully awake or asleep. She sleeps fitfully. When awake, she stares out the window blankly.

She's going to be okay once we get to Zambi.

Or not.

I should find a hospital.

She's going to be okay.

Drive faster.

Focus.

I feel like a retreating army, fleeing the city I was certain I would capture. I'm running. But I'm not running away. I'm running toward life with Elissa. Hour after hour I replay all the stupidity in my life, all of the wasted time chasing and not being present. I want nothing more than to be present, to be with Elissa, to create. I want to leave the darkness and rage behind. Yet all of the crap I'd been running from is still looming on the horizon.

Hank snores while I drive across the hot, dry Spanish border. Elissa looks peaceful in her nest, still asleep. We're near Pamplona. I don't recognize who I was there. I pull over to pee. I try, once again, to rearrange behind my seat, my backpack jamming into my lower back. I pull out the backpack, open it up, grab the three yellow legal pads that contain *Coffee and Absinthe.* I don't need to look at them to know that there isn't a true word or feeling on those pages. I throw them into the ditch. The backpack fits better now. I wonder if someone will find the notebooks. I hope they will be of use, like the poet's pages in *La Bohème,* good for starting a fire.

Strange how long drives all blur into one. For a second I am not in Spain but in Oklahoma, with my father, this high blue summer sky melding with that one, a black wall suddenly appearing on the horizon, maybe sixty or seventy miles off to the west, and as we drive closer the front looming larger and larger, the radio issuing tornado warnings, my father calmly joining other cars stopped under an overpass to wait out the moving wall.

All of my selfish blackness is swirling ahead of me. I keep the car pointed straight at it.

62

"Sweet is the memory of past troubles."

—Cicero

Soundtrack: The Merseybeats, "Sorrow," 1966

I DRIVE THROUGH my second straight dawn, over the Spanish border into Portugal, static childhood memories flickering. A large living room filled with people, laughing and smoking and drinking. I am waist-high to them, carrying trays of drinks. It's our living room, but I can't picture my parents there, especially not together. My mother lighting candles clipped to the branches of a small Christmas tree. Shrimp swimming between my toes by the Danish docks where my father and I will catch a ferry across the North Sea. My father eats raw shrimp from the baskets stacked on the deck. We sleep folded up in our tiny European car. In these fragments there are no families, no couples.

What if Elissa and I had had a child with us in Berlin? We wouldn't have been so cavalier, right? A child would have made us more serious about our art. Like my parents. How did they do it? How did they try to make meaningful creative lives for themselves while simultaneously being parents? At the height of the Cold War, four thousand miles away from home? My God they were crazy. And brave. They must have been terrified all of the time. Especially once they split. Why has it taken me so long to realize this?

Outside of Zambujeira, salt air mixed with red dust is blowing into the open windows. I drive straight to Xica's bar.

Elissa hops out and hugs Xica. "How was Berlin?" Xica asks.

"Surreal," Elissa says, and something else which I miss because I am stunned she's talking. She hasn't said anything—nothing—during the entire forty-hour drive from Berlin to Zambujeira.

"Elissa," I say, and she looks at me with what I'm guessing is supposed to be a reassuring smile, though her eyes are still unfocused. "You think you will be okay here?"

"Of course," Elissa says, sounding weirdly chipper. My head feels like it is going to fall off; I could lie down right here in the road. I want to feel relief. I want nothing more in this world than to believe that she is okay and that we can stay in our happy little fishing village and that she will miraculously recover by breathing in this familiar salt air. But she doesn't look the least bit okay. She looks like a poorly put-together doll—arms and legs slightly spastic, her eyes not tracking.

Down the coast the cliffs are purple, the sun plunging into the lavender-tipped waves. Absinthe hour. That's what I used to believe in—the absinthe hour, history, books, stories, adventure points, outrunning my past.

I cross the square to the phone booth. I ask the operator to patch me through to a U.S. operator, who patches me through to Elissa's parents' house.

"Mom," I say to Elissa's mother. I'm going to throw up.

"What's wrong?" She knows that something bad has happened. She knows that I've failed to protect her daughter.

"Elissa is . . ."

"Is she hurt?"

"No. She's exhausted and I think she's had some kind of a seizure in Berlin. She's okay but really disoriented."

The line crackles with static. I fight the urge to apologize, to explain, to beg for forgiveness.

"Does she need to go to a hospital?" Elissa's mom asks, forcibly calm, all focused on the logistics of caretaking.

"No, home," I reply.

"I'll call the travel agent right away and get you to New York—"

"She needs to come home."

"Home?" Elissa's mom asks. "Here?"

"Yes, home to Delaware."

63

"The meaning of life is to find your gift. The purpose of life is to give it away."

—Pablo Picasso

Soundtrack: Crosby, Stills & Nash, "Helplessly Hoping," 1969

HOME. Not New York, but Delaware, Elissa's childhood home. Her father, as usual, has the stereo cranked up, Crosby, Stills & Nash filling the warm house with familiar music. Elissa's father and mother built this house, their home. Fieldstones and brick; orchids filling the greenhouse; goldfish and frogs in the pond. But it isn't the physical thing that matters; it is the feel of the place. There is no other way to put it than to say that this house is built out of love. This is what you do if you love someone— together you build psychic sanctuaries and within these spaces you share a life.

Or this is what you should do. Or what I should have done.

I was so besotted with romantic visions that I dragged us to Boulder, then Portugal, then Berlin, chasing visions, romantic ghosts. I was looking for creativity outside of myself instead of inside of myself. I wanted to be where I was not. I wanted to be someone—anyone—I was not. My delusion sucked in Elissa, and it has nearly crushed her. I have failed her. And I have failed myself.

Elissa sits next to me on the love seat in her parents' living room, holding my hand. She squeezes it so tightly that her knuckles are white and my fingertips are red. A day removed from Portugal, exhausted and raw. How easy it would be to unlace my fingers, slip out the door, and run. Just run into the unknown. Not this time.

I'm going to let all the pain, failure, and confusion catch up to me. Miserable, yes, but mixed in with the misery is love.

I'm going to let myself be present. I'm going to let myself be. With Elissa. For the first time in my life, I am still. This is the place.

Acknowledgments

Many people helped me through the ten year journey that resulted in this book. For their early and continued support, thank you Elise Cannon, Amy Williams, Michael Hainey, Karen Russell, and my Tin House family. Betsy Lerner believed when few did. Greg Villepique's meticulous insights, both large and small, born out of thirty years of friendship, were invaluable. Jon Raymond also read an early draft with his excellent eye and intellect. Katarina Born offered crucial corrections on all things German. Rachel Kushner, David Shields, and Nick Flynn offered support at just the right time.

Bill Clegg has been there through thick and thin, above and beyond. Thank you for your close attention to every possible thing, from the miniscule to the enormous. I feel honored to work with the incredible literary team at Grove, the house of my publishing hero, Barney Rosset. Thank you Elisabeth Schmitz for your leap of faith and continued guidance, as well as heartfelt thanks to Morgan Entrekin, Judy Hottensen, Amy Hundley, John Mark Boling, and Deb Seager. I will forever be indebted to superhero Corinna Barsan, who patiently edited multiple drafts while repeatedly talking me off of ledges. Thank you to my parents for their love, understanding, and crucial feedback. Thank you also to my in-laws, Connie Schappell and the late Frederick Schappell. My children, Miles and Isadora Schappell-Spillman, are a constant source of inspiration and motivation. Thank you for being yourselves. Lastly, this book would not have been possible without Elissa Schappell. Thank you for pushing and challenging me, and for letting me grow up with you.